SHADOWS OF DECEPTION

Shadows of Deception

QUINN SILVER

Contents

Chapter 1: The Day that Changed the World

The Events of September 11, 2001

The morning of September 11, 2001, began like any other, but by the end of the day, it would be forever etched in the world's memory as one of the darkest moments in modern history. At 8:46 a.m. Eastern Time, the first hijacked plane, American Airlines Flight 11, crashed into the North Tower of the World Trade Center in New York City. At first, it was unclear what had happened. Many people watching the news coverage assumed it was a tragic accident—a commercial jet perhaps lost control or suffered a catastrophic malfunction. But as black smoke billowed from the North Tower, the true horror of the situation would soon become clear.

At 9:03 a.m., a second plane, United Airlines Flight 175, struck the South Tower. This was no accident. The United States was under attack. Within minutes, major news outlets began reporting that the planes had been hijacked, and it became clear that the impacts were intentional acts of terror. Panic began to spread as the scale of the attacks unfolded live on television screens across the country. People in New York watched in terror as flames engulfed the top floors of both towers, and the streets below filled with debris, smoke, and fleeing pedestrians.

Meanwhile, at 9:37 a.m., another plane, American Airlines Flight 77, crashed into the Pentagon, the heart of the U.S. military's operations, just outside Washington, D.C. The attack on the Pentagon further cemented that this was not an isolated incident but part of a coordinated assault on the United States. Government buildings were evacuated, air traffic was grounded across the nation, and cities went into lockdown, as officials struggled to understand the full scope of the threat.

The horror was far from over. At 10:03 a.m., United Airlines Flight 93 crashed into a field near Shanksville, Pennsylvania. This plane had also been hijacked, but thanks to the brave actions of the passengers who fought back against the hijackers, it never reached its intended target, which was believed to be either the White House or the U.S. Capitol. The passengers' heroic actions prevented further devastation, but all 44 people on board perished.

The most shocking and heartbreaking moment of the day came when the South Tower of the World Trade Center collapsed at 9:59 a.m., less than an hour after being struck. The North Tower followed at 10:28 a.m. The sight of these massive buildings—symbols of American economic power—crumbling into dust was broadcast live to millions. The streets of Lower Manhattan were engulfed in a cloud of smoke and debris, and rescue efforts were immediately overwhelmed. Thousands of lives were lost in an instant, and the once-vibrant financial district became a scene of utter devastation.

In the space of just a few hours, nearly 3,000 people were dead, including first responders who had rushed into the towers to save others. The scale of destruction was unprecedented. The attacks on 9/11 were not only an assault on physical structures but also on the American sense of security and identity. The world had changed, and as the dust settled over Ground Zero, the questions of who was responsible and why these attacks happened would dominate public discourse for years to come.

This was the day that the United States, and much of the world, realized that the post-Cold War era of peace and prosperity was an illusion. The attacks of September 11, 2001, reshaped global politics, security, and society in ways that are still felt today. It was also the beginning of an era marked by fear, war, and growing distrust in the government—a distrust that would eventually fuel alternative theories about what really happened on that fateful day.

National and Global Reaction

The immediate aftermath of the September 11 attacks was one of collective shock and profound grief. Across the United States, a sense of disbelief gripped the nation as millions watched the live footage of the burning towers, the gaping hole in the Pentagon, and the smoking wreckage of Flight 93 in Pennsylvania. For many, the events seemed incomprehensible—a nightmare playing out in real-time. The devastation was raw, and the emotional impact deep. The U.S., once perceived as an untouchable superpower, had been attacked on its own soil in a coordinated, catastrophic assault.

The national reaction was swift and visceral. In New York City, people poured into the streets, some covered in dust and debris, others searching for missing loved ones. Hospitals were overwhelmed with the injured, while rescue workers desperately combed through the rubble, hoping to find survivors. Vigils were held in cities across the country, as Americans united in grief and solidarity. The footage of firefighters, police officers, and everyday citizens rushing toward danger, while many fled, became symbolic of the selflessness and heroism that characterized the immediate response.

President George W. Bush addressed the nation from the Oval Office that evening, framing the attacks as a deliberate act of terror and vowing swift retribution. He declared, "America was targeted for attack because we're the brightest beacon for freedom and opportunity in the world. And no one will keep that light from shining." His words resonated with a grieving nation, setting the stage for what would soon become the War on Terror. The president's firm resolve to retaliate comforted many, but it also signaled the beginning of a new era defined by conflict, fear, and sweeping policy changes.

Globally, the reaction was one of solidarity, albeit tinged with underlying political complexities. World leaders expressed their condolences and condemned the attacks. In a rare moment of global unity, nations that were often at odds with the U.S. stood in support of the American people. British Prime Minister Tony Blair declared, "This is not a battle between the United States of America and terrorism, but between the free and democratic world and terrorism." Even countries like Russia and China, which had complicated relationships with the U.S., offered assistance and voiced their support.

On September 12, the world watched as the U.S. Congress gathered on the steps of the Capitol to sing "God Bless America." It was a rare moment of political unity in Washington, a display of resilience and defiance in the face of tragedy. NATO invoked Article 5 for the first time in its history, declaring that the attacks on the U.S. were an attack on all member states, effectively committing its allies to join the fight against those responsible.

Yet, as the days passed, the expressions of solidarity gave way to questions about what would come next. While the world was united in mourning, there were underlying concerns about the U.S. response. In many parts of the Middle East, where resentment toward American foreign policy had simmered for years, there was a fear that this tragic event would lead to more violence, particularly if the U.S. sought revenge in ways that could destabilize the region further. Some governments, though expressing solidarity publicly, were anxious about how the U.S. would use its newfound moral authority to justify military action.

The media played a significant role in shaping both the national and global reaction. Around the clock, news channels broadcast harrowing footage of the attacks, replaying the collapse of the Twin Towers and showing tearful interviews with survivors and family members of victims. The constant media coverage reinforced the sense of shared trauma, making 9/11 not just a national event, but a global one. For many outside the U.S., the attacks were viewed not only as an assault on America but on the very principles of modern civilization.

As the world mourned, a shift began to take place in the public consciousness. The attacks were quickly understood as more than just a random act of violence. They were seen as a declaration of war on the United States and, by extension, the West. Fear began to spread, not just of further attacks, but of the unknown enemy behind this atrocity. Who were these terrorists? Why had they targeted the U.S.? How could they be stopped? These questions would dominate discussions in the days to come, laying the groundwork for the global war on terror.

But in the immediate aftermath, the overwhelming reaction was one of sorrow and solidarity. Memorials sprang up in cities across the globe. In places as far away as London, Sydney, and Tokyo, people gathered outside U.S. embassies to light candles, leave flowers, and offer their condolences. The iconic image of Queen Elizabeth II ordering the U.S. national anthem to be played at Buckingham Palace was one of many poignant moments that underscored the global response to the tragedy.

In the days following 9/11, the world stood still, united in grief and disbelief. It was a day that changed not only America but the entire global order. For a brief moment, it seemed that the world was bound together by shared sorrow and a desire for justice. Yet, as the dust settled and the smoke cleared, the question of how the U.S. would respond loomed large, and with it came the realization that this unity might be fleeting.

The Official Narrative: Terrorism and al-Qaeda

In the hours following the September 11 attacks, the United States government quickly pointed to a shadowy group that many Americans had never heard of: al-Qaeda. Led by Saudi-born Osama bin Laden, al-Qaeda had been on the U.S. intelligence radar for several years, but few could have predicted the scale and audacity of the attacks it was accused of masterminding. By the end of the day, U.S. officials were confident that this group, operating from distant caves in Afghanistan, had orchestrated the deadliest terror attack on American soil.

The official narrative began to form rapidly. According to U.S. authorities, al-Qaeda operatives had hijacked four commercial airplanes, transforming them into weapons of mass destruction. The 19 hijackers were mostly Saudi nationals, and they had been living in the United States for months, quietly preparing for the attack under the noses of American law enforcement and intelligence agencies. These men were part of a broader network of Islamic extremists who had been radicalized by bin Laden's ideology, which called for violent jihad against the West, particularly the United States, for its military presence in the Middle East and support of Israel.

At the center of this narrative was Osama bin Laden, a figure who had risen to prominence during the Soviet-Afghan War in the 1980s. Bin Laden, once a U.S. ally in the fight against Soviet forces, had turned against America in the 1990s. From his base of operations in Afghanistan, he had declared a holy war against the U.S. in a series of fatwas, accusing it of oppressing Muslims worldwide. His anger was fueled by the presence of American troops in Saudi Arabia—home to Islam's holiest sites—and the U.S. support for Israel in its conflicts with Palestinians. For bin Laden, the United States represented a global force of corruption, and al-Qaeda's mission was to strike at the heart of this perceived evil.

According to the U.S. government's narrative, the 9/11 attacks were the culmination of years of meticulous planning by al-Qaeda. Intelligence agencies would later reveal that al-Qaeda had been behind a number of previous attacks, including the 1993 bombing of the World Trade Center, the 1998 U.S. embassy bombings in Africa, and the 2000 attack on the USS *Cole*. Each of these earlier attacks had been a precursor, testing the waters for what would eventually become the most devastating assault on American soil.

Within days of the 9/11 attacks, the U.S. government released a list of the 19 hijackers and quickly identified key figures within al-Qaeda who had orchestrated the plot. Khalid Sheikh Mohammed, a high-ranking al-Qaeda operative, was named as the mastermind behind the attacks, while bin Laden was singled out as the financier and ideological leader. Intelligence gathered in the months following the attacks would reveal that the plot had been in development for several years, with key operatives training in flight schools in the U.S. and carefully planning the timing and targets of the hijackings.

President George W. Bush wasted no time in addressing the nation, framing the attacks as an act of war. In a somber speech delivered on the evening of September 11, he declared that "freedom itself was attacked this morning by a faceless coward," and that the U.S. would "hunt down and punish those responsible." His words set the tone for the aggressive military and political response that would follow. The attacks were not just seen as acts of terror, but as a direct assault on American values and freedom. This framing would soon justify a new kind of warfare—one that would stretch across borders and redefine global security for decades to come.

Within days, the U.S. had formally accused al-Qaeda and Osama bin Laden of being responsible for the attacks, and attention quickly turned to Afghanistan, where the Taliban regime had been harboring bin Laden and his network since the late 1990s. The Taliban's refusal to hand over bin Laden would become the catalyst for the U.S. invasion of Afghanistan in October 2001, marking the beginning of the War on Terror. The invasion, supported by a coalition of NATO allies, aimed to dismantle al-Qaeda, topple the Taliban regime, and capture or kill bin Laden. This war, which began with widespread public support, would eventually become one of the longest and most controversial conflicts in U.S. history.

The official narrative was clear: al-Qaeda, motivated by a radical interpretation of Islam and fueled by grievances against U.S. foreign policy, had carried out the attacks as part of a broader jihad against the West. The 9/11 attacks were framed as the defining battle in this war, and the U.S. response would be both swift and uncompromising. Military action, increased security measures, and a global hunt for terrorists would soon follow, all justified by the need to prevent another catastrophic attack on American soil.

But as this narrative solidified in the days and weeks following the attacks, not everyone was convinced. Early on, some skeptics questioned the speed with which the U.S. government had pinpointed the perpetrators and the motivations behind the attacks. These doubts, although marginal at first, would grow over time, giving rise to alternative theories about who was truly behind the events of 9/11. While the official narrative pointed to al-Qaeda as the sole culprit, these alternative perspectives would soon suggest that there was more to the story than met the eye—a possibility that would be explored in detail in the chapters to come.

The Psychological Impact on the American Public

The September 11 attacks struck at the very heart of American identity, not just in the physical sense but in an emotional and psychological one. For many Americans, the events of that day shattered the illusion of safety and invulnerability that had long been taken for granted. In the span of a few hours, the perception that the United States was an impenetrable fortress—protected by its vast oceans, military strength, and global influence—was irrevocably broken. The emotional toll was immediate, profound, and enduring.

In the hours and days following the attacks, a deep sense of vulnerability took hold across the country. People who had watched the World Trade Center towers fall live on television or experienced the terror in person were haunted by the sheer audacity of the attacks. For many, the shock was accompanied by confusion and fear. How could such a thing happen? How had the world's most powerful nation been caught off guard by an enemy that had seemingly come from nowhere?

As images of the burning towers, the smoke rising from the Pentagon, and the wreckage in Pennsylvania replayed over and over on every television network, a sense of collective trauma emerged. Americans were glued to their screens, unable to turn away from the devastation. The media became an emotional conduit, broadcasting not just the destruction, but the stories of those affected: the firefighters who ran into the towers and never came out, the office workers trapped in upper floors making desperate phone calls to loved ones, and the passengers on United Flight 93 who sacrificed their lives to prevent further carnage.

Grief was the dominant emotion in those early days. The sheer loss of life—nearly 3,000 people killed in the space of a few hours—was incomprehensible. In New York City, grief was palpable in the streets as people posted pictures of missing loved ones on walls and telephone poles, hoping against hope that they might be found alive. Funerals and memorial services became a daily occurrence, not just in New York but across the country. Every American knew someone—directly or indirectly—who had been affected by the tragedy. The collective mourning was raw and widespread, a national wound that would take years to heal.

But grief soon gave way to other emotions: anger and a desire for justice. Americans, still reeling from the shock, began to demand answers and, more importantly, retribution. Who had done this, and why? In the aftermath of 9/11, there was a powerful urge to strike back, to show the world that such an attack would not go unpunished. In this way, patriotism surged. American flags flew from homes, cars, and businesses across the country. It became a symbol not just of national pride but of defiance—an assertion that, despite the attack, the country would rise again.

This surge in patriotism was accompanied by a strong rallying around President George W. Bush. His immediate response to the attacks, particularly his address to the nation on the evening of September 11, reassured many Americans that the government was in control and would do whatever was necessary to protect the country. When Bush stood atop the rubble at Ground Zero three days later, bullhorn in hand, and declared, "I can hear you, the rest of the world hears you, and the people who knocked these buildings down will hear all of us soon," it was a defining moment. His words encapsulated the national mood—a mixture of grief, anger, and resolve.

This wave of patriotism and the call for justice soon transformed into widespread public support for military action. When the U.S. invaded Afghanistan in October 2001 to dismantle al-Qaeda and overthrow the Taliban regime that had sheltered its leaders, the American public was overwhelmingly in favor. The desire to prevent another attack was visceral, and many saw military intervention as the only way to achieve that goal. There was little patience for nuanced discussions about the root causes of terrorism or the potential long-term consequences of war. In the immediate aftermath of 9/11, fear and anger drove public opinion, and the overwhelming sentiment was that the U.S. needed to strike hard and fast.

The psychological impact of 9/11 also manifested in a dramatic shift in how Americans viewed their own safety and security. The sense of invulnerability that had once defined the American experience was replaced by an omnipresent fear of further attacks. This fear was reinforced by the government's frequent warnings of more potential terrorist plots. The Department of Homeland Security was created, and the public became accustomed to the now-iconic color-coded terror alert system, which gauged the level of threat the nation faced on any given day.

This heightened sense of danger extended into daily life. Airports were transformed almost overnight, with new security measures that dramatically changed the experience of travel. Long lines, intensive screenings, and the visible presence of armed guards became the new normal. Suspicion, particularly toward people of Middle Eastern descent, spiked, and the rise of Islamophobia became an unfortunate consequence of the national trauma. The attacks had not only instilled a deep fear of terrorism but had also fostered a culture of suspicion and paranoia that would persist for years.

The psychological wounds of September 11 went far beyond fear and anger. For many, the attacks created a lingering sense of existential uncertainty. If such an unprecedented and catastrophic event could happen once, what was stopping it from happening again? The security measures that followed—ranging from airport screenings to the expansion of government surveillance under the Patriot Act—were meant to reassure the public, but they also reinforced the idea that the threat was always looming.

In the years that followed, the psychological impact of 9/11 would continue to shape the American psyche. It changed how Americans viewed themselves, their government, and the world. The trauma of that day was not something that could be easily forgotten, and the emotional scars left by the attacks would shape public opinion, policy, and culture for years to come. September 11, 2001, was not just a day of physical destruction; it was a day that fundamentally altered the way Americans lived, thought, and felt about their place in the world.

The War on Terror and the Shift in U.S. Policy

In the days following the September 11 attacks, it became clear that the U.S. response would go far beyond immediate recovery and grief. What began as an effort to bring the perpetrators to justice rapidly evolved into a global campaign that would reshape U.S. foreign and domestic policy for years to come. The phrase "War on Terror," first used by President George W. Bush, signified the beginning of an era defined by military intervention, heightened security, and a profound reorientation of America's role in the world.

On September 20, 2001, President Bush addressed a joint session of Congress, delivering a speech that would outline the broad strokes of this new war. "Our war on terror begins with al-Qaeda," he declared, "but it does not end there. It will not end until every terrorist group of global reach has been found, stopped, and defeated." These words set the tone for a far-reaching and open-ended military campaign, not just against the individuals responsible for 9/11 but against terrorism as a global threat. The U.S. would now pursue a policy of preemptive action, targeting terrorist organizations before they could strike.

The immediate focus of the War on Terror was Afghanistan, where al-Qaeda had established a safe haven under the protection of the Taliban regime. On October 7, 2001, less than a month after the attacks, the U.S. launched Operation Enduring Freedom, a military invasion aimed at toppling the Taliban and dismantling al-Qaeda's operations. The U.S. military, with the support of NATO allies, swiftly took control of key Afghan cities, driving the Taliban from power and forcing al-Qaeda into hiding. Although bin Laden and other top leaders escaped, the invasion was initially hailed as a success. The war in Afghanistan, however, would prove far more complex and drawn-out than anyone anticipated, evolving into the longest conflict in U.S. history.

But the War on Terror did not stop in Afghanistan. In 2002, attention shifted to Iraq, where President Bush and key members of his administration began to assert that Saddam Hussein's regime posed an imminent threat to U.S. security. Citing intelligence reports that suggested Iraq was developing weapons of mass destruction (WMDs) and had ties to terrorist organizations like al-Qaeda, the U.S. government argued that Hussein's regime needed to be removed before it could pose a direct danger. This rationale would soon lead to one of the most controversial military decisions in modern history: the U.S. invasion of Iraq in 2003.

The Iraq War, launched under the banner of the War on Terror, was framed as a necessary step in protecting the U.S. from future attacks. However, the war's justification quickly came under scrutiny. Despite initial confidence in the presence of

WMDs, no such weapons were found, leading to widespread criticism that the invasion had been based on faulty intelligence and exaggerated claims. The connection between Saddam Hussein and al-Qaeda also proved tenuous at best. As the war dragged on, the initial public support that had rallied behind the invasion waned, giving rise to deep divisions within the U.S. over the legitimacy and cost of the conflict.

The shift in U.S. foreign policy during this period extended beyond military intervention. The War on Terror justified a series of sweeping changes in how the government approached security and civil liberties. Domestically, the passage of the USA PATRIOT Act in October 2001 gave the federal government unprecedented authority to surveil, detain, and investigate individuals suspected of ties to terrorism. The act expanded the powers of law enforcement agencies to conduct wiretaps, search personal records, and monitor communications without traditional legal oversight. These measures, intended to prevent future attacks, sparked intense debate over the balance between national security and personal freedom. Critics argued that the PATRIOT Act and similar policies eroded civil liberties and opened the door to government overreach.

Another significant shift in U.S. policy was the use of enhanced interrogation techniques, which many viewed as torture. In the wake of 9/11, detainees captured in the War on Terror were held in facilities like Guantanamo Bay and secret CIA black sites, where harsh interrogation methods were employed in an effort to extract intelligence. These practices, which included waterboarding, stress positions, and sleep deprivation, were justified by the government as necessary for protecting the nation from further attacks. However, reports of abuse and the legal ambiguity surrounding the detainees' rights led to widespread condemnation, both domestically and internationally.

The moral and legal implications of these practices would become a defining controversy of the post-9/11 era.

Beyond the battlefield and the domestic front, the War on Terror fundamentally reshaped global politics. It fostered a climate of fear and suspicion that permeated international relations, particularly between the West and the Muslim world. U.S. military interventions in the Middle East were viewed by many in the region as acts of aggression, fueling anti-American sentiment and contributing to the rise of insurgent groups and extremist ideologies. Far from quelling terrorism, the War on Terror appeared to exacerbate it, as new groups like the Islamic State (ISIS) emerged in the power vacuums left by the U.S.-led interventions.

The impact of the War on Terror on U.S. foreign policy was also felt in the erosion of America's global standing. Once seen as a beacon of democracy and human rights, the U.S. faced growing criticism from allies and adversaries alike for its handling of the wars in Afghanistan and Iraq, its treatment of detainees, and its expansive surveillance programs. The invasion of Iraq, in particular, strained relationships with key allies who had opposed the war, such as France and Germany, and led to questions about the legitimacy of U.S. leadership on the global stage.

Domestically, the War on Terror led to a profound transformation in American society. A new culture of fear took hold, where terrorism was perceived as an ever-present threat, and national security became a top priority. The expansion of government surveillance, the militarization of law enforcement, and the emphasis on securing borders and infrastructure were all part of this new normal. The years following 9/11 saw a shift in public attitudes toward privacy and civil liberties, with many Americans willing to sacrifice certain freedoms in exchange for a sense of safety.

The legacy of the War on Terror is complex and far-reaching. It redefined the U.S. approach to foreign policy, created new conflicts, and sparked a debate about the balance between security and freedom that continues to this day. While the War on Terror was launched in response to the attacks of September 11, it evolved into something far greater—an expansive and ongoing struggle that has reshaped the world in ways that could not have been foreseen in the immediate aftermath of the attacks. For many, it has raised enduring questions about the true cost of security and the moral and political implications of waging a seemingly endless war.

Chapter 2: Historical Precedents for Government Co

The Gulf of Tonkin Incident

On August 2, 1964, reports came in that two U.S. Navy destroyers, the *USS Maddox* and the *USS Turner Joy*, had been attacked by North Vietnamese forces in the Gulf of Tonkin, off the coast of Vietnam. Just two days later, another report surfaced claiming that these same ships had been targeted in a second, unprovoked attack. The Lyndon B. Johnson administration seized on this event as a clear act of aggression by North Vietnam, portraying it as the beginning of hostile actions that demanded a swift military response. Within days, President Johnson went before Congress, calling for immediate measures to defend U.S. interests in Southeast Asia. Congress obliged, passing the Gulf of Tonkin Resolution on August 7, 1964, granting the president broad powers to wage war in Vietnam.

This resolution marked the official start of full-scale U.S. involvement in the Vietnam War. It was presented to the American public as a necessary response to unprovoked aggression, a matter of national security, and a defense of democratic values. However, as the war dragged on and casualties mounted, questions began to arise about the legitimacy of the Gulf of Tonkin incident itself. Over time, evidence emerged that the details of the alleged attacks had been exaggerated, manipulated, and in some cases, outright fabricated to justify the escalation of the war.

The initial reports of the August 2 attack on the *USS Maddox* were based on radar and sonar readings, which suggested that North Vietnamese torpedo boats had fired upon the destroyer. In reality, the Maddox had been conducting reconnaissance missions close to North Vietnamese waters as part of a covert intelligence-gathering operation. While there was some exchange of fire between the Maddox and a few North Vietnamese patrol boats, the incident was far less significant than it was made out to be. The second attack, which allegedly occurred on August 4, turned out to be even more dubious. Radar signals and sonar pings were misinterpreted as enemy torpedoes, and it was later revealed that no actual North Vietnamese boats were present during this so-called "attack." Despite this, both incidents were used to create a sense of imminent threat that demanded immediate military action.

The Johnson administration's presentation of the Gulf of Tonkin events to Congress and the public played a pivotal role in securing support for the Vietnam War. The media uncritically reported the official story, with headlines proclaiming that the U.S. had been attacked without provocation. This narrative was used to frame North Vietnam as the aggressor and the U.S. as a defender of freedom, setting the stage for a decade-long conflict that would cost the lives of over 58,000 Americans and millions of Vietnamese.

Years later, documents and recordings were declassified that confirmed what many had long suspected: the Gulf of Tonkin incident had been, at best, a misunderstanding, and at worst, a deliberate manipulation of the facts. The Johnson administration had been looking for a reason to escalate its involvement in Vietnam, and the Gulf of Tonkin provided the perfect pretext. Secretary of Defense Robert McNamara, in private conversations, acknowledged that there was significant doubt about whether the second attack had occurred at all. Despite this uncertainty, the administration pressed forward, knowing that the political momentum was on their side.

The Gulf of Tonkin incident became a textbook example of how governments can use or manufacture crises to justify military intervention. By inflating the threat posed by North Vietnam, the Johnson administration was able to secure public and congressional support for a war that many Americans might have otherwise opposed. This manipulation of facts and the rapid escalation that followed would later become a source of deep distrust between the American public and its government, fueling the anti-war movement and leading to widespread skepticism of official narratives.

For those who believe that 9/11 may have been similarly exploited—or even orchestrated—by elements within the U.S. government, the Gulf of Tonkin incident provides a powerful historical precedent. It demonstrates how a government, when faced with the opportunity to advance its strategic goals, can manipulate or distort information to create a sense of urgency and fear. In the case of Vietnam, this distortion led to a long and costly war that many historians now view as both unjustified and unnecessary.

The legacy of the Gulf of Tonkin incident lingers in the collective memory of those who question the official accounts of major national security events. It serves as a reminder that governments, even democratically elected ones, may not always act in the transparent, honest, and accountable manner that the public expects. When viewed in the context of 9/11, the Gulf of Tonkin raises uncomfortable but important questions: How much of what we are told is true? How much of it is shaped by political or military objectives? And most crucially, to what extent are we, as citizens, willing to trust our leaders when they tell us we are under threat?

In exploring these historical parallels, it becomes clear that the idea of governments fabricating or exaggerating events to serve larger political goals is not without precedent. Whether or not the events of September 11, 2001, fit this pattern is a question that continues to divide opinion. But what the Gulf of Tonkin shows us is that skepticism of official narratives is not only justified but sometimes necessary to prevent governments from leading their citizens into unjust wars.

Operation Northwoods

In 1962, a chilling proposal was put forward by senior officials in the U.S. Department of Defense: a plan to stage terrorist attacks on American soil, with the goal of blaming them on Cuba and justifying military intervention. This plan, known as Operation Northwoods, was part of a larger strategy to overthrow Fidel Castro's communist regime, which had become a thorn in the side of U.S. foreign policy during the height of the Cold War. Although the operation was never carried out, the mere fact that such a proposal was seriously considered at the highest levels of government reveals a disturbing willingness to deceive the American public to achieve political and military objectives.

Operation Northwoods was born out of the frustration and desperation that followed the failed Bay of Pigs invasion in 1961. The U.S. had already attempted to oust Castro by supporting Cuban exiles in a poorly executed invasion that ended in disaster, severely damaging American credibility and emboldening the Castro regime. In response, the U.S. military and intelligence agencies began exploring more aggressive tactics to justify military action against Cuba, believing that only direct intervention could remove Castro from power.

The details of Operation Northwoods were laid out in a document drafted by the Joint Chiefs of Staff and presented to Secretary of Defense Robert McNamara. The plan called for a series of false-flag operations designed to create the illusion that Cuba posed a direct threat to the United States. These operations included ideas that, in hindsight, seem almost unbelievable in their audacity. The military proposed staging bombings in U.S. cities, orchestrating hijackings of American airplanes, and even sinking a U.S. naval vessel—all while making it appear that Cuba was behind these acts of terror. One of the more extreme suggestions involved painting a U.S. aircraft to look like a Cuban MIG fighter jet and using it to attack civilian or military targets, which would then be blamed on the Cuban government.

Perhaps the most shocking aspect of Operation Northwoods is how methodically and coldly the proposal outlined the steps required to deceive the American people and the international community. The plan included specific scenarios for how to stage the attacks and manipulate public opinion. For instance, it recommended producing fake lists of casualties, releasing doctored photographs of wrecked planes, and using the media to disseminate false information. The goal was clear: to create a wave of outrage and fear that would rally public support for a U.S. invasion of Cuba.

Fortunately, Operation Northwoods never advanced beyond the planning stage. When the proposal reached President John F. Kennedy, he rejected it outright, refusing to endorse such extreme measures. However, the existence of the plan was kept secret for decades, only coming to light in the 1990s when declassified documents revealed its full scope. For conspiracy theorists and skeptics of government transparency, Operation

Northwoods became a symbol of the lengths to which the U.S. government was willing to go in pursuit of its geopolitical goals.

The significance of Operation Northwoods cannot be overstated. It serves as a concrete example of a government contemplating the use of false-flag terrorism—attacks that are designed to appear as though they are carried out by an enemy, but are actually orchestrated by the government itself. The fact that high-ranking officials in the U.S. military seriously considered such a plan raises profound ethical questions about the potential for abuse of power in times of national crisis.

For those who believe that the attacks on September 11, 2001, may have been orchestrated or allowed to happen by elements within the U.S. government, Operation Northwoods is often cited as historical precedent. The logic goes like this: If the U.S. government was willing to stage fake terrorist attacks in the 1960s to justify military action against Cuba, could it not be possible that a similar strategy was employed decades later, using 9/11 as a pretext for the invasions of Afghanistan and Iraq? While there is no concrete evidence linking Operation Northwoods to 9/11, the plan's existence demonstrates that the U.S. government has, in the past, entertained extreme measures to manipulate public opinion and justify war.

One of the more unsettling parallels between Operation Northwoods and 9/11 is the use of civilian casualties as a means to achieve political ends. The planners of Operation Northwoods were willing to sacrifice innocent American lives to create the appearance of a Cuban threat. Similarly, those who subscribe to the 9/11 inside job theory argue that the U.S. government may have allowed—or even facilitated—the attacks to justify a broader military and political agenda. While these claims remain speculative, Operation Northwoods provides a historical basis for questioning the official narrative and considering the possibility of government deception in times of crisis.

Moreover, Operation Northwoods sheds light on the darker side of Cold War politics, where the fear of communism and the drive for geopolitical dominance often led to extreme and unethical proposals. The Cold War was a time when covert operations, disinformation, and propaganda were routine tools of statecraft. In such an environment, the line between protecting national security and manipulating the truth became increasingly blurred. Operation Northwoods reflects this mindset—a willingness to sacrifice the truth, and potentially human lives, for the sake of national security.

In retrospect, Operation Northwoods serves as a stark reminder of the potential for government overreach in the name of national security. It also raises important questions about the transparency and accountability of those in power. How can the public trust that their government will act in their best interests when such plans are conceived behind closed doors? What mechanisms are in place to prevent the abuse of power? And most importantly, what role does public skepticism play in holding governments accountable?

While Operation Northwoods was ultimately rejected by President Kennedy, its existence offers a troubling glimpse into how far governments might be willing to go to achieve their objectives. In the context of 9/11 and the wars that followed, this historical precedent underscores the importance of vigilance, transparency, and a questioning of official narratives. It reminds us that, while governments are charged with protecting their citizens, they are also capable of contemplating—and sometimes executing—deception on a massive scale.

COINTELPRO and Government Surveillance

From the 1950s to the 1970s, the FBI operated a covert program known as COINTELPRO (Counter Intelligence Program), aimed at surveilling, infiltrating, and undermining domestic political organizations. While its stated goal was to protect national security and prevent subversion, COINTELPRO became infamous for its unconstitutional methods and its targeting of groups that challenged the political status quo. The program's existence, initially secret, was only revealed in the 1970s, shocking the public and exposing the dark side of government surveillance in the United States. COINTELPRO's tactics and disregard for civil liberties serve as a stark reminder of how easily government power can be abused in the name of security and control, raising uncomfortable questions about the potential for similar abuses in modern times.

COINTELPRO began as a way to disrupt communist activity during the Cold War, but it quickly expanded to target a wide array of groups that the FBI considered radical or subversive. Civil rights organizations like the Southern Christian Leadership Conference (SCLC) and the Student Nonviolent Coordinating Committee (SNCC), as well as groups advocating for Black liberation, such as the Black Panther Party, became prime targets. Antiwar activists, feminist groups, and even environmental organizations were also monitored under the program. Anyone who challenged government policies, advocated for social change, or represented marginalized communities was viewed as a potential threat. COINTELPRO's broad scope demonstrated the government's willingness to view dissent as dangerous, treating political activism as something to be controlled and contained.

Under the direction of FBI Director J. Edgar Hoover, COINTELPRO employed a wide range of tactics to disrupt and discredit these movements. The FBI used informants to infiltrate organizations, collecting information and sometimes provoking internal conflicts. Agents planted false rumors, forged documents, and leaked damaging information to the press in order to create distrust and chaos within activist groups. In some cases, they actively sought to incite violence, hoping that internal strife or external pressure would lead to the collapse of these movements. These tactics were designed to be covert and deniable, leaving no clear evidence of government involvement.

Perhaps the most infamous target of COINTELPRO was Dr. Martin Luther King Jr., the leader of the civil rights movement. Hoover considered King a threat, not only because of his influence in the struggle for racial equality but also due to his vocal opposition to the Vietnam War and his advocacy for broader social and economic reforms. The FBI waged a sustained campaign to discredit King, wiretapping his phones, bugging his hotel rooms, and gathering information about his personal life. In one of the most shocking moves, the FBI even sent King an anonymous letter encouraging him to commit suicide, threatening to expose private information about his extramarital affairs. The extent of this surveillance and harassment highlighted the lengths to which the government was willing to go to silence dissent, even when it came from a leader advocating nonviolent social change.

The revelations about COINTELPRO, which became public in the 1970s after activists broke into an FBI office and leaked documents, sparked outrage across the country. Congressional hearings, led by Senator Frank Church, exposed the full extent of the FBI's illegal activities and led to widespread reforms. These included stricter oversight of intelligence agencies and new regulations on government surveillance. However, despite these reforms, the legacy of COINTELPRO remains a cautionary tale about the dangers of unchecked government power.

For those who believe that 9/11 may have been exploited—or even orchestrated—by elements within the U.S. government, COINTELPRO serves as a key example of how easily government agencies can justify invasive surveillance and covert operations under the guise of protecting national security. While COINTELPRO primarily targeted domestic groups, its methods—secret surveillance, infiltration, and disinformation—mirror the kinds of tactics that conspiracy theorists argue could have been employed in relation to the events of 9/11. The expansion of government surveillance powers after 9/11, particularly through the USA PATRIOT Act, further echoes the fears raised by COINTELPRO: that government agencies, in the name of security, may operate beyond the bounds of the Constitution and violate the rights of citizens.

In the wake of 9/11, the U.S. government implemented sweeping surveillance measures, many of which were justified by the need to prevent future terrorist attacks. The PATRIOT Act, passed in 2001, granted broad new powers to law enforcement and intelligence agencies, including the ability to conduct warrantless wiretaps, search private records, and monitor internet activity. While these measures were framed as necessary to combat terrorism, critics warned that they could be used to target political activists, journalists, and ordinary citizens with no ties to terrorism. The historical precedent of COINTELPRO gave weight to these concerns, showing that once the government gains new surveillance powers, they can be misused to stifle dissent and infringe upon civil liberties.

COINTELPRO also demonstrates how the government's definition of a "threat" can shift over time. While the program initially targeted communists during the Red Scare, it later expanded to include civil rights leaders, anti-war protesters, and other social justice activists. This shifting focus reflected the government's broader anxieties about maintaining social order and political control. Similarly, the post-9/11 War on Terror has raised concerns about the way "terrorism" is defined and used to justify government actions. The fear is that, just as COINTELPRO expanded its scope, the War on Terror could also be used as a pretext to target groups that challenge the government, even if they have no connection to terrorism.

The history of COINTELPRO serves as a stark reminder of the potential for government overreach, especially when fear and national security are invoked. The program's existence, once a closely guarded secret, was a betrayal of the public trust, and its exposure led to a widespread reassessment of the balance between security and civil liberties. As we consider the events of 9/11 and their aftermath, COINTELPRO stands as a warning: governments, even those in democratic societies, can abuse their power, and it is the responsibility of the public to remain vigilant, questioning official narratives and demanding accountability.

In the context of 9/11, COINTELPRO raises uncomfortable questions: If the government could secretly wage war against its own citizens under the guise of protecting national security, what else might it be capable of? Could the same justifications that led to the erosion of civil liberties during the COINTELPRO years be used again in the wake of a national tragedy? For skeptics of the official 9/11 narrative, COINTELPRO offers a historical precedent for how the government might manipulate events or use crises to advance a hidden agenda. While the circumstances may be different, the core lesson remains the same: unchecked government power is dangerous, and transparency and accountability are essential to preserving democracy.

The Iran-Contra Affair

In the 1980s, the United States government became embroiled in one of the most infamous political scandals in its history—the Iran-Contra affair. This complex, covert operation involved the secret sale of arms to Iran, a nation that was, at the time, under an arms embargo and considered an adversary of the U.S. What made this scandal particularly egregious was that the profits from these arms sales were then funneled to support the Contras, a rebel group fighting to overthrow the socialist government in Nicaragua, despite the fact that Congress had explicitly banned such support. The Iran-Contra affair is a stark example of how the U.S. government has been willing to operate outside legal and ethical boundaries to achieve its geopolitical aims, deceiving both Congress and the American public in the process.

The roots of the Iran-Contra affair trace back to two distinct foreign policy challenges facing the Reagan administration. First, the Islamic Revolution in Iran had dramatically shifted the political landscape in the Middle East, turning Iran from a key U.S. ally into a sworn enemy. In 1979, Iranian revolutionaries seized the U.S. embassy in Tehran, holding 52 Americans hostage for 444 days. In response, the U.S. imposed sanctions and an arms embargo, effectively isolating Iran. Despite this, Iran remained a crucial player in the region, especially given its ongoing war with Iraq, another country with which the U.S. had a complicated relationship.

Second, in Central America, the Reagan administration was deeply invested in preventing the spread of communism. Nicaragua, under the Sandinista government, had established itself as a socialist regime, which alarmed the Reagan administration, particularly in the context of Cold War tensions. The Contras, a rebel group fighting against the Sandinistas, were seen by the Reagan administration as a vital tool in pushing back against communist influence in the region. However, Congress, wary of getting entangled in another costly and morally questionable conflict, passed the Boland Amendment, which prohibited further U.S. assistance to the Contras.

Faced with these two challenges, the Reagan administration, led by key figures in the National Security Council, devised a secret plan that violated both U.S. law and official policy. Under the guidance of National Security Advisor Robert McFarlane, Lieutenant Colonel Oliver North, and CIA Director William Casey, the U.S. began selling arms to Iran, hoping that the sales would secure the release of American hostages held by Hezbollah, a militant group with ties to Iran. At the same time, the proceeds from these arms sales were diverted to fund the Contras in Nicaragua, circumventing Congress's explicit prohibition on such funding.

The operation was hidden from both Congress and the American public. The Reagan administration justified its actions under the guise of national security, arguing that the U.S. needed to keep its Cold War enemies in check. However, as with many covert operations, the truth eventually surfaced. In 1986, a Lebanese newspaper exposed the arms-for-hostages deal, leading to a full-blown investigation in the United States. What followed was a scandal that rocked the Reagan administration and revealed the lengths to which the government was willing to go to pursue its foreign policy objectives, even if it meant breaking the law.

The Iran-Contra affair demonstrated several troubling patterns in how the U.S. government operated. First, it showed a blatant disregard for the rule of law. By violating the Boland Amendment, key figures in the administration deliberately bypassed Congress, undermining the checks and balances that are supposed to prevent executive overreach. The affair also revealed the ease with which the government could deceive both the public and lawmakers, keeping covert operations hidden under the veil of national security. The idea that arms were being sold to a hostile nation like Iran, while illegal funding was sent to a rebel group in Central America, was shocking to many Americans, who felt betrayed by their government.

Second, the Iran-Contra affair illustrated the power of secrecy in government operations. The entire scandal was predicated on the fact that key actors in the Reagan administration were able to operate without oversight or accountability. The covert nature of the operation meant that decisions were being made in back rooms, shielded from the scrutiny of Congress and the public. This pattern of secrecy raised concerns about how many other covert operations might have been happening without public knowledge, and to what extent the government could be trusted to act in the best interest of its citizens when left unchecked.

For those who believe that 9/11 may have been orchestrated or exploited by the U.S. government, the Iran-Contra affair offers a compelling historical precedent. It shows that the government has, in the past, been willing to deceive both Congress and the public to pursue its own geopolitical objectives. It also demonstrates how easy it is for those in power to justify illegal actions under the guise of national security. Just as the Reagan administration used the Cold War as a rationale for its covert operations, some argue that the Bush administration used 9/11 to justify military interventions in Iraq and Afghanistan, expanding surveillance powers and launching the War on Terror.

The parallels between the two situations are unsettling. Both involve the manipulation of fear—whether fear of communism during the Cold War or fear of terrorism in the wake of 9/11. Both involve covert operations carried out without the knowledge or consent of the public, and both reveal a pattern of executive overreach in times of crisis. While the Iran-Contra affair is not directly connected to 9/11, it serves as a reminder of how easily governments can exploit crises to push through controversial policies, often at the expense of democratic accountability.

The Iran-Contra affair also demonstrated the resilience of government officials in the face of scandal. Despite the exposure of the operation, many of the key figures involved faced little to no punishment. Oliver North, one of the central figures in the operation, became something of a folk hero to some Americans, despite his role in orchestrating the illegal scheme. While he was initially convicted on several charges, these were later overturned, and North went on to have a successful career as a political commentator. The lack of accountability for those involved in the affair raised concerns about how easily government officials could evade responsibility for illegal actions, a concern that echoes in discussions about the lack of accountability for key players in the 9/11 aftermath.

In the end, the Iran-Contra affair is a stark example of how the U.S. government has engaged in covert, illegal operations to pursue its foreign policy goals. It serves as a reminder that even in a democracy, the government is capable of deceiving its citizens and breaking the law in the name of national security. For those who question the official narrative of 9/11, the Iran-Contra affair offers a historical precedent that fuels skepticism and reinforces the need for transparency and accountability in government actions, especially in times of national crisis.

The Gulf of Tonkin Incident

The Gulf of Tonkin incident, which occurred in 1964, is one of the most striking examples of how a government can manipulate an event to justify military action. This event, often cited by conspiracy theorists as proof of government deception, was a turning point in U.S. involvement in the Vietnam War. It led directly to the passage of the Gulf of Tonkin Resolution, which gave President Lyndon B. Johnson the authority to escalate the war in Vietnam without a formal declaration of war by Congress. The problem, however, is that the Gulf of Tonkin incident—particularly the second attack—may never have happened as it was reported. Decades later, declassified documents and admissions from key officials would reveal that the incident was exaggerated or fabricated, reinforcing the belief that the U.S. government had manipulated the narrative to achieve its geopolitical goals.

The official story of the Gulf of Tonkin incident begins on August 2, 1964, when the USS *Maddox*, a U.S. Navy destroyer, was conducting an intelligence-gathering mission off the coast of North Vietnam. The *Maddox* came under fire from North Vietnamese torpedo boats, leading to a brief skirmish in which the *Maddox* returned fire and successfully drove off the attackers. Two days later, on August 4, reports surfaced of a second attack on the *Maddox* and another destroyer, the USS *Turner Joy*. This second incident, which supposedly took place under stormy weather conditions, was later used by President Johnson as the basis for escalating U.S. military involvement in Vietnam.

In a televised address to the nation, President Johnson described the attacks as unprovoked and a clear act of aggression by North Vietnam. He presented the Gulf of Tonkin incident as an example of communist hostility that needed to be met with a strong U.S. response. Johnson asked Congress for the authority to take "all necessary measures" to repel further attacks and to prevent further aggression. In the political climate of the time, with the Cold War in full swing and the fear of communism spreading throughout Southeast Asia, Congress quickly passed the Gulf of Tonkin Resolution on August 7, 1964. This resolution effectively gave Johnson a blank check to escalate the war, leading to the deployment of hundreds of thousands of American troops to Vietnam and marking the beginning of full-scale U.S. involvement in the conflict.

However, the truth about the Gulf of Tonkin incident is far murkier than the official narrative suggested. Almost immediately, doubts began to surface about whether the second attack had ever occurred. The crew of the *Maddox* and the *Turner Joy* reported conflicting accounts of what happened on the night of August 4. Radar and sonar signals that were initially interpreted as enemy torpedoes were later questioned, with some crew members suggesting that they may have been false readings caused by the rough seas and poor weather conditions. Despite these uncertainties, military officials and the Johnson administration moved forward with the assumption that the attack had taken place.

Over time, evidence began to emerge that cast further doubt on the official version of events. Declassified NSA documents from the 2000s revealed that the second attack likely never happened. Internal communications from the time show that U.S. intelligence officials had serious doubts about whether North Vietnamese forces had engaged the American ships. Some reports even indicated that no North Vietnamese boats were in the area at the time of the supposed second attack. Despite this, President Johnson and his administration chose to present the incident as a definitive act of aggression to justify military escalation.

One of the most damning pieces of evidence came from a recorded phone conversation between President Johnson and then-Secretary of Defense Robert McNamara. In the recording, Johnson expresses doubts about the second attack, stating that "those damn, stupid sailors were just shooting at flying fish." Yet, despite these doubts, the administration proceeded with its narrative, and Congress quickly authorized the use of force. This deliberate decision to present an uncertain and likely fabricated incident as fact has become a textbook example of how governments can manipulate events to serve their political and military objectives.

The Gulf of Tonkin incident is a pivotal example for those who question the official narrative of 9/11. Just as the Johnson administration used the Gulf of Tonkin to justify deeper involvement in Vietnam, skeptics argue that the Bush administration used the events of September 11, 2001, to justify the invasion of Afghanistan, the subsequent war in Iraq, and the expansion of surveillance powers through legislation like the PATRIOT Act. In both cases, a traumatic national event was used as a catalyst for significant policy changes, with long-lasting consequences.

The Gulf of Tonkin incident also raises broader questions about the role of deception in shaping public opinion and policy. At the time, the American public and Congress were largely unaware of the doubts surrounding the second attack. They trusted the government's account of events, and this trust was used to push through a resolution that would lead to a decade-long, devastating conflict. In hindsight, the incident serves as a cautionary tale about the dangers of unchecked executive power and the manipulation of intelligence to achieve a predetermined outcome.

In the years since the Vietnam War, the Gulf of Tonkin incident has become a symbol of government deceit, particularly in the realm of foreign policy. It highlights the ease with which a government can manufacture or exaggerate a threat to justify military action. This historical precedent is often cited by those who believe that 9/11 was either orchestrated or allowed to happen by elements within the U.S. government as a pretext for advancing broader geopolitical objectives in the Middle East. While the circumstances of 9/11 and the Gulf of Tonkin differ, the underlying concern is the same: that governments can and have used deception to manipulate public opinion and justify war.

Moreover, the aftermath of the Gulf of Tonkin incident and the Vietnam War it helped unleash serves as a reminder of the human cost of such deception. The Vietnam War resulted in the deaths of over 58,000 American soldiers and millions of Vietnamese civilians. The long shadow of that war continues to influence U.S. foreign policy and public skepticism toward government narratives. The legacy of the Gulf of Tonkin incident underscores the importance of critically examining government actions, especially in times of crisis when the stakes are high and the consequences far-reaching.

In conclusion, the Gulf of Tonkin incident is a profound example of how governments can manipulate events to justify military action and shape public opinion. It serves as a historical precedent that fuels skepticism about the official narrative of 9/11, reinforcing the belief that governments are capable of using deception to achieve their geopolitical objectives. The incident reminds us that transparency, accountability, and a healthy dose of skepticism are essential in preserving democratic oversight and preventing the abuse of power, especially in times of national crisis.

Chapter 3: The Official Narrative vs. the Alternat

The Official 9/11 Narrative

On the morning of September 11, 2001, the world witnessed a tragedy that would reshape the political, social, and military landscape of the 21st century. According to the official narrative, as presented by the U.S. government and the 9/11 Commission Report, 19 hijackers associated with the terrorist organization Al-Qaeda carried out a highly coordinated and deadly attack on U.S. soil. The events of that day unfolded rapidly, and the sheer scale of destruction and loss of life shocked the nation and the world.

The attack began at 8:46 AM Eastern Time, when American Airlines Flight 11, a Boeing 767 en route from Boston to Los Angeles, was deliberately flown into the North Tower of the World Trade Center in New York City. The impact instantly killed hundreds of people inside the building and marked the beginning of what would become a catastrophic morning. Just 17 minutes later, at 9:03 AM, United Airlines Flight 175, also a Boeing 767, struck the South Tower of the World Trade Center. Both towers were soon engulfed in flames, and as the world watched in horror, the structural integrity of the buildings began to fail. At 9:59 AM, the South Tower collapsed, followed by the North Tower at 10:28 AM, reducing two of the world's tallest skyscrapers to rubble and leaving a death toll of nearly 3,000 people.

But the devastation was not confined to New York. At 9:37 AM, American Airlines Flight 77, a Boeing 757 that had departed from Washington Dulles International Airport, crashed into the Pentagon in Arlington, Virginia. The impact killed all 59 passengers on board and 125 people inside the Pentagon, further deepening the sense of national crisis. Meanwhile, at 10:03 AM, United Airlines Flight 93, a fourth hijacked plane, crashed into a field near Shanksville, Pennsylvania, after passengers fought back against the hijackers. It is widely believed that the intended target of Flight 93 was either the White House or the U.S. Capitol, but the bravery of the passengers prevented the plane from reaching its destination.

The official narrative, outlined in the 9/11 Commission Report, explains that these attacks were planned and executed by Al-Qaeda, a global terrorist organization led by Osama bin Laden. The hijackers, most of whom were from Saudi Arabia, had been living in the United States for months, some even years, preparing for their mission. They had received flight training and learned how to navigate the planes toward their targets. The report detailed how Al-Qaeda operatives meticulously coordinated the attacks, working in small, isolated cells to avoid detection by U.S. intelligence agencies.

The motivation behind the attacks, according to the U.S. government, was Al-Qaeda's desire to strike at the heart of America as retaliation for U.S. foreign policies in the Middle East, particularly its military presence in Saudi Arabia and its support for Israel. Bin Laden had issued multiple fatwas in the years leading up to 9/11, calling for violent jihad against the United States. The attacks were designed not only to cause mass casualties but also to serve as a symbolic blow against American power and influence.

In the immediate aftermath of the attacks, the U.S. government quickly identified Al-Qaeda and Osama bin Laden as the primary suspects. Within days, the Bush administration declared a "War on Terror," vowing to hunt down those responsible for the attacks and dismantle terrorist networks around the world. On October 7, 2001, the United States, along with its allies, launched military operations in Afghanistan to overthrow the Taliban regime, which had provided safe haven to bin Laden and Al-Qaeda.

The 9/11 Commission, formed in late 2002 to investigate the events of September 11, sought to provide a comprehensive account of how the attacks were carried out and how they could have been prevented. The Commission's final report, released in 2004, concluded that the attacks were a result of a failure in intelligence gathering, coordination between agencies, and a lack of preparedness for the kind of asymmetric threat posed by Al-Qaeda. The report did not implicate any members of the U.S. government in facilitating or allowing the attacks to happen but rather emphasized the systemic failures that allowed the plot to succeed.

For many Americans, this official narrative became the accepted explanation of 9/11. It was a straightforward, if devastating, account of how a well-funded and ideologically motivated terrorist group had exploited weaknesses in U.S. security to carry out a devastating attack. The narrative also fit neatly into the broader context of the post-Cold War world, where the primary threat to U.S. security shifted from state actors like the Soviet Union to non-state actors like terrorist organizations. In the years that followed, the War on Terror would become the defining mission of U.S. foreign policy, shaping military, diplomatic, and domestic security strategies for decades.

However, from the very beginning, there were those who questioned the official narrative. Skeptics pointed to what they saw as inconsistencies in the 9/11 Commission Report and raised concerns about the U.S. government's role in the lead-up to the attacks. While the mainstream media and much of the public accepted the official story, a growing number of alternative theories began to emerge, challenging key aspects of the narrative. These alternative views, ranging from questions about the collapse of the Twin Towers to allegations of government complicity, would form the basis of a larger movement that sought to re-examine the events of that fateful day.

But the official narrative, as laid out by the U.S. government, remains the most widely accepted account of 9/11. For millions of Americans, it provided a clear explanation of an otherwise incomprehensible event, one that justified the subsequent military actions in Afghanistan and Iraq, as well as the sweeping changes in domestic security policy. The tragedy of 9/11 became a pivotal moment in U.S. history, one that still reverberates in the collective memory of the nation and the world. The attacks were not only a massive loss of life but also a symbolic attack on American values, power, and security, giving rise to a new era of global conflict and domestic fear.

Questioning the Official Story

From the moment the dust began to settle after the attacks of September 11, 2001, questions started to arise. While the majority of Americans accepted the official account provided by the U.S. government and reinforced by the media, a growing number of individuals and groups began to voice doubts. These doubts centered not only on the sequence of events but also on the broader narrative of how and why the attacks occurred. This skepticism, which started with individual voices, soon coalesced into a movement of people who sought to re-examine the official story of 9/11.

One of the first areas of concern was the failure of the U.S. intelligence community to prevent the attacks. How could 19 hijackers, many of whom had been flagged by intelligence agencies, carry out such a coordinated assault without raising alarm? Critics of the official narrative pointed to a series of warning signs that seemed to have been ignored or mishandled. For instance, in the months leading up to 9/11, there had been reports of unusual activity by some of the hijackers, such as suspicious flight training and travel patterns. Even before that, U.S. intelligence had been tracking Osama bin Laden and Al-Qaeda's growing threat for years, yet the plot went undetected.

The 9/11 Commission Report, while thorough in many respects, left some of these questions unresolved. It acknowledged that the attacks were the result of an "intelligence failure," a conclusion that seemed insufficient to some. For skeptics, this explanation felt too simplistic for an event of such magnitude. How could the most powerful intelligence apparatus in the world, one that had successfully countered numerous threats during the Cold War, fail so spectacularly? Was it merely incompetence, or was something more deliberate at play?

These early doubts gave rise to a key question: Could elements within the U.S. government or intelligence community have known about the attacks in advance and allowed them to happen? This idea, known as the "LIHOP" (Let It Happen on Purpose) theory, suggested that certain actors may have seen the attacks as an opportunity to advance specific political or military goals, such as justifying military interventions in the Middle East or expanding domestic surveillance powers. While this theory remained speculative, it tapped into a broader mistrust of government, particularly in light of past events where the U.S. government had either misled the public or acted deceptively, such as the Gulf of Tonkin incident during the Vietnam War.

Another area of skepticism focused on the collapse of the World Trade Center towers, particularly the collapse of World Trade Center 7 (WTC 7), a 47-story building that was not hit by a plane yet fell in a manner consistent with controlled demolition. For many, this was one of the most puzzling aspects of the day. The official explanation, as provided by the National Institute of Standards and Technology (NIST), was that WTC 7 collapsed due to fires caused by debris from the nearby Twin Towers. However, to those skeptical of the official narrative, the speed and symmetry of the collapse raised red flags. How could a building collapse so neatly and completely due to fire alone, especially when no steel-framed skyscraper had ever collapsed in such a manner before?

This line of inquiry spurred numerous investigations by independent engineers, architects, and scientists, many of whom found the official explanation lacking. These experts argued that the structural failure of the Twin Towers and WTC 7 bore more resemblance to a controlled demolition than to the natural progression of a fire-induced collapse. Some even suggested that explosives or other pre-planned mechanisms could have been used to bring the buildings down. While these theories remained controversial, they sparked ongoing debate and deepened public skepticism about the completeness of the official account.

The Pentagon attack also came under scrutiny. Flight 77, which struck the Pentagon at 9:37 AM, was said to have caused significant damage to the west side of the building, leaving a relatively small entry hole and scattering debris. Yet, some questioned how a Boeing 757, with a wingspan of over 120 feet, could have caused such localized damage. Skeptics pointed to the lack of visible plane wreckage in early photographs of the scene and questioned whether a commercial airliner had indeed hit the Pentagon. These doubts gave rise to alternative theories suggesting that a missile or smaller aircraft could have been involved, though these claims have been thoroughly debunked by independent investigators. Still, the lingering questions about the Pentagon attack fueled the growing movement of 9/11 skeptics.

Additionally, there was widespread confusion and frustration over the U.S. military's failure to intercept any of the hijacked planes. Standard protocol called for fighter jets to be scrambled in the event of a hijacking, yet on 9/11, four commercial airliners were able to deviate from their flight paths for extended periods without interception. The 9/11 Commission Report attributed this to communication failures between the Federal Aviation Administration (FAA) and the North American Aerospace Defense Command (NORAD), as well as confusion over whether the hijackings were part of a military exercise being conducted that day. For skeptics, this explanation was unsatisfactory. How could the most advanced air defense system in the world fail so completely?

All these unanswered questions and perceived inconsistencies in the official story laid the foundation for a broader movement of 9/11 skepticism. What started as individual doubts soon grew into organized efforts to re-examine the events of September 11. Families of victims, engineers, architects, political analysts, and ordinary citizens joined together to demand further investigation. This movement, often referred to as the "9/11 Truth Movement," sought to challenge the official narrative and raise awareness about what they believed were critical omissions and contradictions in the U.S. government's account of the attacks.

At its core, the questioning of the official story was driven by a fundamental desire for transparency and accountability. For many, the idea that a few extremists could carry out such a devastating attack without more government foreknowledge or involvement seemed improbable. The skepticism surrounding the official 9/11 narrative was not merely about rejecting the facts but about addressing deeper concerns regarding government secrecy, intelligence failures, and the potential for manipulation of public perception in times of crisis.

As the movement gained momentum, it would force a wider conversation about 9/11, one that extended beyond the tragic events of that day to questions of power, control, and the responsibility of governments to tell the full truth—even in the most painful of circumstances.

The Role of the Media

In the aftermath of September 11, 2001, the role of the media became crucial in shaping the public's perception of the attacks. From the first horrifying images of planes crashing into the World Trade Center to the continuous coverage of the aftermath, the media was central to how people experienced and understood the tragedy. However, as time passed, some began to question the media's handling of the story. Critics argued that the media, in its coverage, largely parroted the official narrative without critical scrutiny, leaving many important questions unanswered and failing to explore alternative explanations.

On the morning of the attacks, major news networks like CNN, Fox News, and MSNBC went into live, nonstop coverage. The urgency of the situation meant that reporters relied heavily on official sources, such as government spokespeople, law enforcement, and military officials. Initial reports were chaotic and filled with speculation, but as the day wore on, a cohesive narrative emerged. Al-Qaeda, led by Osama bin Laden, was quickly identified as the perpetrator, and this explanation became the dominant story across all networks.

In the immediate days and weeks after 9/11, the media's coverage remained focused on the human impact of the tragedy, the heroism of first responders, and the swift governmental response. The narrative of a terrorist attack orchestrated by foreign extremists was presented as fact, with little questioning of the details. For most Americans, who were glued to their television screens, this framing made sense in the face of such overwhelming devastation. The images of burning buildings and collapsing towers were seared into the national consciousness, leaving little room for dissenting perspectives. In times of crisis, the public typically looks to the media for guidance, and the media delivered a message of unity, mourning, and resolve.

However, the speed and uniformity with which the media accepted and promoted the official story raised eyebrows for some. Within hours of the attacks, news outlets were already broadcasting information about the 19 hijackers and their links to Al-Qaeda. This led some critics to wonder how such detailed information had been gathered so quickly, especially considering the failure of U.S. intelligence to prevent the attacks. To skeptics, the media's rapid adoption of the official narrative seemed almost too smooth, as if the story had been prepared in advance. The question was: How did the media, which struggled to gather information in real time, so quickly align with the government's version of events?

Moreover, the media's role in reinforcing the official narrative extended beyond just reporting the facts. In the days following the attacks, the tone of the coverage became overtly patriotic. American flags adorned news studios, and anchors often made impassioned calls for unity and action. This atmosphere left little room for critical analysis. Anyone who questioned the official account risked being labeled unpatriotic or insensitive to the suffering of the victims. As the Bush administration launched its "War on Terror," the media largely supported these efforts, often framing military intervention in Afghanistan, and later Iraq, as necessary responses to the 9/11 attacks.

The media's reliance on government and military officials as primary sources further limited the scope of reporting. These officials, many of whom were involved in shaping U.S. policy, had a vested interest in presenting the attacks in a way that justified future actions. Journalists rarely challenged these narratives, and stories questioning the official account were often relegated to the fringes of the news cycle or ignored altogether. Mainstream outlets, such as The New York Times and The Washington Post, generally stayed within the parameters set by the government's version of events, lending further legitimacy to the official narrative.

At the same time, independent journalists and alternative media outlets began to explore discrepancies in the official story. Websites, documentaries, and small publications became platforms for those who sought to question the mainstream media's portrayal of 9/11. Early efforts by independent journalists to scrutinize the collapse of the Twin Towers, the unusual behavior of U.S. air defense systems, and the lack of clear evidence for certain claims were dismissed by mainstream outlets as conspiracy theories. These alternative viewpoints were often mocked or marginalized, which further discouraged any broader media discussion of inconsistencies.

In particular, the collapse of World Trade Center 7, a building that was not hit by a plane but still fell in what appeared to be a controlled demolition, received little attention in the mainstream media. Despite being a critical piece of the puzzle for those questioning the official narrative, WTC 7's collapse was rarely discussed on major news networks. Similarly, concerns about the military's failure to intercept the hijacked planes, despite the standard practice of scrambling fighter jets in such situations, were not thoroughly examined in mainstream coverage.

One of the key criticisms of the media's role in 9/11 is that it failed to investigate these anomalies with the rigor and persistence that would typically be expected in the face of such a monumental event. Critics argue that, by uncritically accepting the government's narrative, the media became complicit in shaping a one-dimensional understanding of 9/11. This lack of journalistic inquiry allowed the official story to go largely unquestioned by the general public for years.

As time passed, more independent investigators, engineers, scientists, and political commentators began to challenge the official account in various ways. Documentaries such as *Loose Change* gained widespread attention on the internet, raising doubts about the official story and bringing these questions to a broader audience. While mainstream media outlets eventually covered some of these alternative theories, they were often framed as fringe ideas without merit, further reinforcing the dominance of the government's version of events.

The role of the media in shaping the public's understanding of 9/11 remains a subject of intense debate. On one hand, news organizations fulfilled their role of informing the public during a national emergency, providing essential coverage that helped Americans process the shock and trauma of the attacks. On the other hand, critics argue that the media's close alignment with the government's narrative limited critical inquiry and suppressed legitimate questions about how the attacks unfolded and why they were not prevented. For those seeking a deeper understanding of 9/11, the media's handling of the story is seen as a missed opportunity to uncover the full truth about one of the most significant events in modern history.

Discrepancies in the Physical Evidence

One of the most contentious aspects of the 9/11 debate revolves around the physical evidence from that day—particularly the destruction of the World Trade Center towers and the Pentagon. While the official narrative attributes the collapse of the Twin Towers and World Trade Center 7 (WTC 7) to fire and structural damage caused by the impact of the planes, critics argue that the evidence does not fully support these conclusions. The speed, manner, and completeness of the buildings' collapse have fueled alternative theories, with many questioning whether the official explanation can account for the totality of the events.

The most prominent aspect of this skepticism focuses on the collapse of the Twin Towers. According to the official explanation, the impact of the planes severely damaged the structural integrity of the buildings, while the jet fuel ignited a series of fires that weakened the steel support columns, ultimately causing the towers to collapse. The National Institute of Standards and Technology (NIST), which conducted the official investigation, concluded that the combination of structural damage and intense heat from the fires caused the buildings to fail. However, this account left several unresolved questions that continue to puzzle skeptics.

One of the most debated aspects of the Twin Towers' collapse is the speed at which they fell. Both towers collapsed in near free-fall speed, meaning they fell almost as fast as an object would fall through the air. This led some to question how buildings with intact lower floors could have fallen so quickly if the upper floors were collapsing from structural failure alone. In a normal structural collapse, resistance from the lower floors would slow down the fall, yet the towers disintegrated from top to bottom in a matter of seconds. This observation has led some engineers, architects, and demolition experts to argue that the collapse more closely resembled controlled demolitions, where explosives are used to bring down buildings in a precise, vertical manner.

This theory was further fueled by the fact that both towers collapsed into their own footprints, with very little of the building structure remaining intact. The near-total pulverization of the concrete and steel was seen by skeptics as highly unusual. In most building collapses, large portions of the structure remain standing or fall to the side, but the World Trade Center towers were almost entirely reduced to dust and rubble. Eyewitness accounts from firefighters and other first responders reported hearing explosions inside the buildings prior to the collapse, adding to the speculation that something other than fire may have contributed to the destruction.

The collapse of World Trade Center 7 (WTC 7) has been another focal point of controversy. Unlike the Twin Towers, WTC 7 was not hit by a plane, yet it collapsed in a similarly dramatic fashion—straight down, into its own footprint—just seven hours after the towers fell. The official explanation given by NIST was that fires, ignited by debris from the nearby collapse of the North Tower, caused the building to weaken and collapse. However, critics argue that fires alone could not have caused such a symmetrical and complete failure, particularly in a steel-framed building. Prior to 9/11, no steel skyscraper had ever collapsed due to fire, and the way in which WTC 7 fell has led many to believe that it was brought down through controlled demolition.

This theory gained traction because of the precision with which WTC 7 collapsed. Videos of the event show the building falling in a manner consistent with planned demolitions, where the building is brought down in a controlled and deliberate way. In addition, the presence of molten steel in the rubble of both the Twin Towers and WTC 7 has raised further questions. Numerous witnesses, including firefighters and cleanup workers, reported seeing pools of molten metal weeks after the collapse, which led to speculation about the use of thermite, a chemical compound capable of cutting through steel. While NIST dismissed these claims, arguing that the molten metal could have been caused by normal fires, skeptics have pointed out that the temperatures required to melt steel are far higher than those typically produced by building fires.

The Pentagon attack also raised significant questions about the physical evidence—or the lack thereof. Flight 77, a Boeing 757, crashed into the Pentagon at 9:37 AM, creating a relatively small hole in the side of the building. This led to immediate speculation about how a large commercial airplane, with a wingspan of over 120 feet, could have caused such limited damage. Photographs of the Pentagon shortly after the crash showed very little plane wreckage, which raised doubts about whether a Boeing 757 had indeed hit the building. Critics argued that if a plane of that size had struck the Pentagon, there should have been more visible debris, such as large sections of fuselage, engines, or wings.

Additionally, the lack of clear video footage showing the plane hitting the Pentagon has fueled conspiracy theories. While numerous security cameras were in place around the Pentagon, only a few frames of footage were released, and these images do not clearly show a commercial airplane. Skeptics argue that the government has withheld crucial evidence that could clarify exactly what happened, and some have even suggested that the damage to the Pentagon was caused by a missile or smaller aircraft rather than Flight 77. Although these theories have been largely discredited by independent investigations, the initial lack of transparency regarding the release of evidence fed suspicion and distrust.

Moreover, Flight 93, which crashed in a field in Pennsylvania after passengers fought the hijackers, has also been the subject of scrutiny. According to the official narrative, the plane disintegrated on impact, leaving behind a large crater and minimal debris. However, some witnesses reported seeing debris scattered over a wide area, leading to speculation that the plane may have been shot down by the military, rather than crashing as a result of the passengers' struggle with the hijackers. The lack of clarity surrounding these reports, along with inconsistencies in early news coverage, has kept these alternative theories alive, despite official denials.

In sum, the discrepancies in the physical evidence surrounding the 9/11 attacks have been a central point of contention for those skeptical of the official story. While government agencies and independent experts have offered explanations for these anomalies, the sheer scale and complexity of the events, combined with the unusual characteristics of the building collapses and the Pentagon damage, have kept these questions at the forefront of the 9/11 Truth Movement. For those who doubt the official narrative, these physical inconsistencies suggest that a more comprehensive investigation is needed to uncover the full truth behind the attacks.

Government Secrecy and the Fight for Transparency

One of the most significant elements fueling skepticism about the official account of 9/11 is the perception that the U.S. government has not been fully transparent about the events of that day. From the initial response to the attacks to the years-long investigations that followed, critics argue that key pieces of information have been withheld, redacted, or obscured, making it difficult for the public to form a complete understanding of what really happened. The secrecy surrounding many aspects of 9/11 has led to a growing distrust in government, with some people believing that this lack of transparency suggests a deliberate cover-up.

Immediately following the attacks, the government's response was swift but not always forthcoming. For example, it took over a year for the Bush administration to agree to establish an official commission to investigate 9/11, despite public pressure from families of the victims and others who wanted answers. Even when the 9/11 Commission was finally created, the process was hampered by numerous challenges. Key witnesses, including then-President George W. Bush and Vice President Dick Cheney, testified behind closed doors, and their statements were not made available to the public. In addition, many documents related to intelligence activities before and after 9/11 were heavily classified or redacted when released, further fueling suspicions that the full story was not being told.

One of the most controversial areas of government secrecy involves the classified sections of the 9/11 Commission Report, particularly the infamous "28 pages" that were initially withheld from the public. These pages, which were eventually declassified in 2016, detailed possible connections between the 9/11 hijackers and high-ranking officials within the Saudi Arabian government. While the release of the 28 pages did not conclusively prove Saudi involvement in the attacks, it raised serious questions about the relationship between the U.S. and Saudi Arabia, and whether diplomatic or economic considerations influenced the decision to withhold this information. For skeptics, the fact that such critical information was hidden for over a decade only reinforced the belief that the government was concealing uncomfortable truths about the attacks.

Another point of contention centers around the destruction of evidence related to the World Trade Center attacks. In the months following 9/11, much of the debris from the Twin Towers was quickly removed and disposed of, with large quantities of steel being shipped to recycling plants overseas. This rapid cleanup, critics argue, may have destroyed important evidence that could have shed light on the true cause of the buildings' collapse. For instance, some engineers and demolition experts believe that closer examination of the steel could have provided more insight into whether explosives or other devices were used to bring the buildings down. The government's decision to prioritize the removal of debris over a thorough forensic investigation has been seen by some as an attempt to cover up evidence that could challenge the official narrative.

The secrecy surrounding military and intelligence activities in the lead-up to 9/11 has also drawn significant attention. One of the most pressing questions that remains unanswered is how U.S. intelligence agencies, which had been tracking Al-Qaeda for years, failed to prevent the attacks. In the months before 9/11, multiple intelligence agencies, including the CIA and FBI, received warnings about potential attacks on U.S. soil, yet these warnings were not acted upon. Internal memos, such as the now-famous Presidential Daily Briefing titled "Bin Laden Determined to Strike in U.S.," have since been declassified, revealing that the U.S. government had information suggesting a major attack was imminent. Despite this, no significant action was taken to thwart the plot.

For many, the failure to act on this intelligence points to either gross incompetence or something more sinister. Some members of the 9/11 Truth Movement have suggested that elements within the U.S. government may have deliberately ignored these warnings to allow the attacks to occur, thus providing a pretext for the subsequent wars in Afghanistan and Iraq. While there is no definitive evidence to support this theory, the lack of transparency from intelligence agencies has kept such suspicions alive. The CIA and FBI's unwillingness to fully disclose their activities and internal communications from that time has only deepened the sense that the public is not being told the whole story.

In addition to intelligence-related secrecy, there have been ongoing concerns about the lack of transparency regarding the financial aspects of 9/11. One area that has garnered particular attention is the issue of insider trading in the days leading up to the attacks. In the week before 9/11, there was an unusual spike in "put options" on airline stocks, particularly those of American Airlines and United Airlines, the two carriers involved in the attacks. A put option is a financial instrument that allows investors to profit when a company's stock price falls, leading some to speculate that individuals with foreknowledge of the attacks placed these bets to capitalize on the impending disaster. The 9/11 Commission looked into these allegations but ultimately concluded that there was no evidence of insider trading. However, many skeptics remain unconvinced, pointing to the lack of detailed investigations into certain financial transactions and the swift dismissal of this line of inquiry.

In the years since 9/11, various Freedom of Information Act (FOIA) requests have been filed by journalists, activists, and researchers seeking access to classified or unreleased documents related to the attacks. While some documents have been declassified, many requests have been denied, and significant portions of important documents remain redacted. This ongoing battle for transparency has become a central focus for those who believe that the full truth about 9/11 has yet to be revealed. Whether it is the details of intelligence failures, the potential involvement of foreign governments, or the destruction of physical evidence, the secrecy surrounding these issues has only deepened the public's mistrust of the official narrative.

The fight for transparency has been particularly driven by the families of 9/11 victims, many of whom have spent years demanding answers and accountability. Organizations like the "Jersey Girls" – a group of widows who lost their husbands in the attacks – have been at the forefront of efforts to pressure the government to release more information. Their tireless advocacy played a key role in pushing for the creation of the 9/11 Commission, and they continue to seek greater transparency regarding the events leading up to and following the attacks. These families, along with other activists, have argued that the American people deserve to know the full truth about 9/11, not only for the sake of historical accuracy but also to ensure that such a tragedy never happens again.

Ultimately, the secrecy and lack of transparency surrounding 9/11 have left many unanswered questions. While the official narrative may provide a plausible explanation for the attacks, the gaps in the government's account, the destruction of evidence, and the refusal to release critical documents have led a significant portion of the public to believe that more remains to be uncovered. For those who question the official story, the fight for transparency is about more than just solving the mysteries of 9/11—it's about holding the government accountable and ensuring that the truth is never hidden from the public.

Chapter 4: The Collapse of the Twin Towers

The Official Explanation

The official explanation for the collapse of the Twin Towers, provided by the 9/11 Commission and the National Institute of Standards and Technology (NIST), is rooted in the devastating effects of the airplane impacts, combined with the resulting fires. On the morning of September 11, 2001, two commercial airplanes, American Airlines Flight 11 and United Airlines Flight 175, were hijacked and flown into the North and South Towers of the World Trade Center. According to the official reports, the impacts severely compromised the structural integrity of both buildings, setting off a chain reaction that led to their eventual collapse.

The NIST report, which remains the cornerstone of the official explanation, begins by focusing on the immediate consequences of the plane impacts. Each plane, weighing more than 100 tons and traveling at speeds of approximately 500 miles per hour, tore through multiple floors of the towers. The collisions caused immense damage to the buildings' steel support columns and dislodged fireproofing materials that were critical for protecting the structural elements. In the South Tower, Flight 175 hit between the 77th and 85th floors, while in the North Tower, Flight 11 struck between the 93rd and 99th floors. These impacts destroyed a significant portion of the load-bearing columns on the perimeter of the towers, severely weakening the buildings' overall stability.

However, the impacts alone did not cause the collapse of the towers. The key factor that NIST emphasizes in its findings is the role of the fires ignited by the planes' jet fuel. Upon impact, the planes' fuel tanks ruptured, spreading thousands of gallons of highly flammable jet fuel throughout multiple floors. The ensuing fires, which raged uncontrollably in both towers, burned at temperatures estimated to reach up to 1,800°F (1,000°C). Although the jet fuel itself burned off within minutes, it ignited the contents of the buildings—office furniture, paper, carpeting, and other materials—which sustained the fires for more than an hour in the South Tower and nearly two hours in the North Tower.

These fires were catastrophic for the steel framework of the buildings. Steel, while incredibly strong, loses its structural integrity when exposed to extreme heat. According to the NIST report, the prolonged exposure to high temperatures caused the steel columns and trusses that supported the floors to weaken and warp. As the steel buckled, the floors above the impact zones began to sag, causing immense pressure on the remaining, already-compromised structure. In both towers, the combination of the structural damage caused by the planes and the heat-induced weakening of the steel eventually led to a critical failure.

NIST concluded that once the upper floors of the towers began to collapse, the massive weight of the falling sections initiated a progressive, or "pancake," collapse. This theory posits that as each floor gave way, it fell onto the floor below, creating an unstoppable chain reaction that brought the entire building down in a matter of seconds. The official investigation suggests that this progressive collapse happened so rapidly because the buildings' support systems were unable to withstand the downward force of the upper sections. As each floor failed, it added to the momentum of the collapse, resulting in the near free-fall speed at which both towers ultimately fell.

The pancake theory became a central explanation for the collapse, describing how the failure of a single floor could cause a cascading effect that would bring down the entire structure. The NIST report rejects the idea that explosives were involved, emphasizing that the buildings' collapse was the result of a unique combination of unprecedented factors: the severe impact of the planes, the widespread damage to the structural system, and the intensity of the fires.

However, the official explanation has not gone without criticism. Some have questioned the integrity of the investigations and pointed to potential gaps in the evidence. Despite these criticisms, the 9/11 Commission and NIST maintain that their findings represent the most comprehensive analysis of the event. Their explanation—rooted in the destructive power of the airplane impacts, the subsequent fires, and the resulting progressive collapse—continues to be the prevailing account of why the towers fell.

In sum, the official narrative offered by the government and supported by independent engineering analyses is that the Twin Towers collapsed as a direct result of the severe structural damage caused by the planes, compounded by the intense fires that followed. The official reports underscore that no buildings of this size and construction had ever experienced such extreme conditions, making the collapse of the towers an unprecedented event in modern history.

Structural Design of the Towers

To understand how the Twin Towers collapsed, it is crucial to first examine their unique structural design. The World Trade Center towers, completed in the early 1970s, were hailed as marvels of modern engineering. They represented not only the pinnacle of architectural achievement but also symbolized New York City's prominence in global commerce. At 110 stories each, the North and South Towers stood as some of the tallest buildings in the world, showcasing an innovative design that allowed for vast, open office spaces and unparalleled strength. However, the very design that made them revolutionary also played a critical role in their eventual downfall.

At the heart of the towers' design was a concept known as the "tube within a tube" structure. The towers were built with a central core of 47 steel columns that housed elevators, stairwells, and utility shafts. Surrounding this core was an exterior steel framework consisting of closely spaced vertical columns connected by horizontal beams. This outer "tube" of steel columns acted as the primary load-bearing system for the building, supporting the weight of the floors and protecting the structure against lateral forces like wind. The outer columns were spaced just three feet apart, creating a dense latticework that provided immense structural stability.

The architects and engineers behind the towers, led by Minoru Yamasaki and Leslie Robertson, designed this "tube" structure to maximize floor space by minimizing the need for internal columns. This innovative approach allowed for vast, uninterrupted office floors that stretched up to 60 feet between the outer walls and the central core, making the towers highly desirable for commercial use. The design also distributed the weight of the building more evenly than traditional skyscrapers, where internal columns would typically bear the majority of the load. The result was a building that was both strong and flexible, able to sway gently in the wind without compromising its integrity.

One of the most notable features of the World Trade Center's design was its ability to withstand external forces, including high winds and even the impact of an airplane. In fact, during the planning stages in the 1960s, the possibility of a commercial airliner crashing into the towers was considered by the design team. Robertson himself once remarked that the towers were engineered to survive the impact of a Boeing 707, the largest commercial plane at the time. The expectation was that if a plane accidentally hit one of the towers, the building would absorb the impact, much like how a screen absorbs the force of a punching fist. The external steel columns were designed to act as a protective cage, distributing the impact and minimizing damage to the overall structure.

However, while the towers were designed to withstand an accidental impact, they were not designed to endure the catastrophic combination of a high-speed collision and the subsequent fires fueled by thousands of gallons of jet fuel. The structural engineers at the time did not fully account for the explosive energy released by the collision of a modern jumbo jet, nor did they anticipate the intense heat generated by prolonged fires. These factors, which were central to the events of 9/11, overwhelmed the buildings' original design parameters.

The steel columns in both the central core and the outer framework were coated with a fireproofing material intended to protect them in the event of a fire. This fireproofing was expected to prevent the steel from reaching temperatures high enough to weaken it significantly. However, the violent impacts of American Airlines Flight 11 and United Airlines Flight 175 dislodged much of this fireproofing material, leaving the steel exposed to the intense heat generated by the burning jet fuel and office contents. As the fires burned, the unprotected steel began to weaken, which led to the gradual failure of the floor trusses and the eventual collapse of the buildings.

Another critical aspect of the towers' design was their reliance on the floor trusses to connect the outer steel framework to the central core. These lightweight trusses spanned the distance between the core and the outer walls, supporting each floor's concrete slabs. While they were more than adequate to handle the normal loads of a typical office day, they were vulnerable to the intense heat generated by the fires. As the steel trusses heated up, they expanded and sagged, pulling on the outer walls and contributing to the instability of the buildings. In the South Tower, this phenomenon occurred more quickly due to the plane's impact being lower on the building, allowing the fire to spread rapidly across multiple floors.

It is important to note that while the design of the Twin Towers was considered cutting-edge for its time, it was also highly unorthodox. The decision to use the exterior columns as the primary load-bearing system, combined with the open floor plans and lightweight trusses, made the buildings remarkably efficient and cost-effective, but also left them vulnerable in ways that were not fully appreciated until 9/11. The very design elements that allowed the towers to rise so high and function so efficiently—open floors, external columns, and lightweight steel trusses—ultimately contributed to their catastrophic collapse when faced with a highly unusual set of circumstances.

In retrospect, the design of the World Trade Center towers was a double-edged sword. On the one hand, it allowed for a bold, unprecedented architectural achievement that transformed the New York skyline and redefined what was possible in high-rise construction. On the other hand, the inherent vulnerabilities in that design, when exposed to the extreme conditions of the 9/11 attacks, played a crucial role in the rapid collapse of both towers.

Eyewitness Accounts and Explosive Theories

As the world watched in horror on September 11, 2001, many of those present at the World Trade Center provided eyewitness accounts that would later become critical to both the official investigation and the formation of alternative theories. Among the most controversial of these accounts were numerous reports from first responders, survivors, and bystanders who claimed to have heard explosions before and during the collapse of the Twin Towers. These testimonies have been cited by proponents of the theory that the towers were brought down not by the impacts of the planes and the resulting fires alone, but by controlled demolitions using pre-planted explosives.

On that fateful day, firefighters and emergency personnel were some of the first to arrive at the scene. Many of them later reported hearing loud, booming sounds that seemed to resemble explosions. For instance, firefighter Richard Banaciski, in an interview following the attack, recalled, "It was like a boom, boom, boom—like a demolition going off." Other firefighters, such as Battalion Chief Orio Palmer, reported hearing explosions as they climbed the stairwells of the South Tower shortly before its collapse. These accounts, along with similar reports from survivors fleeing the buildings, have fueled speculation that explosive devices may have been planted inside the towers prior to the attacks.

The idea that controlled demolitions could have brought down the towers gained further traction when experts in the demolition industry began weighing in. Many noted that the way the towers collapsed—seemingly straight down into their own footprints—bore a striking resemblance to the way buildings fall during planned demolitions. Controlled demolitions are carefully engineered to take out key structural supports in a precise sequence, ensuring that the building collapses inward rather than toppling over, which minimizes damage to the surrounding area. The sudden, symmetrical collapse of the towers, along with the speed at which they fell, led some to believe that explosives could have been strategically placed to achieve this effect.

Proponents of the controlled demolition theory point to several pieces of circumstantial evidence to support their claims. One key argument revolves around the sounds of explosions heard by witnesses. These theorists argue that the loud bangs and booms reported by firefighters and others could not be explained solely by the structural failures outlined in the official explanation. They assert that the sound of explosives detonating would align with these accounts, particularly the reports of explosions heard in the basement levels of the towers before the buildings began to fall.

Another piece of evidence often cited by supporters of the explosive theory is the discovery of molten steel at Ground Zero. Some workers at the site, as well as firefighters and engineers, reported seeing pools of molten metal beneath the rubble weeks after the attacks. Theorists argue that the extreme temperatures required to melt steel could not have been generated by the fires alone, which NIST and other official reports claim did not exceed 1,800°F. Instead, they suggest that thermite—a highly incendiary chemical compound used in demolitions—could explain the presence of molten steel. Thermite burns at temperatures of up to 4,500°F, which would be more than sufficient to melt steel and could account for the molten metal found in the debris.

These explosive theories also draw on the work of physicists and engineers who have analyzed the collapse dynamics of the Twin Towers. Some researchers, such as Steven Jones, a former physics professor at Brigham Young University, argue that the rapid, nearly free-fall speed at which the towers collapsed could not have occurred without the assistance of pre-planted explosives. Jones and others have published papers asserting that the collapse of the towers was inconsistent with the natural progression of structural failure due to fire and impact damage. They claim that the buildings' cores, made of 47 massive steel columns, would have provided more resistance to the falling upper sections, slowing the collapse if it had occurred due solely to fire and damage. Instead, they argue, the speed of the collapse suggests the kind of sudden, simultaneous failure characteristic of controlled demolitions.

Despite these claims, there are significant counterarguments from engineers and experts who have refuted the explosive theory. NIST's investigation, which remains the most comprehensive study of the events, specifically addressed the reports of explosions and found no evidence to support the idea that explosives were used. According to NIST, the loud booms heard by witnesses can be explained by the collapse of floors within the buildings as the fire-weakened steel structure gave way. As the floors fell onto one another, the resulting impact would have produced sounds similar to explosions. Furthermore, NIST's analysis of the collapse mechanics concluded that the combination of impact damage and fire-induced weakening was sufficient to explain the rapid and symmetrical collapse of both towers.

The presence of molten metal, while still a subject of debate, has also been explained by official sources as the result of fires fueled by various materials found within the towers, such as office furniture, carpeting, and electrical systems. These fires, combined with the friction generated during the collapse, could have produced localized areas of intense heat capable of melting certain metals, though not necessarily steel.

In the end, the explosive theories surrounding the collapse of the Twin Towers remain one of the most contentious aspects of 9/11. While the official explanation continues to hold that the buildings fell as a result of structural damage and fire, the testimonies of eyewitnesses and the analysis of independent experts continue to raise questions. For many, the idea that explosives were involved fits into a broader narrative of government complicity in the attacks, adding yet another layer of mystery to the tragic events of that day. Whether these theories will ever be definitively proven or debunked, they remain a critical part of the ongoing debate over what truly happened on September 11, 2001.

The Speed of the Collapse and Free-Fall Debate

One of the most puzzling aspects of the collapse of the Twin Towers is the extraordinary speed at which they fell. Both buildings came down in approximately 10 seconds each, a rate of collapse that has been compared to free fall. This rapid descent, occurring with almost no visible resistance, has fueled significant controversy, especially among those who question the official narrative. The speed of the collapse is often cited by proponents of alternative theories, particularly the theory that explosives were used to bring down the towers, as it challenges the expected outcome of a natural structural failure.

The official investigation by the National Institute of Standards and Technology (NIST) offers a detailed explanation for why the towers fell so quickly. According to NIST, once the upper floors of each tower began to collapse, the immense weight of the falling sections created a downward force so powerful that it overwhelmed the floors below. The collapse started in the impact zone, where the structural steel had been compromised by both the plane impacts and the intense fires. As the upper portion of each tower began to fall, it initiated a progressive collapse in which each floor pancaked onto the one below, accelerating the collapse as it progressed.

NIST's explanation emphasizes the concept of "progressive collapse," where the failure of one part of a structure leads to the failure of the rest in quick succession. Once the upper sections began to fall, the floors beneath had no chance of resisting the combined weight and momentum of the upper floors. The steel columns and trusses, already weakened by the heat of the fires, gave way with little resistance. This phenomenon, according to NIST, explains the near free-fall speed of the towers' collapse. The official narrative asserts that the unique combination of structural damage, fire, and the immense weight of the buildings led to a rapid collapse.

However, skeptics of the official explanation argue that the near free-fall speed of the collapse suggests an absence of resistance that is inconsistent with a purely structural failure. In a natural collapse, they argue, the lower floors of the building—many of which were completely undamaged by the plane impacts or fire—should have provided significant resistance to the falling upper sections. This resistance would have slowed the collapse, resulting in a more drawn-out process. The fact that both towers fell at a rate close to free fall, they claim, is evidence that the lower floors were somehow weakened or destroyed before the collapse reached them.

The free-fall debate is one of the key arguments made by advocates of the controlled demolition theory. They point out that in a controlled demolition, explosives are used to eliminate the structural support of a building in a carefully orchestrated sequence, allowing the structure to fall straight down at a high speed. In their view, the sudden, symmetrical, and rapid collapse of both towers is more indicative of a controlled demolition than of a progressive structural failure caused by fire and impact damage.

Physicists and engineers critical of the official narrative have focused on the issue of resistance in their analyses. They argue that the towers' central steel cores, made up of 47 massive columns, should have provided considerable resistance, slowing the collapse as the falling upper sections encountered them.

The fact that both buildings collapsed at nearly the same speed from top to bottom, without any significant pauses, has led these theorists to suggest that explosives or some other form of intervention may have been used to weaken the core columns before the collapse reached the lower floors. They also argue that the lower sections of the towers were largely undamaged by fire and should have been strong enough to at least slow the descent.

NIST's response to the free-fall argument is based on the specific nature of the damage caused by the planes and the fires. In the South Tower, United Airlines Flight 175 struck the building between the 77th and 85th floors, while in the North Tower, American Airlines Flight 11 hit between the 93rd and 99th floors. In both cases, the impact zones spanned multiple floors, and the fires spread rapidly through these areas. The damage to the steel columns in the impact zones was severe, and the fires, which burned for over an hour in both towers, further weakened the structural integrity of the remaining steel. NIST asserts that once the upper sections began to fall, the weakened steel columns in the lower floors were unable to withstand the force of the collapse.

Furthermore, NIST's analysis emphasizes the role of the floor trusses in the rapid collapse. The lightweight trusses that supported the concrete floors were connected to both the outer steel framework and the central core. As the trusses heated up, they began to sag, pulling on the outer walls and causing the floors to fail in a cascading manner. This cascading effect, according to NIST, explains why the collapse progressed so quickly. The falling upper sections essentially crushed the lower floors in a domino-like fashion, with each floor adding to the weight and momentum of the collapse.

Despite NIST's detailed explanation, the speed of the collapse remains a focal point for critics. The controlled demolition theory, while rejected by official investigations, continues to resonate with those who believe that the free-fall-like speed of the collapse cannot be fully explained by fire and structural damage alone. The debate over the speed of the collapse and the role of resistance highlights the broader struggle between the official narrative and alternative theories, with each side presenting technical arguments in support of their conclusions.

Ultimately, the question of how the Twin Towers could collapse at such a rapid pace remains one of the most hotly debated aspects of 9/11. While the official explanation attributes the speed to a combination of structural damage, fire, and the unique design of the towers, alternative theorists see the near free-fall speed as evidence of something more deliberate. The competing interpretations of the collapse reflect the broader tension between those who accept the official version of events and those who continue to question whether the full truth about 9/11 has been revealed.

The Collapse of World Trade Center 7

One of the most controversial and least understood aspects of the 9/11 attacks is the collapse of World Trade Center 7 (WTC 7), a 47-story building located just north of the Twin Towers. Unlike the North and South Towers, WTC 7 was not hit by a plane, yet it collapsed at 5:20 p.m. on the afternoon of September 11, hours after the main attacks. The sudden collapse of this building has fueled widespread speculation, particularly among conspiracy theorists who argue that its fall could not have been caused by fire alone. To this day, WTC 7 remains a focal point for those who believe the 9/11 attacks involved more than just the planes and fires.

WTC 7 housed several government offices, including the Secret Service, the Securities and Exchange Commission (SEC), and the Mayor's Office of Emergency Management. It was built in the mid-1980s and was considered a modern, reinforced structure. On the morning of 9/11, the building sustained some damage from the debris that fell when the North Tower collapsed. However, this damage was relatively minor compared to the complete destruction of the Twin Towers. WTC 7 was primarily affected by fires that ignited inside the building, allegedly caused by the collapse of the North Tower.

The National Institute of Standards and Technology (NIST) conducted a detailed investigation into the collapse of WTC 7, releasing its final report in 2008. According to NIST, the building's collapse was the result of a unique combination of factors, including the prolonged fires and the failure of a critical structural component. The fires in WTC 7 burned uncontrolled for nearly seven hours, as the sprinkler system was disabled due to water line failures caused by the collapse of the adjacent towers. These fires weakened the building's steel structure, specifically a key girder on the 13th floor. NIST's report concluded that the failure of this girder triggered a chain reaction of structural failures, ultimately causing the entire building to collapse.

NIST's explanation of the collapse of WTC 7 is the only official account of the event, but it has been met with skepticism from many quarters. One of the main points of contention is the fact that WTC 7 is the only known high-rise building to have ever collapsed solely due to fire. Critics argue that the fires, while intense, should not have been sufficient to bring down a building of WTC 7's size and design. The building's steel structure, they contend, should have withstood the heat of the fires for a much longer period, and the collapse should have been more gradual, rather than the sudden, near-free-fall descent that was observed.

Adding to the controversy is the fact that WTC 7's collapse looked remarkably similar to a controlled demolition. The building fell symmetrically into its own footprint, a characteristic often seen in buildings that are brought down intentionally by explosives. This observation has led to widespread speculation that explosives were used to demolish WTC 7, just as some believe they were used to bring down the Twin Towers. In fact, several demolition experts, including those who have watched footage of the collapse, have remarked on its resemblance to a controlled demolition. The sudden, uniform descent of the building, combined with the fact that it was not struck by a plane, has fueled alternative theories suggesting that WTC 7's collapse was a planned event.

Theories surrounding the collapse of WTC 7 often point to certain inconsistencies and unexplained details. For example, a BBC news broadcast on the afternoon of 9/11 reported the collapse of WTC 7 over 20 minutes before it actually happened. In the live report, the news anchor stated that the building had already collapsed, while WTC 7 was still visible standing in the background. This premature announcement has been seized upon by conspiracy theorists as evidence that the collapse was premeditated, possibly part of a larger plan. The BBC later explained this as a simple error in the chaos of the day, but for many, the incident remains suspicious.

Another element of intrigue is the presence of several government agencies in WTC 7. The building housed offices for the SEC, which was reportedly investigating several major financial scandals at the time. Some have speculated that the destruction of records in the collapse may have conveniently erased evidence of wrongdoing. While no concrete evidence has emerged to support these claims, the fact that WTC 7 housed important government offices has only added to the suspicions surrounding its collapse.

Despite the questions and theories, NIST's report remains the definitive explanation for the collapse of WTC 7. The agency's investigation concluded that the combination of structural damage from falling debris and the prolonged fires was sufficient to bring down the building. NIST also addressed the "free-fall" argument raised by skeptics, acknowledging that the building did indeed experience a period of free fall during its collapse. However, NIST attributed this to the failure of the internal structure, which caused the outer walls to fall without resistance for a brief moment.

Still, for many, the collapse of WTC 7 remains an unresolved mystery. The building's sudden and dramatic fall, combined with the lack of a direct impact from an airplane, has left open the possibility of alternative explanations. Theories of controlled demolition, government cover-ups, and pre-planned destruction persist, fueled by the questions that continue to linger around WTC 7. Whether or not these theories are ever proven, WTC 7's collapse remains one of the most enigmatic and controversial aspects of the events of September 11, 2001.

The collapse of WTC 7, like the destruction of the Twin Towers, is a subject of ongoing debate that reflects the broader tensions surrounding the official account of 9/11. For some, the explanation of structural failure and fire is sufficient to close the case. For others, the unusual circumstances of the collapse, coupled with the building's high-profile tenants and the way it fell, point to deeper and more troubling possibilities.

Chapter 5: Follow the Money

Financial Gains from the Attacks

The September 11, 2001 attacks had profound economic and financial repercussions, not just for the average American or the global markets, but especially for certain industries and corporations that saw unprecedented profits in the aftermath. Among the most significant beneficiaries were military contractors, defense companies, and private security firms, all of which experienced massive growth as the United States launched the War on Terror. This rise in profits was fueled by an influx of government spending on defense, security, and military operations, sparking a financial bonanza for those tied to the military-industrial complex.

Immediately following the attacks, the U.S. government dramatically increased its defense budget. Between 2001 and 2003, the Department of Defense's budget ballooned by nearly $100 billion, with much of the additional funding going to military operations in Afghanistan and later Iraq. This surge in defense spending was accompanied by large government contracts being awarded to private military contractors and defense firms. Companies such as Lockheed Martin, Boeing, Raytheon, and General Dynamics saw their stock prices soar as the demand for military equipment, surveillance systems, and advanced weaponry sky-rocketed.

Lockheed Martin, the world's largest defense contractor, reaped significant financial rewards in the post-9/11 environment. The company was awarded billions in government contracts to produce fighter jets, missile defense systems, and unmanned drones. In the years following the attacks, Lockheed's revenue grew by over 50%, a clear indication of how the War on Terror became a major economic engine for the company. Other major contractors like Boeing and Northrop Grumman similarly saw their profits rise as they capitalized on the increased demand for military technology and aircraft.

One of the most high-profile beneficiaries of the post-9/11 defense boom was Halliburton, a company once headed by Vice President Dick Cheney. Halliburton's subsidiary, Kellogg Brown & Root (KBR), was awarded no-bid contracts to provide logistical support to U.S. troops in Iraq and Afghanistan. These contracts, which covered everything from building military bases to supplying food and water to soldiers, were worth billions of dollars. The company's revenue surged, particularly as KBR became the primary contractor for rebuilding infrastructure in Iraq, including oil facilities, roads, and government buildings.

Critics have pointed out the cozy relationship between Halliburton and key figures in the Bush administration, particularly Dick Cheney, who had been the company's CEO before becoming Vice President. Although Cheney claimed to have severed all ties with Halliburton, his former position raised ethical concerns, especially as the company continued to receive lucrative contracts. The perception of conflict of interest added to the growing belief that the wars in Afghanistan and Iraq were as much about enriching defense contractors as they were about combating terrorism.

Beyond defense contractors, the private security industry also experienced rapid growth in the wake of 9/11. Companies like Blackwater (later known as Academi) became household names as they took on roles traditionally reserved for the military. Private security firms were hired to protect diplomats, provide security for oil fields, and even participate in combat operations. These firms charged the U.S. government hefty fees for their services, leading to a boom in the private military industry. By outsourcing many aspects of military operations to private companies, the U.S. government fueled a multi-billion-dollar industry that continues to thrive.

The economic aftermath of 9/11 also saw increased spending on domestic security, which led to massive profits for companies involved in surveillance, intelligence gathering, and cybersecurity. The passage of the USA PATRIOT Act expanded the government's ability to monitor communications and gather data on potential threats, creating a surge in

demand for technologies that could aid in these efforts. Companies specializing in surveillance systems, data analysis, and cybersecurity, such as Booz Allen Hamilton and Palantir Technologies, saw their profits soar. These firms were contracted by the government to develop sophisticated software and tools capable of monitoring vast amounts of digital information, tracking potential threats, and analyzing patterns of behavior. The post-9/11 environment created a thriving marketplace for surveillance technologies, leading to a new era of mass data collection and intelligence gathering that benefited many private companies.

Another significant financial ripple from the attacks was felt in the energy sector, particularly in oil and gas. As U.S. foreign policy increasingly focused on the Middle East, the region's vast oil reserves came into sharper focus. The wars in Afghanistan and Iraq had geopolitical and economic consequences, with many arguing that securing energy resources was a primary motivation behind the U.S. invasion of Iraq. Iraq, which holds one of the largest oil reserves in the world, became a central theater not only for military operations but also for corporate interests seeking to capitalize on the country's resources. In the post-invasion period, several multinational oil companies, including ExxonMobil, BP, and Chevron, secured lucrative contracts to develop Iraq's oil fields, profiting immensely from the nation's reconstruction.

For these corporations, 9/11 was not just a tragic event but a catalyst for unprecedented financial growth. The military-industrial complex, which President Dwight D. Eisenhower warned about in his 1961 farewell address, expanded dramatically in the years following the attacks, as war, reconstruction, and domestic security became highly profitable enterprises. The surge in defense and security spending created a web of corporate interests deeply entwined with government policy, leading to significant economic gains for those positioned to benefit from the U.S. response to 9/11.

Critics have long argued that the financial beneficiaries of 9/11 played a role in shaping U.S. foreign policy, with some going so far as to suggest that the attacks provided a pretext for wars that were motivated as much by profit as by national security concerns. This perspective, while often dismissed by mainstream narratives, has persisted in part because of the enormous economic windfalls reaped by certain industries and individuals in the wake of the attacks. The phrase "follow the money" is often invoked to highlight how these financial gains might indicate deeper, more troubling motivations behind the decisions made in the aftermath of 9/11.

In conclusion, while the world mourned the loss of nearly 3,000 lives and grappled with the fear of future terrorist attacks, certain corporations experienced an era of financial prosperity.

The massive influx of government spending on defense, private security, and reconstruction efforts allowed a select group of companies to thrive, raising questions about the intersection of war, profit, and political power. For those examining the financial consequences of 9/11, the trail of money points to the significant influence that these economic forces may have had on the direction of U.S. policy in the years that followed.

Insider Trading Allegations

One of the most intriguing and controversial aspects of the financial aftermath of 9/11 is the allegation of insider trading leading up to the attacks. In the days and weeks prior to September 11, there was an unusual surge in the purchase of "put options" on the stock of major airlines, including American Airlines and United Airlines — the very airlines whose planes were hijacked during the attacks. These put options, which allow investors to profit when a stock's value declines, sparked immediate suspicion and raised questions about whether certain individuals or groups had advance knowledge of the attacks.

Put options are a financial instrument used by investors to hedge against potential losses or to speculate on a decline in stock prices. In the case of 9/11, the sheer volume of put options placed on American Airlines and United Airlines stocks far exceeded normal trading patterns, and they were concentrated in the days immediately preceding the attacks. This prompted investigators to consider whether these transactions indicated that someone had inside information about the impending disaster.

The most striking example was the unusually high number of put options placed on United Airlines on September 6, 2001, and American Airlines on September 10, 2001. The volume of put options on these stocks was several times higher than usual, suggesting that certain investors were anticipating a significant drop in the airlines' stock prices. This trading activity became even more suspicious when, in the aftermath of the attacks, both airlines' stock values plummeted, resulting in massive profits for those who had purchased the put options.

Investigators, including the Securities and Exchange Commission (SEC), launched an inquiry into these trades shortly after 9/11. The SEC worked alongside other financial regulatory bodies to analyze the trading data, track down the individuals involved, and determine whether any illegal activity had occurred. They scrutinized not only the put options on airline stocks but also other suspicious trades in industries that were directly affected by the attacks, such as insurance companies, financial institutions, and defense contractors.

Despite the apparent red flags, the official investigation into the alleged insider trading did not result in any conclusive findings of wrongdoing. The SEC ultimately concluded that the unusual trading activity could not be definitively linked to foreknowledge of the attacks. According to the Commission, many of the trades were traced to institutional investors and hedge funds that were making routine portfolio adjustments or hedging against broader economic downturns. Additionally, the stock market had been volatile in the months leading up to 9/11, due in part to concerns about a potential recession, which may have contributed to the spike in trading activity.

Nevertheless, skeptics have remained unconvinced by these explanations. Some point out that the timing of the put options and their concentration in the airline industry is too coincidental to dismiss as mere chance. They argue that the individuals responsible for the trades may have been tipped off by insiders within the government, intelligence agencies, or even within terrorist networks, who were aware of the impending attacks and sought to profit from the catastrophe.

Adding fuel to the fire of suspicion, some theorists have highlighted the fact that no individuals were publicly charged or named in connection with the suspicious trades, despite the extensive investigation. The lack of transparency around the results of the inquiry has only deepened doubts about the official explanation. For many, the absence of accountability or clarity reinforces the belief that there was a deliberate effort to cover up the involvement of powerful individuals or entities who had foreknowledge of 9/11.

Moreover, the investigation was hampered by the sheer complexity of tracking financial transactions across global markets. The stock exchanges involved in the trading were not limited to the United States, and the investigation required cooperation from regulatory bodies in multiple countries. In some cases, the individuals behind the trades used offshore accounts and shell corporations to obscure their identities, making it difficult to determine who ultimately benefited from the put options.

Beyond the airline industry, there were also suspicious trading activities reported in other sectors, particularly in companies that stood to gain from the chaos following the attacks. For example, some financial firms that handled the insurance claims related to the World Trade Center and Pentagon damages saw unusual trading patterns. Likewise, defense contractors and companies involved in homeland security experienced a surge in stock activity shortly before 9/11, raising questions about whether investors had inside information about the impending war and the expansion of defense budgets that followed.

The insider trading allegations continue to be a focal point for those who believe there was a deeper conspiracy behind the 9/11 attacks. For them, the unusual financial activity in the stock market is evidence that certain individuals or entities had prior knowledge of the attacks and sought to profit from the destruction. The idea that these trades were made in the days leading up to one of the most devastating events in modern history has fueled the belief that 9/11 was not just a tragic act of terrorism but also a financial opportunity for those in the know.

Despite the official narrative that downplays the significance of the insider trading allegations, they remain a lingering question in the broader debate about what truly happened on September 11. Whether these trades were the result of foreknowledge or mere coincidence, they serve as a reminder of the complex financial landscape surrounding the attacks — a landscape that, for many, suggests there is still much more to the story than meets the eye.

The Role of Saudi Money

One of the most contentious and controversial aspects of the 9/11 attacks is the question of who financed the operation, and a significant part of this debate centers on Saudi Arabia. Over the years, a growing body of evidence has suggested that the Saudi government—or at least certain influential individuals within it—may have played a direct or indirect role in funding the 9/11 hijackers. These claims have been bolstered by both government investigations and independent research, leading many to question the official narrative about the attackers' financial backing.

At the center of these allegations are the 28 classified pages from the 9/11 Commission Report, which for years were kept secret by the U.S. government. These pages, finally declassified in 2016, revealed troubling connections between several of the 9/11 hijackers and individuals with ties to the Saudi government. The hijackers, 15 of whom were Saudi nationals, received financial support from individuals linked to the Saudi royal family and government officials. This revelation has led to widespread speculation that elements within the Saudi government may have had prior knowledge of the attacks, or at the very least, helped facilitate the hijackers' ability to operate within the United States.

One of the most striking examples of this is the case of Omar al-Bayoumi, a Saudi national living in California who provided financial and logistical support to two of the 9/11 hijackers, Nawaf al-Hazmi and Khalid al-Mihdhar. Al-Bayoumi was reportedly a "ghost employee" of the Saudi Civil Aviation Authority, collecting a salary for a job he never performed. He was also suspected of having close ties to Saudi intelligence. Despite these red flags, al-Bayoumi met with Hazmi and Mihdhar shortly after their arrival in the U.S., helped them find an apartment, and provided them with financial assistance, raising serious questions about his role in the attacks.

Further complicating matters is the involvement of the Saudi Embassy in Washington, D.C., which has long been suspected of indirectly supporting the hijackers. Reports suggest that several hijackers received financial support from individuals connected to the embassy, including payments from Princess Haifa bint Faisal, the wife of Saudi Ambassador Prince Bandar bin Sultan. These payments, funneled through a Saudi intermediary, allegedly ended up in the hands of Hazmi and Mihdhar, though the Saudis have consistently denied any wrongdoing, claiming the funds were part of a charitable donation.

The declassified 28 pages also highlighted the presence of a well-established network of Saudi nationals in the U.S. who provided assistance to the hijackers. This network, which included diplomats, businessmen, and religious figures, appeared to operate under the radar of U.S. authorities, providing the hijackers with financial support, housing, and transportation. While the exact extent of this network's involvement in the 9/11 plot remains unclear, its existence raises significant concerns about how deeply the Saudi government—or at least certain elements within it—may have been involved.

In addition to the direct financial ties, there are broader questions about the ideological and financial support Saudi Arabia has provided to extremist groups over the years. For decades, the Saudi government has funded the spread of Wahhabism, a strict, ultraconservative interpretation of Islam that has inspired jihadist movements around the world. This funding, which has included the construction of mosques and schools that promote radical ideologies, has been linked to the rise of groups like al-Qaeda. Osama bin Laden himself, a Saudi national, came from a wealthy and influential Saudi family with close ties to the royal family, further complicating the narrative of Saudi Arabia's role in the attacks.

The U.S. government's response to the allegations of Saudi involvement has been mixed. On the one hand, officials have been careful not to accuse the Saudi government outright, likely due to the close diplomatic and economic ties between the two countries. Saudi Arabia has long been a key ally in the Middle East, particularly due to its vast oil reserves and strategic importance in the region. The U.S. has relied on Saudi oil and its cooperation in maintaining stability in the region, making the prospect of publicly implicating the kingdom in the 9/11 attacks politically and economically problematic.

However, the declassification of the 28 pages, combined with ongoing lawsuits from 9/11 victims' families seeking to hold Saudi Arabia accountable, has kept the issue in the public eye. These lawsuits, filed under the Justice Against Sponsors of Terrorism Act (JASTA), allow U.S. citizens to sue foreign governments for their involvement in terrorist attacks on U.S. soil. While Saudi Arabia has vehemently denied any involvement in 9/11 and has sought to have the lawsuits dismissed, the legal battle continues, with new evidence and testimonies surfacing over the years.

For those who question the official narrative of 9/11, the role of Saudi money and influence in the attacks is a critical piece of the puzzle. The financial and logistical support provided by individuals linked to the Saudi government, combined with the ideological backing of extremist groups, suggests a far more complex web of involvement than the U.S. government has publicly acknowledged. While the 9/11 Commission ultimately concluded that there was no conclusive evidence of Saudi government complicity in the attacks, the lingering questions about Saudi Arabia's financial ties to the hijackers have continued to fuel suspicions of a cover-up.

In the end, the issue of Saudi involvement in 9/11 remains unresolved. The declassified pages of the 9/11 Commission Report shed light on troubling connections, but they also raise more questions than they answer. For many, the possibility that the U.S. government has downplayed or ignored Saudi involvement due to political and economic considerations is a compelling reason to continue investigating the role of Saudi money in the worst terrorist attack in American history. The relationship between the U.S. and Saudi Arabia, shaped by oil, diplomacy, and strategic interests, may hold the key to understanding the full story behind 9/11.

The Missing Pentagon Trillions

One of the most baffling and underreported financial mysteries surrounding the events of September 11, 2001, involves the Pentagon's announcement of $2.3 trillion in unaccounted funds—just one day before the attacks. On September 10, 2001, then-Secretary of Defense Donald Rumsfeld made a stunning revelation: the Pentagon's financial records were in such disarray that they could not account for an astronomical sum of money, estimated at $2.3 trillion. This news, which should have dominated headlines, was overshadowed almost immediately by the events of the following day, leading many to wonder whether the announcement and the attacks were somehow connected.

Rumsfeld's disclosure came as part of a broader initiative to reform Pentagon accounting practices. He admitted that the Department of Defense's financial systems were outdated, inefficient, and prone to errors, making it nearly impossible to track how and where money was being spent. The Pentagon had been under scrutiny for years due to its opaque budgeting processes and massive expenditures, but this admission—of trillions of dollars simply missing—was unprecedented in its scope. Yet, within 24 hours, the attacks on the World Trade Center and the Pentagon itself shifted the public's focus entirely, leaving the question of the missing trillions largely ignored by the media.

What makes this revelation even more suspicious is the fact that one of the targets on 9/11 was the Pentagon itself. The section of the Pentagon that was struck by American Airlines Flight 77 housed the offices of the Pentagon's budget analysts, many of whom were involved in investigating the missing trillions. The attack killed 125 military personnel and civilians in the building, including many of the very analysts tasked with examining the Defense Department's financial discrepancies. The destruction of that particular section of the Pentagon, coupled with the timing of Rumsfeld's announcement, has led to widespread speculation that the attack may have been orchestrated, at least in part, to derail investigations into the missing funds.

The financial black hole at the Pentagon was not a new phenomenon. Over the years, the Department of Defense had repeatedly come under fire for its inability to pass an audit, despite being the recipient of the largest portion of the federal budget. Billions of dollars in contracts were routinely awarded to private companies without proper oversight, and many expenditures were either untraceable or labeled as "classified," making it difficult for investigators to follow the money. The Pentagon's vast bureaucracy and the sheer scale of its operations made accountability a significant challenge, but the $2.3 trillion figure announced by Rumsfeld represented a financial anomaly on a scale never before seen.

After the 9/11 attacks, much of the focus on the Pentagon's financial mismanagement faded into the background as the U.S. entered a period of heightened military activity. The War on Terror led to an even greater influx of money into the Defense Department, with little oversight or accountability, as the government prioritized rapid military response over bureaucratic efficiency. In the years that followed, the Pentagon continued to struggle with its financial records, and further investigations into the missing trillions were either stalled or deprioritized amid the chaos of the post-9/11 world.

Some skeptics have pointed to the missing trillions as evidence of a deeper conspiracy involving the military-industrial complex. The theory suggests that powerful interests within the defense sector may have been involved in a scheme to siphon off money for black-budget projects or other covert operations, using the chaotic aftermath of 9/11 as cover. The destruction of records and the deaths of key budget analysts in the Pentagon attack have only added fuel to this theory, as many believe that the investigation into the missing funds was intentionally derailed.

The idea of black-budget projects—secret programs funded by untraceable government money—is not new. For decades, the U.S. government has been known to funnel money into classified projects, often related to national security or advanced military technology, without public disclosure. The missing trillions at the Pentagon have led some to believe that a portion of these funds may have been diverted to such projects, with the 9/11 attacks serving as a convenient distraction to cover up the financial irregularities.

In the years since 9/11, the Pentagon's financial problems have persisted, with various reports revealing that the Department of Defense continues to struggle with accounting for its expenditures. Despite numerous efforts to reform its financial systems, the Pentagon has repeatedly failed audits, and large sums of money remain unaccounted for. In 2018, the Pentagon underwent its first-ever comprehensive audit, and the results were disheartening: the auditors found that the Defense Department could not account for more than $6.5 trillion in spending over the previous two decades. This staggering figure has only deepened the mystery surrounding the Pentagon's finances and has led to renewed calls for greater transparency and accountability.

For those who question the official narrative of 9/11, the missing Pentagon trillions represent a crucial piece of the puzzle. The timing of Rumsfeld's announcement, the destruction of key financial offices in the Pentagon, and the ongoing inability of the Defense Department to account for its spending all point to a potential cover-up of epic proportions. Whether the missing funds were used to finance covert operations, black-budget projects, or other nefarious activities, the fact remains that trillions of taxpayer dollars vanished without a trace—and the events of September 11 conveniently overshadowed any serious investigation into the matter.

The mystery of the missing Pentagon trillions continues to haunt the post-9/11 world, serving as a stark reminder that, even in times of national crisis, there are financial interests and unanswered questions lurking beneath the surface. While the official story of 9/11 focuses on the terrorist plot and the tragic loss of life, the financial irregularities surrounding the attacks suggest that there may be much more to the story than we have been told. The missing trillions, for many, are not just a footnote to the tragedy, but a key element in understanding the broader forces at play during one of the most pivotal events in modern history.

Profiting from War — The Military-Industrial Complex

The aftermath of 9/11 saw a dramatic expansion in U.S. military operations, with the War on Terror becoming the defining global conflict of the early 21st century. As American forces invaded Afghanistan and later Iraq, one sector experienced a massive windfall: the military-industrial complex. This term, coined by President Dwight D. Eisenhower in his 1961 farewell address, refers to the powerful alliance between the military, defense contractors, and the government. In the wake of 9/11, this complex grew exponentially, with defense companies, private contractors, and related industries raking in billions of dollars in profits. For many critics, this immense financial gain suggests that powerful interests may have had a vested interest in the wars that followed, and even the attacks themselves.

Before 9/11, defense spending in the U.S. had been steadily declining since the end of the Cold War. The attacks, however, created an immediate justification for a massive increase in military expenditures. Almost overnight, the defense budget surged, with hundreds of billions of dollars allocated to military operations in Afghanistan, Iraq, and other global theaters. The Pentagon became the beneficiary of an almost limitless flow of taxpayer money, with much of it funneled into contracts with private defense companies, security firms, and contractors specializing in everything from arms manufacturing to logistics and surveillance technology.

The first and most obvious beneficiaries were the major defense contractors, often referred to as the "Big Five"—Lockheed Martin, Boeing, Northrop Grumman, General Dynamics, and Raytheon. These companies, already dominant players in the defense industry, saw their stock prices soar in the months and years following 9/11. Contracts for weapons systems, aircraft, surveillance equipment, and military technologies ballooned as the U.S. geared up for sustained military operations. Lockheed Martin, for example, secured massive contracts for fighter jets, missile defense systems, and intelligence technologies, all critical to the War on Terror. The company's stock value more than doubled between 2001 and 2005, as did its profits.

In addition to the traditional defense contractors, the rise of private military companies (PMCs) marked a significant shift in the nature of modern warfare. Companies like Blackwater (later rebranded as Academi), DynCorp, and Halliburton's subsidiary KBR became integral to U.S. military operations, providing private security, logistical support, and even combat services in Iraq and Afghanistan. Blackwater, in particular, gained infamy for its role in Iraq, where its contractors were involved in numerous controversial incidents, including the 2007 Nisour Square massacre in Baghdad. Despite these scandals, the demand for private contractors soared, with companies securing lucrative contracts worth billions of dollars.

Halliburton, a company with close ties to Vice President Dick Cheney, became emblematic of the blurred line between government and private profit in the post-9/11 era. Cheney, who had served as Halliburton's CEO before becoming vice president, was instrumental in shaping U.S. foreign policy in the early years of the War on Terror. His role in pushing for the invasion of Iraq and his connections to Halliburton raised significant ethical questions about conflict of interest and war profiteering. Halliburton's subsidiary KBR received multi-billion-dollar contracts to provide logistical support to U.S. troops in Iraq, including everything from food services to building bases, and was accused of overcharging the government and engaging in corrupt practices.

For critics of the military-industrial complex, these financial connections are not coincidental but part of a broader pattern of profit-driven war. The idea is simple: wars create demand for military hardware, services, and technology, and defense companies stand to make enormous profits from prolonged conflicts.

The longer and more widespread the war, the more lucrative the contracts. In this light, the military-industrial complex has a vested interest in perpetual warfare, incentivizing the government to engage in and sustain military conflicts for financial gain.

The wars in Afghanistan and Iraq, both of which were direct outcomes of 9/11, became extraordinarily profitable for private industry. The Iraq War, in particular, sparked intense debate about the motivations behind the U.S. invasion. Officially, the U.S. government cited the threat of weapons of mass destruction (WMDs) and ties between Saddam Hussein and al-Qaeda, though both claims were later discredited. Critics argued that the true motivation behind the war was less about national security and more about securing oil resources and enriching defense contractors. The war cost trillions of dollars, with much of that money flowing to private companies with close ties to the U.S. government.

In addition to defense contractors, the tech industry also profited immensely from the post-9/11 world. The rise of the surveillance state, fueled by the Patriot Act and other counterterrorism measures, created new opportunities for tech companies specializing in data collection, cybersecurity, and surveillance technologies. Companies like Palantir, a data analytics firm co-founded by billionaire Peter Thiel, became central players in the U.S. government's efforts to track and prevent terrorist activities. Palantir's technology was used by the CIA, NSA, and other intelligence agencies to sift through vast amounts of data, looking for patterns and connections that might reveal terrorist networks. The company's government contracts grew significantly after 9/11, and its influence on U.S. intelligence operations continues to this day.

The confluence of government policy, private profit, and military operations has led many to question whether 9/11 was exploited—or even orchestrated—by elements within the U.S. government and private industry to justify endless war and generate massive profits for the military-industrial complex. While such claims remain speculative, the undeniable fact is that the events of 9/11 set off a chain reaction of financial benefits for certain sectors of the economy, with defense contractors and private military companies at the forefront. The intertwining of war and profit, as Eisenhower warned decades earlier, has only grown more entrenched in the post-9/11 era.

In conclusion, the financial gains reaped by the military-industrial complex in the wake of 9/11 have fueled suspicions that the attacks served as a catalyst for enriching a select group of companies and individuals. The wars in Afghanistan and Iraq, coupled with the expansion of the surveillance state, created a financial bonanza for defense contractors, private military companies, and tech firms. Whether through design or coincidence, the attacks provided the perfect justification for a surge in military spending that continues to this day. For many, the undeniable financial benefits accrued by the military-industrial complex serve as a stark reminder of the dangerous intersection between war and profit.

Chapter 6: Who Benefited from 9/11?

The U.S. Government and Expanded Executive Power

The immediate aftermath of the 9/11 attacks transformed the political landscape of the United States, granting the federal government unprecedented authority. One of the most significant beneficiaries of the 9/11 attacks was the U.S. government itself, particularly the executive branch. The terror and uncertainty that gripped the nation created an atmosphere in which swift and sweeping action was not only accepted but expected. This environment of urgency allowed the government to implement a series of measures that fundamentally expanded its power, some of which remain in place today.

The most notable legislation to emerge from this period was the **USA PATRIOT Act**, passed on October 26, 2001, just six weeks after the attacks. This sweeping bill was designed to give law enforcement and intelligence agencies greater powers to prevent future terrorist activities. But in doing so, it significantly eroded many civil liberties that had been protected under the Constitution. The Patriot Act enabled the government to conduct wide-ranging surveillance on U.S. citizens, including wiretapping phone calls, accessing email records, monitoring financial transactions, and even searching homes without the owner's knowledge or consent, all under the banner of national security. The act's most controversial provision, Section 215, allowed the government to collect "any tangible things" deemed relevant to a terrorism investigation, which later justified the bulk data collection programs revealed by Edward Snowden in 2013.

While the Patriot Act was the most well-known example of expanded governmental authority, it was far from the only one. In the days following 9/11, the **Authorization for Use of Military Force (AUMF)** was passed by Congress, granting the president broad authority to use "all necessary and appropriate force" against those responsible for the attacks. This vague and open-ended language allowed President George W. Bush, and subsequent presidents, to engage in military operations around the globe without the need for further congressional approval. The AUMF became the legal foundation for the wars in Afghanistan and Iraq, as well as drone strikes and other military actions in countries like Pakistan, Yemen, and Somalia. Even today, the AUMF continues to be used to justify U.S. military interventions, often with little oversight or transparency.

Another significant expansion of executive power came through the establishment of the **Department of Homeland Security (DHS)** in 2002. This new federal agency consolidated 22 previously separate government entities, including the Coast Guard, Secret Service, and Immigration and Naturalization Service (INS), into one vast organization tasked with protecting the U.S. from future terrorist attacks. The creation of DHS not only centralized national security functions but also gave the executive branch greater control over immigration policies, border security, and disaster management. The Transportation Security Administration (TSA), now a familiar part of air travel in the U.S., was also formed under DHS, changing the way Americans travel and perceive security threats.

In addition to these structural changes, **executive orders** became a powerful tool for presidents to bypass the usual legislative process, especially in matters of national security. Post-9/11, a series of executive orders authorized secret military tribunals for terror suspects, established detention centers like Guantanamo Bay, and permitted enhanced interrogation techniques, many of which would later be classified as torture. These measures, often carried out without judicial oversight, highlighted the growing power of the executive branch in defining and pursuing the War on Terror.

The implications of this expansion were profound. The American public, traumatized by the attacks and eager for protection, largely supported these measures in the early 2000s. However, as the years went by, concerns grew about the erosion of civil liberties and the abuse of executive authority. The surveillance programs initiated after 9/11 sparked debates about privacy rights, and Guantanamo Bay became a symbol of the extrajudicial detentions that many felt undermined the rule of law.

In retrospect, it is clear that the U.S. government leveraged the fear and uncertainty following the 9/11 attacks to expand its reach far beyond what had previously been considered acceptable in a democracy. While these powers were granted in the name of protecting the nation from terrorism, they also laid the groundwork for a more intrusive government. The expansion of executive authority after 9/11 set a precedent for future administrations, creating a legacy of power that endures to this day. Whether these measures were a necessary response to an unprecedented threat or an opportunistic grab for power remains a subject of debate. What is undeniable, however, is that the U.S. government emerged from 9/11 with far greater authority, fundamentally changing the relationship between the state and its citizens.

The Military-Industrial Complex and Defense Contractors

In the wake of the 9/11 attacks, the military-industrial complex — a term coined by President Dwight D. Eisenhower to describe the close relationship between the government, the military, and defense contractors — became one of the primary beneficiaries of the War on Terror. With the U.S. launching large-scale military operations in Afghanistan and Iraq, the demand for military hardware, private security, and support services exploded. As a result, defense contractors saw their profits soar as they secured billions of dollars in contracts for everything from weapons systems to logistics.

Before 9/11, the defense industry had been in a period of relative stagnation. The end of the Cold War had brought a reduction in military spending, and companies that depended on defense contracts were struggling to maintain growth. The events of September 11, however, changed that trajectory overnight. Within days of the attacks, Congress passed emergency funding for military operations, and the Pentagon began awarding contracts to defense firms. The subsequent wars in Afghanistan and Iraq, coupled with the global War on Terror, created a bonanza for defense contractors.

The so-called **"Big Five" defense contractors**—Lockheed Martin, Boeing, Northrop Grumman, General Dynamics, and Raytheon—were among the biggest winners. These companies quickly became indispensable to the military's efforts, providing everything from fighter jets and missile systems to surveillance technologies and military communications. Lockheed Martin, the largest defense contractor in the world, secured massive contracts for its F-22 and F-35 fighter jets, as well as missile defense systems. Boeing supplied helicopters and military transport aircraft, while Northrop Grumman played a critical role in developing unmanned aerial vehicles (UAVs), or drones, which became a cornerstone of U.S. counterterrorism efforts. These companies saw their stock prices soar, with their revenues closely tied to the duration and intensity of military engagements.

Beyond traditional defense contractors, the post-9/11 era saw the rise of **private military companies (PMCs)**, which played an increasingly prominent role in U.S. military operations. Companies like Blackwater (later rebranded as Academi), DynCorp, and Halliburton's subsidiary KBR became essential providers of security, logistics, and support services. These firms filled gaps left by an overstretched military, often taking on roles traditionally performed by soldiers. Blackwater, in particular, gained notoriety for providing private security in Iraq, where its contractors were involved in controversial incidents, including the infamous 2007 Nisour Square massacre, in which 17 Iraqi civilians were killed. Despite public outcry, private military companies continued to receive lucrative contracts, with little oversight and accountability.

Halliburton, a major energy and defense contractor, played a significant role in the reconstruction efforts in both Afghanistan and Iraq. The company, which had ties to Vice President Dick Cheney (who had served as its CEO before joining the Bush administration), was awarded billions of dollars in contracts to provide services ranging from building military bases to supplying food and fuel for U.S. troops. KBR, a Halliburton subsidiary, became the military's go-to contractor for logistics, benefiting enormously from the Iraq War. Halliburton's close ties to the government, along with allegations of overcharging and mismanagement, made the company a focal point of criticism for those who believed the war was driven, at least in part, by profit motives.

The **sheer scale of defense spending** in the years following 9/11 was staggering. Between 2001 and 2010, the U.S. defense budget more than doubled, from $287 billion to over $700 billion annually. Much of this increase was directed toward defense contractors and private firms, who provided everything from weapons systems to security services. The wars in Afghanistan and Iraq, as well as counterterrorism operations in countries like Pakistan, Yemen, and Somalia, ensured a steady stream of income for the military-industrial complex. By some estimates, U.S. defense contractors earned over $4 trillion in the two decades following the 9/11 attacks, with much of that money flowing to a small number of well-connected companies.

Critics of the military-industrial complex argue that this **profiteering from war** distorted U.S. foreign policy, encouraging military interventions that were not necessarily in the national interest but served the financial interests of defense companies. The profit motive, they argue, incentivized prolonged military engagements, with contractors benefiting from the ongoing need for military equipment and services. This concern was encapsulated in President Eisenhower's 1961 warning about the dangers of a military-industrial complex that, if left unchecked, could wield undue influence over government policy. The post-9/11 era seemed to confirm many of Eisenhower's fears, as the war on terror became not only a military campaign but also a business opportunity.

Another critical factor in the growth of the military-industrial complex was the role of **lobbyists**. Defense contractors employed vast armies of lobbyists to ensure continued government spending on military operations and defense projects. These lobbyists worked closely with members of Congress and the executive branch to shape policy, ensuring that defense budgets remained high. In many cases, former government officials, military officers, and even former members of Congress took lucrative jobs as lobbyists or executives within the defense industry, creating a revolving door between the government and the private sector. This close relationship between lawmakers and defense contractors raised concerns about conflicts of interest and the undue influence of money on U.S. military policy.

In conclusion, the military-industrial complex was one of the primary beneficiaries of the 9/11 attacks and the subsequent War on Terror. The demand for military hardware, security services, and logistical support created a windfall for defense contractors, who reaped enormous profits from government contracts. The close relationship between the government and the defense industry, along with the role of private military companies, reshaped the way wars were fought and financed. The military-industrial complex's influence on U.S. foreign policy became more pronounced, as defense spending surged and military engagements expanded globally. In the years following 9/11, it became clear that war, for many, had become a profitable enterprise.

Energy Interests and the Geopolitical Reordering of the Middle East

One of the most significant, though less overt, beneficiaries of the 9/11 attacks was the global energy sector, particularly companies and governments that stood to gain from the geopolitical reshuffling of the Middle East. The immediate response to the terrorist attacks—military intervention in Afghanistan and Iraq—had profound implications for the control and distribution of energy resources, especially oil. The Middle East, long known for its vast oil reserves, was at the heart of U.S. foreign policy well before 9/11. However, the attacks provided an unprecedented opportunity to assert greater control over these resources under the guise of national security and counterterrorism.

The invasion of **Iraq in 2003** was arguably the most striking example of how energy interests shaped post-9/11 military actions. While the official rationale for the war was Saddam Hussein's alleged possession of weapons of mass destruction (WMDs), many analysts and critics argued that securing Iraq's vast oil reserves was a significant, if not primary, motivating factor. Iraq possesses some of the largest untapped oil fields in the world, and control over these resources would not only benefit the U.S. and its allies economically but also strategically, by reducing dependency on other oil-producing nations, particularly those in the OPEC cartel.

Prior to the invasion, Iraq's oil industry had been largely closed off to Western companies due to sanctions and Saddam's nationalization of the oil fields in the 1970s. However, the removal of Saddam Hussein and the subsequent occupation opened up Iraq's oil sector to foreign investment, particularly by U.S. and British energy companies. Companies like **ExxonMobil**, **Chevron**, and **BP** were among the first to sign contracts to develop Iraq's oil fields, positioning themselves to benefit from the reconstruction of the country's energy infrastructure. **Halliburton**, the energy and defense contractor formerly led by U.S. Vice President **Dick Cheney**, also secured lucrative contracts to rebuild Iraq's oil facilities and provide logistical support to U.S. forces.

While the war in Iraq was officially framed as a necessary intervention to protect the U.S. from future terrorist attacks and to liberate the Iraqi people from a tyrannical regime, the economic benefits of controlling Iraq's oil were undeniable. In fact, some members of the Bush administration, including Cheney, had long advocated for increased U.S. access to Middle Eastern oil, and 9/11 provided the pretext to pursue this agenda. **Paul Wolfowitz**, one of the key architects of the Iraq War, famously stated that Iraq's oil wealth would help fund the country's reconstruction, further tying the military intervention to energy interests.

Beyond Iraq, the broader **geopolitical reordering of the Middle East** following 9/11 also served energy interests. Afghanistan, though not a major oil producer, held strategic importance for energy companies looking to build pipelines to transport oil and natural gas from Central Asia to global markets. The planned **Trans-Afghanistan Pipeline**, which would transport natural gas from Turkmenistan through Afghanistan and Pakistan to the Indian Ocean, was a long-standing project that had stalled due to political instability. The U.S. invasion of Afghanistan and the removal of the Taliban opened the door for renewed discussions about the pipeline, though the project has yet to be fully realized.

The war on terror also **reshaped alliances** in the Middle East, particularly in relation to energy politics. The U.S. maintained its close relationship with **Saudi Arabia**, the world's largest oil producer, despite evidence that 15 of the 19 hijackers involved in the 9/11 attacks were Saudi nationals. Saudi Arabia's strategic importance as an energy supplier and its influence within OPEC meant that the U.S. could not afford to jeopardize its relationship with the kingdom. In fact, the U.S. deepened its ties with Saudi Arabia in the years following 9/11, providing military aid and support for the kingdom's own security concerns, in exchange for continued access to oil.

At the same time, the U.S. used the War on Terror as an opportunity to weaken or destabilize regimes that were seen as hostile to Western energy interests. The overthrow of Saddam Hussein in Iraq, the continued pressure on **Iran** over its nuclear program, and the destabilization of **Libya** during the Arab Spring all had the effect of reshuffling the political landscape of the region, often to the benefit of Western energy companies. In many cases, countries that were previously closed off to foreign oil companies became more accessible, as new governments, eager for reconstruction aid and investment, opened their energy sectors to outside interests.

The 9/11 attacks also had broader implications for the global energy market. The uncertainty caused by the attacks, combined with the wars in Afghanistan and Iraq, led to **volatile oil prices** in the early 2000s. While this was a challenge for consumers and industries dependent on cheap energy, it was a boon for oil companies and energy traders who profited from price spikes. The instability in the Middle East, a region that produces a significant portion of the world's oil, meant that energy markets remained on edge, with prices fluctuating based on geopolitical events.

In conclusion, while the 9/11 attacks were framed as a tragedy that necessitated a global response to terrorism, they also provided a convenient pretext for pursuing energy interests in the Middle East. The invasion of Iraq, in particular, highlighted the connection between military intervention and access to oil, as U.S. and British companies benefited from the opening of Iraq's energy sector. The broader geopolitical reordering of the region, coupled with volatile energy markets, further underscored the role of oil and gas in shaping post-9/11 policies. For the energy sector, the War on Terror created new opportunities for profit and influence, while for many in the region, it reinforced the perception that U.S. foreign policy was driven by a desire to control the world's most valuable resource.

Wall Street and Financial Institutions

Another group that benefited significantly from the aftermath of the 9/11 attacks was Wall Street and the broader financial sector. Although the financial markets experienced immediate turbulence and shock following the attacks, with the New York Stock Exchange closing for four days, the longest shutdown since the Great Depression, financial institutions quickly rebounded and found ways to profit from the new economic realities shaped by the War on Terror. The attacks, and the government's response to them, created opportunities for investment firms, banks, and insurers to capitalize on war spending, security infrastructure, and financial deregulation.

In the immediate aftermath of 9/11, **defense stocks surged**, driven by the anticipation of massive military spending. Investors flocked to companies poised to benefit from the War on Terror, including defense contractors, security firms, and infrastructure companies. Wall Street analysts quickly identified the sectors that would see increased government contracts, and hedge funds, private equity firms, and institutional investors began to shift their portfolios to take advantage of the coming wave of defense and security spending. Companies like Lockheed Martin, Boeing, and Raytheon, whose stock prices had been stagnant before the attacks, saw significant gains as the government ramped up defense spending in the years that followed.

Beyond the defense sector, **financial institutions** also found ways to profit from the reconstruction and privatization efforts in Iraq and Afghanistan. U.S. banks and investment firms became key players in the rebuilding process, securing contracts for everything from infrastructure development to the privatization of state-owned enterprises. As Iraq's economy began to open up to foreign investment following the invasion, banks like JPMorgan Chase and Citigroup established footholds in the country, advising the Iraqi government on economic reforms and managing reconstruction funds. These banks, often acting in coordination with the U.S. Treasury and the International Monetary Fund (IMF), were instrumental in reshaping Iraq's post-war economy, ensuring that American and multinational corporations had access to lucrative business opportunities.

The **insurance industry** also experienced profound effects from 9/11. In the immediate aftermath of the attacks, insurance companies faced enormous losses, particularly in property and casualty insurance related to the destruction of the World Trade Center. However, the industry quickly adapted, with insurance companies raising premiums across the board, particularly for terrorism-related coverage. The creation of **terrorism risk insurance** became a new and profitable market for insurers, as businesses, governments, and institutions sought to protect themselves against future attacks. The U.S. government's passage of the **Terrorism Risk Insurance Act (TRIA)** in 2002 provided a backstop for insurance companies, ensuring that the federal government would cover the most significant losses in the event of another major terrorist attack, thereby encouraging insurers to continue offering coverage while reducing their exposure to catastrophic losses.

Another major financial shift came from the **Federal Reserve's monetary policy** in response to the economic uncertainty following the attacks. In the months after 9/11, the Fed aggressively cut interest rates, reducing the federal funds rate from 3.5% to 1.75% by the end of 2001. These rate cuts, intended to stabilize the economy and prevent a recession, had far-reaching consequences for the financial sector. Lower interest rates spurred borrowing, particularly in the housing market, and led to an increase in speculative investments as investors sought higher returns in a low-interest-rate environment. This period of easy money helped fuel the housing boom of the early 2000s, laying the groundwork for the subprime mortgage crisis and the financial collapse of 2008. For the time being, however, Wall Street profited immensely from the surge in lending, securitization of mortgages, and the creation of complex financial products designed to generate returns in the low-rate environment.

The post-9/11 world also saw a **deregulation of financial markets**, justified in part by the need for flexibility in combating terrorism and financing military operations. The **Bank Secrecy Act** and **Patriot Act** both included provisions aimed at preventing terrorist financing, which, paradoxically, also contributed to the rise of shadow banking and unregulated financial practices. The Patriot Act's anti-money laundering (AML) provisions required banks and financial institutions to report suspicious activity, but these regulations also created opportunities for firms to develop new methods of compliance that often blurred the lines between legal and illegal financial activities. Meanwhile, Wall Street lobbied for and secured the loosening of certain regulations, particularly those related to the trading of derivatives and the securitization of debt, allowing banks and investment firms to take on greater risks while maximizing profits.

Wall Street also benefited from **government contracts related to homeland security**. As the Department of Homeland Security (DHS) expanded its reach, financial institutions became key partners in building the infrastructure to track and combat terrorist financing. This new market for financial services led to the development of sophisticated data tracking systems, risk management tools, and compliance software. Investment in **cybersecurity** and **financial intelligence** became a growth area, with companies offering specialized services to both the government and private sector clients. Firms specializing in risk assessment, data analytics, and financial intelligence saw significant growth as they helped both the U.S. government and private corporations navigate the new security landscape.

Additionally, **private equity firms** took advantage of the climate of uncertainty by acquiring distressed assets and companies affected by the post-9/11 economic downturn. These firms, which specialize in buying undervalued companies, restructuring them, and selling them for profit, capitalized on the volatility in the markets. Private equity firms were able to purchase assets at discounted prices, particularly in industries hit hard by the attacks, such as airlines, hospitality, and real estate. Many of these firms later profited handsomely as the economy recovered and asset values rebounded.

In sum, while Wall Street and the financial sector faced immediate challenges in the wake of 9/11, the broader economic landscape that emerged from the attacks provided significant opportunities for profit. Defense stocks surged, financial institutions profited from reconstruction efforts in Iraq and Afghanistan, and the insurance industry adapted to create new revenue streams from terrorism coverage. Lower interest rates and deregulation further fueled speculative investment, setting the stage for future financial crises while providing short-term gains for Wall Street. The financial sector, much like other industries, found ways to thrive in the post-9/11 world, benefiting from the economic and geopolitical shifts that followed the attacks.

The Role of Media and Corporate Interests

The media landscape following 9/11 changed dramatically, with major news outlets, entertainment conglomerates, and corporate media entities playing a pivotal role in shaping public perception of the attacks, the War on Terror, and the broader global narrative. As the U.S. embarked on military campaigns in Afghanistan and Iraq, the media became both a tool for disseminating the official government narrative and a beneficiary of the heightened attention and advertising revenue that came with round-the-clock coverage of the war. The role of corporate media in benefiting from the post-9/11 environment is a crucial, if less visible, element of understanding who profited from the attacks.

In the days following 9/11, the American public was glued to their televisions, radios, and newspapers, desperate for information about what had happened, who was responsible, and what would happen next. The attacks were the most significant event to occur on U.S. soil in decades, and the media, both print and broadcast, experienced a surge in viewership, readership, and ratings. Major networks like **CNN**, **Fox News**, and **MSNBC** saw unprecedented spikes in their ratings, as people turned to these channels for real-time updates and analysis. This increased attention resulted in a flood of advertising dollars, as corporations sought to reach massive audiences tuning in to coverage of the unfolding global crisis.

The **24-hour news cycle**, which had already become a norm in the wake of the first Gulf War and the rise of cable news, was now in full effect, with networks dedicating entire days to the aftermath of the attacks and the subsequent wars in Afghanistan and Iraq. The extended coverage not only kept viewers hooked but also stoked fear and anxiety, ensuring that people remained engaged and reliant on the news media for updates on new threats, terror alerts, and government actions. This environment of perpetual fear and uncertainty, which was often fueled by sensationalized reporting and a constant barrage of breaking news, played into the hands of corporate media entities looking to maintain high ratings.

Fox News, in particular, emerged as one of the primary beneficiaries of the post-9/11 media landscape. Known for its staunch support of the Bush administration's policies and its hawkish stance on the War on Terror, Fox News cultivated a loyal audience that embraced its pro-military, pro-government messaging. The network's viewership grew significantly in the years following 9/11, making it the highest-rated cable news network. By framing the War on Terror in black-and-white terms, where the U.S. and its allies were righteous defenders of freedom and democracy against an evil enemy, Fox News created a narrative that resonated with a large segment of the American public, reinforcing the administration's justifications for military intervention. This narrative was not only politically expedient but also financially profitable, as the network's ratings soared and its advertising revenue grew.

The **media's relationship with the government** became more intertwined in the years following 9/11, as the Bush administration relied heavily on news outlets to help shape public opinion in favor of the wars in Afghanistan and Iraq. In some cases, the media willingly played along, echoing the administration's talking points and uncritically reporting on claims of weapons of mass destruction in Iraq, despite growing evidence to the contrary. This failure to question the official narrative was not just a journalistic oversight; it was also driven by corporate interests. Many media companies were owned by larger conglomerates with diverse business interests, including defense contracts and other investments tied to the war effort.

General Electric (GE), for example, which owned **NBC** at the time, was one of the largest defense contractors in the U.S., supplying military equipment and technology to the Pentagon. This dual role as a media company and defense contractor raised questions about whether NBC's reporting on the wars in Afghanistan and Iraq was influenced by its parent company's financial interests. While it is impossible to definitively prove that GE's defense contracts directly affected NBC's editorial decisions, the potential for conflicts of interest was clear, as the parent company stood to profit from the very wars that its news division was covering.

Beyond the news, the broader **entertainment industry** also benefited from the post-9/11 environment. Hollywood, in particular, capitalized on the surge of patriotism and interest in military-themed content. Movies like **"Black Hawk Down"**

(2001), **"We Were Soldiers"** (2002), and **"The Hurt Locker"** (2008) tapped into the public's appetite for stories about American heroism and military valor, with many of these films receiving support from the Pentagon in exchange for access to military equipment and personnel for filming. This close relationship between Hollywood and the military-industrial complex, known as the **Pentagon-Hollywood** alliance, helped to shape public perceptions of the War on Terror by glorifying the U.S. military and reinforcing the idea that America's actions abroad were just and necessary.

In addition to films, the rise of **reality TV** post-9/11 reflected a shift in entertainment preferences, with shows like **"Cops"** and **"Border Patrol"** reinforcing themes of law enforcement, security, and the fight against crime and terrorism. These programs, while often seen as mere entertainment, played a role in shaping public attitudes toward government surveillance, police power, and the need for security at all costs. By focusing on the threat of crime and terrorism, reality TV contributed to a culture of fear that aligned with the government's messaging about the need for heightened security measures, such as the **Patriot Act** and increased airport screenings.

The **media's role** in the post-9/11 world extended beyond simply informing the public. Corporate media entities actively profited from the fear, anxiety, and uncertainty generated by the attacks and the War on Terror. By sensationalizing the news, prioritizing profits over journalistic integrity, and promoting narratives that supported government policies, the media became both a beneficiary and a participant in the events that followed 9/11. This symbiotic relationship between the government, the military, and the media created a feedback loop that not only served the interests of those in power but also ensured that corporate media conglomerates reaped substantial financial rewards from the tragedy and its aftermath.

Chapter 7: The Role of the Media

Media Coverage on 9/11 and Immediate Aftermath

On the morning of September 11, 2001, as the first plane hit the North Tower of the World Trade Center, news channels across the United States shifted focus to what seemed at first like a tragic accident. Within minutes, images of smoke billowing from the tower dominated the airwaves. It wasn't until the second plane struck the South Tower that the gravity of the situation became clear: this was no accident. This was an attack on American soil, one that would define a generation. As millions of Americans watched the unfolding horror live on television, the media became the primary source of information, emotion, and understanding during those first chaotic hours.

In the immediate aftermath, the media's role as both an informer and a shaper of perception became crucial. The live coverage of the attacks was unprecedented. Major news networks—CNN, Fox News, NBC, ABC, and others—shifted to 24-hour coverage, running continuous updates, interviews, and speculation as the events of the day unfolded. The **footage of the collapsing Twin Towers**, replayed incessantly, became the symbol of the tragedy, embedding itself in the national psyche. The **plumes of ash**, **fireballs from the impact**, and the horrific scenes of people jumping from the burning towers were broadcast in an unending loop, creating a visceral, emotional connection to the event for viewers across the globe. For many, the media coverage wasn't just a report of what had happened—it was the event itself, experienced in real time through the lens of the news cameras.

This barrage of imagery and the accompanying commentary served not only to inform but to **shape the emotional response** of the public. News anchors, struggling to grasp the scope of the tragedy, spoke in tones of shock, disbelief, and grief, mirroring the emotions of viewers. The words "unprecedented" and "horrific" were used repeatedly to describe the events, framing 9/11 as an attack that would irrevocably change the world. The sheer **scale of the destruction**, the **loss of life**, and the audacity of the attackers made it clear to the American public that this was not just another terrorist incident—it was a national trauma.

In the hours that followed, as details slowly trickled in, news outlets tried to make sense of who could be responsible. Initial reports were fragmented, as many speculated that it was the work of Osama bin Laden, based on intelligence hints and previous terrorist threats. However, the **uncertainty** of those early hours added to the growing fear. Was there more to come? Were other cities under threat? The lack of immediate answers fueled a sense of **vulnerability**, which the media both reflected and amplified. Journalists and commentators spoke of the potential for further attacks, and the **nationwide grounding of airplanes** added to the aura of unease.

As the day progressed, it wasn't just New York that dominated the news cycle. The attack on the Pentagon and the crash of **United Airlines Flight 93** in Pennsylvania broadened the scope of the narrative, transforming what had initially been seen as a tragedy centered in New York City into a full-scale national crisis. The media's coverage expanded in response, focusing on the **global implications** of the attacks. The **comparisons to Pearl Harbor** came swiftly, as pundits and analysts began to frame the events of 9/11 not just as a terrorist attack, but as a defining moment in American history—one that would demand a military and governmental response on a scale not seen in decades.

The immediate media coverage also played a role in shaping the national mood of **unity and patriotism**. As Americans watched firefighters, police officers, and first responders risk their lives at Ground Zero, the news began to highlight stories of heroism and resilience. The **selflessness of the rescue workers** became a focal point of the coverage, serving as a counterbalance to the overwhelming destruction. News anchors often praised the bravery of those on the front lines, and stories of ordinary citizens stepping in to help began to emerge. The media's emphasis on these narratives of courage and community helped to foster a sense of **national solidarity** in the face of a shared trauma.

However, in its effort to provide real-time updates, the media sometimes contributed to confusion. In the frantic rush to report every new development, conflicting information was often aired. Early reports, for instance, suggested there might be additional planes targeting other major cities. This added to the fear and uncertainty of the moment, as Americans struggled to determine what was real and what was speculative. The rapid pace of updates sometimes led to **errors and misreporting**, as news organizations sought to be the first to break stories in a competitive landscape.

Despite these challenges, the media's coverage of 9/11 was comprehensive, continuous, and in many ways, cathartic. For many Americans, watching the news became a way to process the events as they unfolded. The media offered not only information but a collective space for mourning, shock, and reflection. In those first days, as the rubble of the Twin Towers still smoldered, the media framed the attacks as a moment of reckoning for the nation. The emotional intensity of the coverage, combined with the **sense of national vulnerability**, laid the groundwork for what would follow—a rallying cry for unity, resilience, and, ultimately, retribution.

The Media as a Conduit for the Government's War on Terror Narrative

In the weeks and months following the attacks of September 11, 2001, the media became a key player in communicating and amplifying the Bush administration's War on Terror narrative. The shock and horror of the event had left the public reeling, desperate for answers, and looking to the government for reassurance and direction. The media, acting as the main intermediary between the government and the people, played a significant role in shaping the public's understanding of the attacks and the subsequent responses. As the nation sought to come to terms with the events, the administration's messaging was delivered to the public through a largely compliant and unquestioning media apparatus, creating a unified front that paved the way for war.

President George W. Bush's **speeches** during this time were widely broadcast, and his message was clear: America had been attacked by terrorists who hated freedom and democracy, and the only response was to strike back with force. Bush's first major address, given just nine days after the attacks, introduced the term **"War on Terror,"** which would come to define U.S. foreign and domestic policy for years to come. In this speech, Bush framed the conflict in stark, binary terms, declaring, "Either you are with us, or you are with the terrorists." This message was repeated in media reports, talk shows, and news broadcasts, creating a powerful narrative of **good vs. evil** that resonated with a traumatized and angry public. The media's constant reiteration of this message helped to cement it in the national consciousness, making it the lens through which many Americans viewed the post-9/11 world.

The **language of the War on Terror** quickly became ubiquitous in news reporting, with terms like "terrorist networks," "rogue states," and "Islamic extremists" repeated across various platforms. The media adopted and amplified the government's messaging, often without critical examination. Anchors and reporters echoed the administration's talking points, portraying the War on Terror as a righteous cause in defense of American values. The message was clear: the United States had been attacked by shadowy forces, and it was the government's duty to hunt them down and eliminate them, wherever they might be. The **simplified and emotionally charged narrative** made it easy for the public to understand and support the administration's actions, even as these actions involved complex geopolitical strategies and long-term consequences.

As the Bush administration began planning military operations in **Afghanistan** and later **Iraq**, the media continued to play a critical role in shaping public opinion. The invasion of Afghanistan in October 2001 was presented as a necessary and justified response to the 9/11 attacks. News outlets extensively covered the administration's claims that the **Taliban** regime in Afghanistan was harboring **Osama bin Laden** and his al-Qaeda network. The media coverage largely reflected the government's narrative that Afghanistan was a safe haven for terrorists and that military intervention was the only solution to eliminate the threat. The rapid fall of the Taliban government in the early stages of the invasion was portrayed as a major victory, reinforcing the idea that military force was the appropriate and effective response to terrorism.

The **Iraq War**, launched in 2003, represented an even greater example of the media's role in disseminating government propaganda. From late 2002 onward, the Bush administration began a sustained campaign to convince the American public that Iraq posed an imminent threat. Central to this campaign was the assertion that **Saddam Hussein** possessed **weapons of mass destruction** (WMDs) and that he could supply these weapons to terrorists. These claims were reported extensively in the media, often without sufficient skepticism or fact-checking. Major newspapers like **The New York Times** ran stories citing anonymous government sources, which further solidified the narrative that Iraq was a grave danger to the United States. This was despite growing doubts from intelligence experts and international inspectors who found no evidence of WMDs.

The **role of television news**, particularly networks like **Fox News**, in promoting the Iraq War cannot be overstated. Fox News, which had aligned itself with the Bush administration's policies, became a leading voice in the push for war, using fear-driven rhetoric and visuals to garner support for the invasion. Anchors and commentators frequently discussed the threat of Iraq in dire terms, warning of the potential for catastrophic attacks if Saddam Hussein remained in power. The network's stance not only helped rally public support for the war but also influenced the coverage of competing networks, many of which were hesitant to challenge the prevailing pro-war sentiment for fear of being seen as unpatriotic. In the months leading up to the invasion, Fox News's ratings soared, showing that its aggressive stance in favor of the war was resonating with viewers.

In addition to television news, **newspapers** and **magazines** played a crucial role in shaping public perception of the War on Terror. Articles in respected publications like **The**

Washington Post and **Time Magazine** often echoed the administration's arguments, presenting the case for war as both morally justified and strategically necessary. Few mainstream media outlets questioned the veracity of the government's claims or explored alternative perspectives in depth. Those who did raise concerns or questioned the evidence, such as **Knight Ridder** reporters, were largely marginalized and ignored by the wider media establishment. The lack of critical reporting and the overwhelming repetition of the government's talking points created an environment in which dissenting voices were drowned out, and public opinion became largely supportive of the war efforts.

The **media's complicity in the government's narrative** extended beyond simply reporting on events. By framing the War on Terror in moralistic and patriotic terms, the media played an active role in shaping public sentiment and reinforcing the belief that military intervention was the only way to protect the United States. This framing stifled debate and critical analysis, limiting the range of acceptable opinions in the public discourse. As the U.S. embarked on its wars in Afghanistan and Iraq, the media's portrayal of these conflicts as necessary and just helped to solidify public support, even as the long-term consequences of these wars were not yet fully understood.

In this way, the media served as a powerful **conduit for the government's messaging**, ensuring that the official narrative of the War on Terror reached millions of Americans without significant opposition. The relentless coverage of the attacks, the wars, and the constant warnings of future threats kept the public in a state of fear and heightened vigilance, making it easier for the government to implement sweeping security measures and launch military interventions with minimal pushback. The media's role in amplifying the War on Terror narrative would have lasting implications, not only for U.S. foreign policy but also for the public's understanding of global events and the limits of government power.

Coverage of Controversial Legislation: The Patriot Act and Civil Liberties

In the wake of the 9/11 attacks, fear gripped the nation. The horror of the event, coupled with the uncertainty about when or if another attack might occur, created a perfect storm for sweeping government actions. Just over a month after the attacks, Congress passed the **USA PATRIOT Act** on October 26, 2001, with overwhelming bipartisan support. The bill was presented as an essential tool to combat terrorism, granting the government expanded powers of surveillance, intelligence gathering, and law enforcement. The media's coverage of the **Patriot Act**—and the broader debate over civil liberties—played a critical role in shaping how the public viewed this legislation. By and large, mainstream media outlets emphasized the necessity of these new powers, framing them as crucial to national security, while largely downplaying the potential risks to individual freedoms.

When the **Patriot Act** was introduced, it was presented to the American people as a necessary and immediate response to the terrorist threat. The media, echoing the government's message, emphasized the Act's primary purpose: to prevent future terrorist attacks by improving coordination between law enforcement and intelligence agencies, removing legal barriers to sharing information, and providing the government with enhanced tools to track and intercept terrorist communications. Reports in newspapers and on television news were quick to highlight the Act's role in tightening national security, with the primary focus on **defending American lives** rather than examining the potential erosion of civil liberties.

Major news outlets, such as **The New York Times** and **The Washington Post**, ran editorials and opinion pieces that reflected the general mood of the time—one of heightened anxiety and fear. The overwhelming narrative in media coverage was that the nation was at war, and extraordinary measures were justified in the face of an extraordinary threat. The notion of temporarily sacrificing certain freedoms in exchange for greater security was treated as an acceptable, even necessary, trade-off by much of the mainstream press. Few outlets critically examined the long-term consequences of granting the government unprecedented power to spy on its own citizens.

Television news networks also played a crucial role in presenting the Patriot Act as an essential response to the 9/11 attacks. **CNN**, **Fox News**, and **MSNBC** aired frequent segments discussing the need for heightened security measures. Interviews with government officials, law enforcement officers, and terrorism experts reinforced the idea that **terrorists were lurking in the shadows**, waiting to strike again. The message was clear: America had been caught off guard on 9/11, and the Patriot Act would help ensure that the country would never be so vulnerable again. The focus was on the Act's effectiveness in identifying and preventing terrorist plots, with minimal attention given to the potential risks of government overreach.

Despite the Patriot Act's sweeping powers, there was little substantial debate in the mainstream media over the implications for **civil liberties**. The Act authorized extensive government surveillance, including the ability to monitor phone and email communications, access financial records, and track internet activity, often without a warrant or judicial oversight. It also allowed for **indefinite detention of non-citizens** suspected of terrorism-related activities and expanded the definition of terrorism to include domestic threats. These provisions represented a significant shift in the balance between civil liberties and national security, yet the media largely framed these measures as necessary to protect the country from further attacks.

Critics of the Patriot Act, including civil liberties organizations like the **American Civil Liberties Union (ACLU)**, warned that the legislation granted the government too much unchecked power and posed a threat to individual privacy rights. However, these voices were often marginalized in mainstream coverage. When opposition to the Act was reported, it was frequently framed as a secondary concern, overshadowed by the pressing need for security in a time of crisis. Media outlets tended to present these criticisms as part of a minor, fringe debate, with the overwhelming consensus being that the government's actions were justified. As a result, many Americans were unaware of the full scope of the powers being granted to the government under the Patriot Act and the potential for abuse.

The limited discussion of **civil liberties** in the media reflected a broader reluctance to challenge the government's actions in the immediate post-9/11 period. Journalists and commentators were wary of appearing unpatriotic or unsupportive of national security efforts. In a time when the country was rallying behind the flag and uniting in grief and anger, questioning the government's approach to fighting terrorism was often viewed with suspicion. This created a chilling effect on critical reporting, particularly when it came to complex issues like the trade-offs between security and privacy.

While the mainstream media largely supported the Patriot Act, **alternative media outlets** and civil rights advocates offered a more critical perspective. Publications like **The Nation** and websites like **Salon** ran pieces that delved into the potential dangers of the legislation. These outlets raised concerns about the expansion of government surveillance and the erosion of constitutional protections, warning that the Patriot Act could lead to a **surveillance state**. However, these voices were drowned out by the overwhelming support for the government's actions in the mainstream media, and their critiques failed to gain traction with the broader public.

In the years following the passage of the Patriot Act, the media would eventually begin to report on the abuses of power that stemmed from the legislation. Stories of warrantless wiretapping, mass data collection by the **National Security Agency (NSA)**, and the detention of individuals without due process began to emerge, leading to greater public awareness of the civil liberties issues at stake. However, in the immediate aftermath of 9/11, the media's focus was overwhelmingly on security, and the public was largely shielded from the full implications of the government's new powers.

The coverage of the Patriot Act serves as a stark example of how the media, during times of national crisis, can become an instrument for advancing government narratives, particularly when the public is gripped by fear and uncertainty. The legislation was framed as a necessary tool in the fight against terrorism, with little attention given to the potential consequences for individual freedoms. In this way, the media played a crucial role in shaping public opinion, creating an environment in which the sacrifice of civil liberties was not only accepted but seen as an essential part of the nation's defense against a shadowy and undefined enemy.

Silencing Dissent and Marginalizing Critics

In the immediate aftermath of the 9/11 attacks, the U.S. media environment became highly charged, with an atmosphere of patriotic fervor that left little room for dissent or critical voices. As the Bush administration rallied support for its policies—both domestic and foreign—the mainstream media, by and large, helped to create an environment where questioning the official narrative was equated with being unpatriotic or, in some cases, even sympathetic to the enemy. This dynamic had a chilling effect on public discourse, limiting the range of perspectives that were given a platform and marginalizing those who dared to challenge the government's actions.

Prominent public figures who voiced concerns about the government's response to 9/11, the rush to war, or the loss of civil liberties were often met with a fierce backlash. For example, when then-**Democratic Congresswoman Barbara Lee** was the only member of Congress to vote against the Authorization for Use of Military Force (AUMF), which gave President Bush broad authority to wage war against terrorism, she faced a torrent of criticism. Lee expressed concern that the AUMF would lead to endless war without sufficient checks on executive power—a concern that would prove prescient—but the media coverage of her vote largely framed her as an outlier, with some outlets suggesting that her stance was unpatriotic. Lee received death threats, and her political future was called into question, despite her thoughtful and principled objections.

Similarly, **celebrities** who spoke out against the wars in Afghanistan and Iraq or questioned the government's narrative faced harsh consequences. Perhaps the most infamous case was that of the **Dixie Chicks**, a popular country music group who were virtually blacklisted from country radio after lead singer Natalie Maines criticized President Bush during a concert in 2003, saying they were "ashamed" that he was from Texas. This offhand comment ignited a firestorm of controversy, with country music stations refusing to play their songs, record sales plummeting, and public outrage leading to boycotts. The media played a significant role in amplifying the backlash, framing the Dixie Chicks as traitors in a time when the country was meant to be united. The episode sent a clear message: those who spoke out against the government or the war effort could expect serious consequences, not just from the public but also from the media itself.

The **mainstream press**, particularly in the run-up to the Iraq War, largely failed to provide a platform for voices of dissent. Those who questioned the legitimacy of the war, the evidence for weapons of mass destruction (WMDs), or the broader War on Terror were often ignored or dismissed. The media's role in this was twofold: first, by not giving adequate attention to critical perspectives, and second, by amplifying and legitimizing the government's justifications for war. Journalists who raised questions about the official narrative were often sidelined or pressured to conform to the dominant pro-war sentiment.

One of the few journalistic outlets that consistently questioned the case for the Iraq War was **Knight Ridder**, a chain of newspapers whose reporters, notably **Jonathan Landay** and **Warren Strobel**, critically examined the Bush administration's claims about Iraq's WMDs. Despite their dogged reporting, which highlighted the lack of concrete evidence and the doubts of intelligence experts, their stories were largely ignored by the larger media outlets. Meanwhile, major newspapers like **The New York Times** and **The Washington Post** ran stories that uncritically accepted the government's assertions, often based on unnamed sources within the administration. This failure of the mainstream press to adequately investigate and challenge the government's claims contributed to the public's overwhelming support for the invasion of Iraq.

The **lack of critical reporting** was also evident on television. News networks like **Fox News**, **CNN**, and **MSNBC** focused heavily on promoting the administration's narrative, often showcasing retired military officers and government officials who supported the war. This created the impression that there was a consensus in favor of the Iraq invasion, with little room for skepticism or alternative viewpoints. In this environment, those who opposed the war were often portrayed as fringe elements or unpatriotic. The relentless focus on the threat posed by Saddam Hussein, coupled with the government's warnings about WMDs, left little space for meaningful debate. As a result, the public was largely shielded from the complexities of the situation, and dissenting voices were drowned out by the drumbeat for war.

The media's role in **silencing dissent** extended beyond the Iraq War. In the broader context of the War on Terror, critical discussions about civil liberties, government overreach, and the long-term consequences of U.S. foreign policy were often marginalized. Voices that questioned the expansion of surveillance powers under the **Patriot Act**, the use of **torture** at places like Guantanamo Bay and Abu Ghraib, or the indefinite detention of terror suspects without trial were largely confined to alternative media outlets and advocacy groups. When these issues were discussed in the mainstream press, they were often framed in a way that minimized their significance or justified them as necessary evils in the fight against terrorism.

The media's complicity in marginalizing dissent was further illustrated by its treatment of **whistleblowers** and critics within the government. Figures like **Thomas Drake**, a former National Security Agency (NSA) official who exposed abuses of government surveillance, and **John Kiriakou**, a former CIA officer who blew the whistle on the agency's use of waterboarding, were vilified in the press. Their actions were often framed as threats to national security, rather than as courageous attempts to expose wrongdoing. The government's aggressive prosecution of whistleblowers under the **Espionage Act**, combined with the media's portrayal of them as traitors, created a hostile environment for those who sought to challenge government secrecy and abuse.

By marginalizing critics and dissenters, the media contributed to a **narrowing of public discourse** during the critical years following 9/11. This stifling of debate had profound consequences, not only for the country's foreign policy but also for the preservation of civil liberties at home. As the government expanded its powers under the banner of the War on Terror, the media's failure to give adequate attention to opposing voices allowed these policies to go largely unchallenged. In this way, the media became an accomplice in the silencing of dissent, creating an environment where criticism of the government was equated with disloyalty and where the complexities of national security were reduced to simplistic narratives of good versus evil.

The Role of Alternative and Independent Media

While the mainstream media largely fell in line with the government's post-9/11 narrative, **alternative and independent media outlets** played a critical role in providing a platform for dissenting voices and challenging the official story. These outlets, often operating on the fringes of the media landscape, became essential spaces for discussions that questioned the U.S. government's actions in the wake of 9/11, the erosion of civil liberties, and the justification for wars in Afghanistan and Iraq. As the mainstream press focused on security, patriotism, and unquestioning support for the government, these alternative platforms became a crucial outlet for those seeking a broader perspective.

Independent media outlets such as **Democracy Now!**, hosted by **Amy Goodman**, and publications like **The Nation** and **CounterPunch** offered an alternative to the largely homogeneous coverage found on major networks and newspapers. These platforms were not afraid to ask tough questions about the motivations behind U.S. foreign policy or to highlight the human rights abuses that resulted from the War on Terror. Democracy Now!, for instance, regularly featured guests who critiqued the expansion of government surveillance, the use of torture, and the unchecked power of the executive branch. This programming offered a stark contrast to the prevailing narratives on major news networks, where criticism of the government was rare, and those who raised concerns were often dismissed as fringe voices.

Independent journalists and online publications also played a significant role in uncovering stories that were neglected by the mainstream press. One of the most important figures in this regard was **Glenn Greenwald**, who, through his work with The Guardian, helped bring to light the revelations of **Edward Snowden** in 2013. Although this occurred several years after the immediate post-9/11 period, Snowden's disclosures about the **NSA's mass surveillance** programs confirmed many of the concerns that had been raised by critics of the Patriot Act and government overreach. Greenwald's reporting demonstrated the value of independent journalism in holding powerful institutions accountable, particularly when the mainstream media had failed to do so.

Online platforms like blogs, independent news websites, and social media also became important vehicles for dissent. The rise of the internet gave ordinary citizens the ability to share information, critique the government's actions, and connect with others who shared their concerns. Websites like **Antiwar.com** provided in-depth coverage and analysis of U.S. military interventions, while other blogs and independent forums questioned the veracity of the government's claims about WMDs and the necessity of the Iraq War. These platforms, often run by small teams or individuals, helped to fill the void left by the mainstream media's failure to scrutinize the government's actions.

One of the key strengths of **alternative media** was its willingness to challenge the official narrative and provide a voice to those who were marginalized in mainstream discourse.

For instance, after 9/11, alternative media outlets were quick to highlight the experiences of **Muslim Americans**, who faced increased scrutiny, racial profiling, and Islamophobia in the wake of the attacks. While the mainstream press often focused on the broader national security implications of the War on Terror, independent media gave space to stories of how these policies were affecting ordinary people, particularly those in vulnerable communities. This kind of coverage was vital in countering the often one-dimensional portrayal of Muslims in mainstream news, where they were frequently framed in the context of terrorism.

Another significant contribution of alternative media was its persistent focus on **civil liberties** and the constitutional implications of the government's actions. Publications like **The Intercept**, launched in 2014 by Greenwald, **Laura Poitras**, and **Jeremy Scahill**, were dedicated to investigative journalism and regularly published stories about government surveillance, abuses of power, and the erosion of civil rights. These outlets served as watchdogs, keeping the public informed about the growing reach of government agencies like the NSA and FBI, and providing a counter-narrative to the mainstream media's focus on security at all costs.

Media activists and organizations also played a role in pushing back against government propaganda and misinformation. Groups like **Fairness & Accuracy In Reporting (FAIR)** worked to highlight the ways in which mainstream media outlets were complicit in promoting pro-government narratives. FAIR's critiques of the media's role in selling the Iraq War, for example, were some of the most incisive analyses of how news organizations had failed to do their job of holding power to account. By monitoring media coverage and providing detailed reports on bias and misinformation, organizations like FAIR offered the public tools to better understand how the media was shaping their perceptions of national security and foreign policy.

Importantly, **alternative media** not only critiqued the U.S. government's actions but also provided platforms for the voices of international activists, scholars, and political leaders who opposed the War on Terror. Figures like **Noam Chomsky**, who was a vocal critic of U.S. imperialism, found space in these outlets to present a different perspective on the events of 9/11 and their aftermath. These voices offered a global context for the U.S. government's actions, drawing attention to the long history of American intervention in the Middle East and the broader geopolitical consequences of the War on Terror. In contrast, the mainstream media often failed to provide this kind of historical or international perspective, instead presenting the U.S. response to 9/11 as a necessary and justified reaction to an unprecedented attack.

Despite the important role of **alternative and independent media** in fostering dissent and critical discourse, these platforms often struggled to reach a broader audience. The dominance of corporate-owned media outlets, coupled with the immense resources at their disposal, meant that alternative voices were often drowned out or relegated to niche audiences. However, the impact of these independent outlets should not be underestimated. Over time, the reporting and analyses produced by alternative media helped to shift public opinion, particularly as the long-term consequences of the Iraq War and the War on Terror became more apparent. As more Americans began to question the official narratives they had been fed, they increasingly turned to these alternative sources for a fuller understanding of the issues.

In the years following 9/11, **alternative media** outlets continued to serve as critical spaces for debate, offering a much-needed counterweight to the government's expansive powers and the mainstream media's often complacent coverage. Their efforts to expose the truth, challenge misinformation, and give voice to the voiceless were essential in preserving a space for democratic discourse at a time when dissent was being systematically silenced. While their reach may have been limited, their influence was significant, providing a foundation for future movements that would continue to demand accountability and transparency from the U.S. government and its media allies.

Chapter 8: Intelligence Failures or Intentional Ig

Early **Warnings and Missed Opportunities**

In the years leading up to September 11, 2001, multiple warnings about an imminent terrorist attack on U.S. soil surfaced within various intelligence circles. As early as 1995, reports of Osama bin Laden's growing influence and ambitions had begun to catch the attention of U.S. intelligence agencies. Despite these early signs, the response from U.S. authorities was limited, fragmented, and, in many cases, dangerously slow. It's this period of overlooked warnings and missed opportunities that lies at the heart of the question: Could 9/11 have been prevented if the available intelligence had been taken more seriously?

One of the most significant early warnings came from the **Philippines** in 1995, where authorities uncovered a plot known as the **Bojinka plot**. This plot, masterminded by **Khalid Sheikh Mohammed**, the eventual architect of 9/11, involved plans to blow up multiple U.S. airliners over the

Pacific and crash a plane into the CIA headquarters. While the Bojinka plot was thwarted, elements of it would later resurface in the 9/11 attacks. Despite this critical discovery, U.S. intelligence agencies failed to fully grasp the implications or connect the dots between this foiled plan and the growing threat posed by bin Laden's network.

As the 1990s progressed, bin Laden's involvement in terrorist activities became more apparent. In 1998, he issued a **fatwa** declaring jihad against the United States, urging Muslims to kill Americans, both military and civilian, wherever they could be found. This fatwa was not just rhetoric—it was a public declaration of intent. Later that year, the **U.S. embassies in Kenya and Tanzania** were bombed, killing hundreds and wounding thousands. These attacks were later traced back to bin Laden and Al-Qaeda. In retaliation, President Bill Clinton ordered missile strikes against suspected Al-Qaeda training camps in **Afghanistan**, but these strikes did little to dismantle the organization or diminish bin Laden's resolve.

Despite these clear signals of bin Laden's increasing ambition to strike at the U.S., the government's response remained inconsistent. Key pieces of intelligence continued to flow into U.S. agencies, but they often went ignored or were not acted upon. For example, in **2000**, the **USS Cole** was attacked by Al-Qaeda in the Yemeni port of Aden, killing 17 American sailors. This attack, coupled with the embassy bombings, should have triggered a more robust investigation into Al-Qaeda's operational capabilities and long-term plans. Instead, the response was relatively muted, with intelligence agencies failing to anticipate the larger-scale attack that was brewing.

Perhaps the most glaring warning came just weeks before the attacks, in the form of the now-infamous **Presidential Daily Brief (PDB)** delivered to President **George W. Bush** on **August 6, 2001**. The briefing, titled "**Bin Laden Deter-**

mined to Strike in U.S.," explicitly warned of bin Laden's desire to carry out attacks within the United States. The PDB mentioned possible hijackings and suggested that the attacks could involve New York City. Yet, despite the specificity and urgency of this warning, the briefing was dismissed by Bush and his administration as a "historical" document rather than an actionable threat. National Security Adviser **Condoleezza Rice** later downplayed the importance of the PDB, describing it as a general assessment of bin Laden's intentions rather than a concrete plan.

In retrospect, this failure to act on the August 6 briefing is seen as one of the most critical missed opportunities in the lead-up to 9/11. Intelligence officials within the **CIA** had been warning of an imminent attack for months, with heightened chatter about a "spectacular" event. **George Tenet**, the CIA Director at the time, famously remarked that "the system was blinking red." Yet, despite this, the warnings were not followed up with any significant preventative measures.

Other notable warnings also went unheeded. For instance, FBI agents had noticed suspicious behavior among individuals later identified as some of the 9/11 hijackers. In **Arizona**, an FBI agent raised concerns in **July 2001** about Middle Eastern men training at American flight schools and suggested that Al-Qaeda might be sending operatives to the U.S. for aviation-related attacks. Similarly, **Zacarias Moussaoui**, who was later revealed to be the "20th hijacker," was arrested in Minnesota in **August 2001** after flight instructors reported his suspicious behavior. FBI agents there believed he was planning to hijack a plane, but their requests to search his laptop were denied by higher-ups in Washington due to concerns over civil liberties and the absence of clear evidence.

The combination of these multiple warnings and the lack of an adequate response raises troubling questions. How could so many signs have been overlooked or dismissed? Was it simple incompetence, or were there other factors at play that led to this collective failure? While hindsight is always 20/20, the repeated failure to act on credible intelligence casts doubt on the official narrative that 9/11 was an unforeseeable event. It is clear that the U.S. government had been warned repeatedly about the possibility of an attack on American soil, but for reasons that remain debated, these warnings were not enough to prevent the tragedy that unfolded on September 11, 2001.

Bureaucratic Failures and Interagency Rivalries

One of the most significant obstacles to preventing the 9/11 attacks was the deep-seated culture of competition and mistrust between U.S. intelligence agencies, most notably the **CIA** and the **FBI**. While both agencies were tasked with gathering intelligence to protect the United States from threats, their historical rivalry and institutional silos made cooperation difficult, if not impossible. This bureaucratic dysfunction was not just a minor administrative hurdle; it had profound consequences that contributed to the inability to stop the 9/11 plot.

The **CIA**, as the agency primarily responsible for foreign intelligence, had been tracking **Osama bin Laden** and his network for years. They had amassed significant intelligence about Al-Qaeda's activities overseas, including details about the group's training camps in Afghanistan and the involvement of bin Laden in various terrorist attacks. The **FBI**, on the other hand, was responsible for domestic intelligence and law enforcement. Its agents were often the first to detect suspicious activities inside the U.S., such as the presence of potential terrorists or criminal conspiracies. Despite this clear division of labor, the two agencies often found themselves at odds, with critical information being withheld from one another.

This rivalry was deeply rooted in their respective histories. The FBI, under **J. Edgar Hoover**, had long maintained a monopoly over domestic intelligence and had little interest in sharing its turf with other agencies. The CIA, created after World War II, was designed to focus on foreign threats, but the boundaries between foreign and domestic intelligence were often blurred, especially as terrorism became a global phenomenon. The end result was a pervasive lack of cooperation between the two agencies, even when their missions intersected. In the years leading up to 9/11, this rivalry became a deadly impediment to the sharing of vital information.

One of the clearest examples of this bureaucratic failure was the case of **Khalid al-Mihdhar** and **Nawaf al-Hazmi**, two of the 9/11 hijackers. The **CIA** had been tracking al-Mihdhar and al-Hazmi since they attended an Al-Qaeda meeting in **Malaysia** in **January 2000**. The agency knew that the two men had ties to bin Laden's network and that they had traveled to the U.S. later that year. Despite this critical intelligence, the CIA did not inform the FBI or other agencies that these known terrorists were in the country. This lack of communication proved to be a devastating oversight, as the FBI, had they known about al-Mihdhar and al-Hazmi's presence in the U.S., could have monitored their activities and potentially disrupted their plot.

Even within the FBI, information was not always shared effectively. The FBI's **Phoenix** office, as mentioned earlier, raised concerns in **July 2001** about Middle Eastern men attending flight schools in the U.S. and suggested that they might be involved in a larger plot. This memo, known as the "**Phoenix Memo**," was sent to FBI headquarters, but it was never acted upon. Similarly, the agents in **Minnesota** who arrested **Zacarias Moussaoui** before 9/11 were frustrated by the lack of support from FBI leadership in Washington. They had requested a warrant to search Moussaoui's laptop, believing him to be involved in a hijacking plot, but their requests were denied, partly due to concerns over the legal ramifications of searching a foreign national's personal property without concrete evidence.

The failure to share this critical intelligence in a timely manner was exacerbated by structural and cultural barriers within these agencies. At the time, there was no unified system for sharing intelligence across agencies. Each agency operated with its own databases, its own networks, and its own internal protocols. There was no centralized repository where information about potential threats could be analyzed and cross-referenced by all relevant parties. Instead, critical intelligence often remained compartmentalized, with no single entity having the full picture. This lack of coordination meant that pieces of the puzzle existed in different places but were never brought together in time to prevent the attacks.

The cultural divide between the **CIA** and **FBI** also played a significant role in these failures. The CIA, focused on covert operations and espionage, was traditionally more secretive and less willing to share its intelligence with other agencies, even when it was in the national interest to do so. The FBI, with its law enforcement focus, was more concerned with gathering evidence for criminal prosecutions, which often led to delays in action while agents built their cases. These differing priorities created a situation where vital intelligence was either delayed, misinterpreted, or withheld altogether, leaving the door open for the 9/11 plot to unfold.

Perhaps the most tragic irony of these interagency failures is that many of the individuals involved were aware of the growing threat from Al-Qaeda. **George Tenet**, the CIA Director, had been sounding the alarm about bin Laden and his network for years. The **National Security Council (NSC)**, led by **Condoleezza Rice**, had held multiple meetings about the increasing likelihood of a terrorist attack in the U.S. Yet, despite this growing awareness, the institutional barriers between agencies, combined with bureaucratic inertia, prevented decisive action.

In the aftermath of 9/11, these failures led to widespread criticism and calls for reform. The **9/11 Commission Report**, which investigated the intelligence lapses leading up to the attacks, concluded that the lack of coordination between the FBI and CIA was a key factor in the failure to prevent the attacks. The report famously stated that "the system was blinking red," but the warnings were lost in a sea of bureaucracy and interagency rivalries. It was this realization that ultimately led to the creation of the **Department of Homeland Security** and the **Office of the Director of National Intelligence (DNI)**, which were designed to streamline intelligence-sharing and coordination across agencies.

In the final analysis, the bureaucratic failures and interagency rivalries that plagued U.S. intelligence in the years leading up to 9/11 were not just matters of inefficiency—they were fundamental flaws that allowed the plot to proceed unchecked. The inability of the FBI and CIA to work together, combined with the structural and cultural obstacles within each agency, contributed directly to the failure to prevent the deadliest terrorist attack in U.S. history. The question that remains is whether these failures were the result of simple incompetence, or whether there were deeper reasons for the lack of cooperation—reasons that go beyond bureaucratic dysfunction and into the realm of deliberate ignorance.

The "Wall" Between Foreign and Domestic Intelligence

One of the most critical structural issues that contributed to the intelligence failures leading up to 9/11 was the so-called "Wall" between foreign and domestic intelligence. This metaphorical barrier, built through a combination of legal frameworks, agency cultures, and political decisions, prevented the seamless sharing of information between agencies like the **CIA**, which focused on foreign intelligence, and the **FBI**, which handled domestic threats. While this separation was intended to protect civil liberties and prevent abuses of power, it had the unintended consequence of hampering the ability of U.S. intelligence agencies to effectively combat terrorism within the country's borders.

The "Wall" was largely a result of historical policies and legal frameworks designed to separate foreign intelligence gathering from domestic law enforcement. The **Foreign Intelligence Surveillance Act (FISA)** of **1978** was a key part of this separation. FISA was enacted in the wake of the **Watergate scandal** and other abuses of power by U.S. intelligence agencies, including the illegal surveillance of political activists and civil rights leaders. The law established strict guidelines for how intelligence agencies could conduct surveillance on U.S. citizens and people inside the country, requiring a special court to approve warrants for such activities. While FISA was an important safeguard for civil liberties, it also created a bureaucratic hurdle that made it difficult for intelligence agencies to share information across the foreign-domestic divide.

The **CIA** and the **FBI** operated under very different mandates. The CIA was prohibited from conducting operations on U.S. soil, focusing instead on gathering intelligence overseas. Meanwhile, the FBI, as the nation's domestic law enforcement agency, had the authority to investigate crimes within the U.S. but was not involved in gathering foreign intelligence. This division of labor worked in theory, but in practice, it created significant blind spots. As terrorism evolved into a global threat that did not respect borders, this rigid separation between foreign and domestic intelligence became a liability. Terrorists like those involved in 9/11 often moved between countries, coordinating attacks overseas while carrying out the final stages of their plots within the U.S. The inability to bridge the gap between foreign and domestic intelligence left the U.S. vulnerable to precisely this kind of threat.

An example of how the "Wall" hindered intelligence efforts is seen in the handling of information about **Khalid al-Mihdhar** and **Nawaf al-Hazmi**, two of the 9/11 hijackers. As mentioned earlier, the CIA had been tracking these two men since they attended an Al-Qaeda summit in **Malaysia** in January **2000**. The agency knew that they had ties to Osama bin Laden's network and that they had entered the U.S. later that year. However, because the information was gathered through foreign intelligence operations, the CIA was hesitant to share it with the FBI or other domestic agencies. The CIA feared that sharing such information might violate FISA rules, which were designed to prevent domestic surveillance abuses. As a result, al-Mihdhar and al-Hazmi were able to live in the U.S. for months without being monitored, even though they were known terrorists.

The "Wall" also played a role in the FBI's failure to act on its own intelligence. Several FBI field offices had uncovered suspicious activities related to Al-Qaeda operatives in the months leading up to 9/11. The **Phoenix Memo**, written by an FBI agent in July 2001, warned of a growing number of Middle Eastern men enrolling in U.S. flight schools and suggested that this could be part of a larger terrorist plot. However, this memo was not acted upon by FBI headquarters, partly because it was seen as lacking direct ties to a foreign intelligence threat. The FBI's domestic focus, combined with the separation between foreign and domestic intelligence, prevented this warning from being escalated or shared with other agencies in a way that might have prevented the attacks.

The lack of collaboration between agencies was further compounded by the fact that the "Wall" was not just a legal or procedural barrier but also a cultural one. Both the CIA and FBI had long-standing traditions of protecting their own information and operating in silos. Even when legal restrictions were not in play, there was a reluctance to share intelligence for fear of compromising ongoing investigations or operations. This culture of secrecy and interagency rivalry meant that even when critical information was available, it was often not passed along to the people who needed it most.

After 9/11, the "Wall" became a focal point of criticism in the investigations that followed. The **9/11 Commission Report** emphasized the detrimental effects of this separation, stating that it "contributed to the government's failure to share critical intelligence across agencies." In response, significant reforms were made to improve information-sharing across the intelligence community. The creation of the **Department of Homeland Security (DHS)** and the **Office of the Director of National Intelligence (DNI)** were direct attempts to dismantle the "Wall" and promote greater coordination between foreign and domestic intelligence agencies. Additionally, new laws such as the **Patriot Act** were passed to loosen the restrictions on intelligence sharing and allow for greater collaboration in counterterrorism efforts.

However, the dismantling of the "Wall" also sparked controversy. While the post-9/11 reforms were aimed at improving security, they also raised concerns about civil liberties. The expansion of surveillance powers under the Patriot Act, for example, has been criticized for infringing on Americans' privacy rights. The debate over how to balance security with civil liberties continues to this day, with some arguing that the removal of the "Wall" has led to overreach by the government and abuses of power.

In the context of 9/11, the existence of the "Wall" stands as a stark example of how well-intentioned safeguards can have unintended consequences. What was designed to protect Americans from government overreach ultimately contributed to the failure to stop one of the deadliest attacks in U.S. history. The inability to share intelligence between foreign and domestic agencies left the U.S. blind to the threat that was already within its borders. While reforms have since been made to address these issues, the lessons of 9/11 continue to shape the debate over how intelligence should be gathered, shared, and used in the fight against terrorism.

Missed Warnings and the "System Blinking Red"

In the months leading up to September 11, 2001, there were numerous warnings that a major terrorist attack against the United States was imminent. Intelligence agencies, both foreign and domestic, had picked up chatter and other indications that Al-Qaeda was planning something significant. Despite these ominous signals, the U.S. government failed to act decisively to prevent the attacks. This period of missed warnings is often referred to as the time when the "system was blinking red," a phrase famously used in the **9/11 Commission Report** to describe the failure of various parts of the intelligence and national security apparatus to connect the dots.

From the spring of 2001 onward, a growing number of reports indicated that Al-Qaeda was planning a major operation, possibly within the United States. **George Tenet**, the Director of the CIA, later testified that the level of concern within his agency had reached a fever pitch. The CIA's Counterterrorism Center was receiving constant streams of information about Al-Qaeda's activities, much of it pointing toward an imminent attack. As early as **June 2001**, Tenet had told senior officials at the **White House** and **Pentagon** that "the system was blinking red." This phrase was intended to convey the urgency of the threat — a metaphorical flashing light signaling that a major crisis was on the horizon.

One of the clearest warnings came in the form of a **Presidential Daily Briefing (PDB)** delivered to **President George W. Bush** on **August 6, 2001**. The title of this PDB, "Bin Laden Determined to Strike in the U.S.," was an explicit warning about Al-Qaeda's intentions. The briefing highlighted historical patterns of Al-Qaeda's attacks, dating back to the bombings of U.S. embassies in Africa in **1998**, and it specifically mentioned reports of bin Laden's desire to carry out attacks on U.S. soil. It even noted that Al-Qaeda members had been detected conducting surveillance of federal buildings in New York and that there were concerns about the possibility of hijackings. Despite the specificity of these warnings, no significant action was taken to bolster domestic security or increase surveillance of known terrorist operatives.

The **FBI**, too, had internal warnings about suspicious activities that could have been related to the 9/11 plot. In addition to the **Phoenix Memo**, which raised concerns about Middle Eastern men attending U.S. flight schools, FBI agents in **Minnesota** had arrested **Zacarias Moussaoui** in August 2001. Moussaoui, a French national of Moroccan descent, was detained after employees at a flight school became alarmed by his erratic behavior and his apparent lack of interest in learning how to take off or land a plane. Although Moussaoui's behavior and background set off alarm bells, the FBI's attempts to investigate him further were stymied by internal bureaucratic hurdles, including the aforementioned "Wall" between foreign and domestic intelligence operations. Agents in Minnesota requested a warrant to search Moussaoui's laptop, suspecting that he might be involved in a terrorist plot, but their request was denied due to lack of sufficient evidence.

In retrospect, these warnings seem glaringly obvious, yet at the time, they were either ignored or dismissed. Part of the problem was the sheer volume of intelligence that was flowing into various agencies. The U.S. intelligence community was constantly receiving threats and information about possible terrorist attacks from around the world. Analysts were tasked with sifting through this information, determining which threats were credible, and prioritizing their responses. In the case of the warnings about a potential Al-Qaeda attack, there was no single piece of intelligence that pointed directly to the specific plot of using hijacked airplanes as weapons. Instead, there were pieces of information scattered across different agencies, none of which on their own seemed sufficient to trigger a full-scale response.

Compounding this problem was the fact that, despite the growing awareness of the threat posed by bin Laden, there was a lack of a coordinated strategy for addressing it. In the years before 9/11, the U.S. government had taken steps to confront Al-Qaeda, including the launch of missile strikes on bin Laden's camps in **Afghanistan** after the embassy bombings in 1998. However, these efforts were piecemeal and reactive, rather than part of a comprehensive strategy to dismantle the terrorist network. Inside the **White House**, there was also a sense of confusion and inertia regarding how to deal with the growing threat. **Condoleezza Rice**, who served as **National Security Advisor** at the time, later admitted that the Bush administration did not view terrorism as the most urgent issue in the months leading up to 9/11, despite the warnings from the CIA and other agencies.

There was also a cultural issue within the intelligence community. The CIA, FBI, and other agencies were accustomed to dealing with more traditional state actors, such as the **Soviet Union** during the **Cold War**. Al-Qaeda, a decentralized, non-state actor with cells operating across different countries, represented a new kind of enemy that did not fit neatly into the existing frameworks for counterintelligence. This made it more difficult for analysts and policymakers to assess the threat and respond effectively. Furthermore, the idea of using hijacked planes as weapons was not widely considered, despite historical precedents such as the **Bojinka Plot** of the 1990s, in which terrorists had planned to crash planes into U.S. landmarks. The innovative nature of the 9/11 plot, combined with the lack of clear precedent, made it harder for intelligence officials to anticipate the attack.

The failure to act on these warnings has been a source of ongoing debate and controversy. Critics argue that the government's inaction in the face of such clear signs of an impending attack constitutes gross negligence. Others suggest that the warnings, while alarming in hindsight, did not provide enough concrete information to prompt a preemptive response. Still, the fact remains that the system was indeed "blinking red," and yet the necessary actions were not taken to prevent the catastrophe that followed.

In the years since 9/11, efforts have been made to improve the ability of the intelligence community to detect and respond to such threats. The creation of the **Department of Homeland Security** and the expansion of the **National Counterterrorism Center** are both aimed at improving coordination between agencies and ensuring that warnings are acted upon more swiftly. However, the missed warnings leading up to 9/11 remain a stark reminder of the consequences of inaction in the face of clear danger. The failure to heed these warnings continues to raise questions about whether the U.S. government could have done more to prevent the attacks, and whether future threats will be met with a more proactive and decisive response.

Was It a Failure or Intentional Ignorance?

The tragic events of 9/11 have prompted endless speculation, not only about the intelligence failures that led to the attack but also about whether these failures were purely accidental or, as some suggest, a result of intentional ignorance. Some argue that key players in the U.S. government might have been aware of the looming threat but chose not to act for reasons ranging from bureaucratic inertia to darker motivations involving political or financial gain. The distinction between incompetence and intentionality is critical because it changes the entire narrative surrounding 9/11 and its aftermath.

The official explanation, as laid out in the **9/11 Commission Report**, is that the attacks were the result of systemic intelligence and communication failures. The report describes a chaotic and uncoordinated intelligence apparatus that, while flooded with warnings about Al-Qaeda, was unable to piece together the clues that could have prevented the attacks. According to this narrative, the failure was one of imagination: U.S. officials simply did not anticipate that terrorists would use hijacked planes as weapons, even though elements of the plot were in plain sight. In this view, the missed opportunities to prevent 9/11 were the result of bureaucratic dysfunction and the inherent difficulties of dealing with a decentralized, non-state actor like Al-Qaeda.

However, there are those who question this narrative and argue that the intelligence failures go beyond mere incompetence. Some point to the pattern of ignored warnings as evidence of something more deliberate. For example, several high-level figures, including **CIA Director George Tenet** and **National Security Advisor Condoleezza Rice**, were repeatedly briefed about the growing threat from Al-Qaeda in the months leading up to 9/11. The August 6, 2001, Presidential Daily Brief (PDB) titled "**Bin Laden Determined to Strike in U.S.**" was one of the most glaring red flags. Critics argue that the lack of action in response to this and other warnings suggests not just negligence but potentially an intentional decision not to intervene.

One of the most contentious aspects of this theory is the idea that certain officials might have had something to gain from allowing the attacks to happen. Some conspiracy theorists suggest that elements within the U.S. government or military-industrial complex might have seen the attacks as a pretext for advancing specific agendas. These agendas could include securing increased funding for defense contractors, justifying the invasion of Afghanistan and Iraq, or expanding domestic surveillance powers under the **Patriot Act**. The immediate aftermath of 9/11 certainly saw a massive shift in U.S. foreign and domestic policy, with defense budgets skyrocketing and the **War on Terror** becoming a central focus of American geopolitical strategy.

Additionally, some point to **Operation Northwoods**, a declassified Cold War-era plan proposed by the U.S. military in the early 1960s, as a historical precedent for the notion that the U.S. government might consider staging or allowing attacks to further its interests. The plan, which was never carried out, involved U.S. operatives staging acts of terrorism on American soil and blaming them on Cuba to justify military action against Fidel Castro's regime. Though this operation was ultimately rejected by President **John F. Kennedy**, it demonstrates that high-level officials have, in the past, considered using false-flag attacks to advance U.S. policy goals. For those who subscribe to the belief that 9/11 was allowed to happen or even orchestrated by elements within the government, Operation Northwoods serves as a chilling reminder of what might be possible.

Proponents of the "intentional ignorance" theory also point to the behavior of top officials on the day of the attacks as suspect. For example, **President George W. Bush** was famously reading to a group of elementary school children when he was informed that the second plane had struck the World Trade Center. Rather than immediately taking decisive action, Bush remained with the children for several minutes, appearing calm and composed. Some argue that this behavior suggests prior knowledge of the attacks, though others counter that the president's reaction was likely a result of shock or a desire to avoid causing panic.

In addition to these theories, there is the fact that several high-ranking officials and military personnel appeared to have been unusually prepared for an event of this magnitude. On the morning of 9/11, a number of military exercises were being conducted that mimicked the real attacks, further complicating the ability of air traffic controllers and NORAD to respond to the hijackings. Some theorists argue that these exercises were not a coincidence but were designed to confuse the response and allow the attacks to proceed unchallenged. Whether these exercises were part of a deliberate effort to stymie the defense of U.S. airspace or simply an unfortunate timing issue remains a matter of debate.

While these theories remain speculative, they raise important questions about the nature of the intelligence failures leading up to 9/11. Were they simply the result of bureaucratic inertia and systemic issues within the intelligence community? Or was there a deliberate effort to ignore the warnings in order to capitalize on the political and financial opportunities that followed the attacks? The answers to these questions are still hotly debated, and the truth may never be fully known.

What is clear, however, is that the U.S. government's response to 9/11 had far-reaching consequences, both at home and abroad. The attacks provided the justification for a sweeping reorganization of U.S. intelligence and military operations, from the creation of the **Department of Homeland Security** to the authorization of the wars in **Afghanistan** and

Iraq. Domestically, the **Patriot Act** expanded the government's surveillance powers in ways that continue to be controversial today. The events of 9/11 were a turning point in modern history, and the decisions made in its aftermath were shaped, at least in part, by the failures — or intentional choices — of the intelligence community in the months leading up to the attacks.

In the end, the debate over whether the 9/11 intelligence failures were due to incompetence or intentional ignorance reflects broader concerns about the transparency and accountability of government institutions. While the official narrative focuses on the structural and systemic issues that led to the attacks, the persistence of alternative theories speaks to a deep mistrust of government explanations. The tragedy of 9/11 and the events leading up to it will likely continue to be the subject of scrutiny, as people seek to understand how such a catastrophic failure could have occurred — and whether it could happen again.

Chapter 9: The Neocon Agenda and the "New American

The Rise of Neoconservatism in the U.S.

The roots of neoconservatism in the United States trace back to the mid-20th century, a period marked by ideological shifts and the emergence of new political philosophies. Originally, neoconservatism arose as a reaction against the liberal and leftist movements of the 1960s. Intellectuals like **Irving Kristol**, often called the "godfather" of neoconservatism, and **Norman Podhoretz** were at the forefront of this movement, which began as a critique of the perceived failures of liberal policies, particularly in the realms of foreign affairs and national defense. These early neoconservatives were former liberals who became disillusioned with what they saw as the pacifism and weakness of the left.

The central tenet of neoconservatism is a belief in the moral responsibility and strategic necessity of American global leadership. The movement advocates for a strong military, an assertive foreign policy, and the use of American power to spread democracy and free-market capitalism worldwide. This belief was a reaction to the perceived failures of containment during the Cold

War and the ineffectiveness of diplomacy when dealing with authoritarian regimes. For neoconservatives, the United States had a duty to act as the world's police force, intervening wherever necessary to protect its interests and promote its values. This idea would later serve as a cornerstone for U.S. foreign policy in the 21st century.

During the **Reagan administration**, neoconservatives began to gain significant influence. The administration's focus on military buildup and its confrontational stance against the **Soviet Union** aligned closely with neoconservative ideals. Figures like **Richard Perle** and **Paul Wolfowitz**, both of whom would become instrumental in the post-9/11 landscape, were prominent voices advocating for a more aggressive approach to American foreign policy. This period saw an increase in defense spending and a renewed emphasis on U.S. military dominance, laying the groundwork for the neoconservative vision of American hegemony.

After the collapse of the Soviet Union, neoconservatism faced a crossroads. The end of the Cold War left the United States as the world's sole superpower, and the movement began to shift its focus. With no major power to contain, neoconservatives argued that America's role should expand beyond merely defending against threats; it should proactively shape the global order. This period saw the development of what would become known as "unipolarity" — the idea that the U.S. should maintain and exercise its dominance unchallenged. Neoconservatives believed that this power, if wielded correctly, could transform unstable regions and prevent the rise of any future rivals.

A crucial aspect of this vision was the use of military intervention as a tool not only to protect U.S. interests but also to spread democracy, particularly in regions where authoritarian regimes posed a threat to stability. Neoconservatives argued that democratic nations were less likely to go to war with each other, subscribing to the theory of "democratic peace." As such, they saw the promotion of democracy as a strategic imperative that could create a more secure and prosperous international order. This belief would become central to their policy prescriptions in the Middle East, where they viewed authoritarianism as the root of extremism and instability.

The Gulf War in the early 1990s provided an opportunity for neoconservatives to further their agenda. The swift and decisive U.S. military action against **Saddam Hussein's** invasion of Kuwait was seen as a vindication of their emphasis on American strength and interventionism. However, the decision not to remove Saddam from power left some neoconservatives dissatisfied. They believed that allowing such an authoritarian figure to remain in power undermined the moral authority and strategic objectives of the United States. This sentiment would linger throughout the 1990s, as they continued to push for a more assertive policy aimed at reshaping the Middle East.

The end of the 1990s marked the emergence of the **Project for the New American Century (PNAC)**, a think tank founded in 1997 by leading neoconservatives like **William Kristol** and **Robert Kagan**. PNAC became the institutional vehicle through which the neoconservative agenda was articulated and promoted. Its members included many individuals who would later occupy influential positions in the **George W. Bush** administration, such as **Dick Cheney**, **Donald Rumsfeld**, and **Paul Wolfowitz**. PNAC's mission was to advocate for a more robust and interventionist American foreign policy, one that would ensure U.S. dominance well into the 21st century. It called for increased defense spending, the modernization of the U.S. military, and a willingness to confront and remove regimes deemed hostile to American interests.

By the turn of the century, the neoconservative vision for America's role in the world had crystallized: the United States should be an unchallenged global power, one that would not hesitate to use its military might to secure its interests and spread its values. This vision would soon collide with the events of September 11, 2001, providing the neoconservative movement with an opportunity to implement its long-held agenda on an unprecedented scale. The seeds of this transformation had been planted over decades, and with the right circumstances, neoconservatives were poised to reshape U.S. foreign policy in ways that would define a generation.

The Project for the New American Century (PNAC)

In 1997, a group of influential neoconservative thinkers and policymakers formed the **Project for the New American Century (PNAC)**, a think tank dedicated to advancing American military strength and global dominance. Among its founders were prominent figures such as **William Kristol**, **Robert Kagan**, and others who had long been associated with neoconservative ideals. PNAC's mission was clear: to promote a vision of American leadership that relied on military power and strategic intervention to maintain U.S. dominance and shape the international order according to American interests and values.

At the heart of PNAC's ideology was the belief that the United States, as the world's sole superpower after the Cold War, had both a responsibility and an opportunity to reshape the global landscape. The organization argued that maintaining a strong military presence was crucial to deterring potential adversaries and securing American interests abroad. It also emphasized the importance of spreading democracy, particularly in regions that were considered unstable or hostile to Western values. PNAC's founders saw the spread of democratic governance as not only a moral imperative but a strategic necessity to create a world order more favorable to U.S. influence.

One of the most significant contributions PNAC made to the policy discourse was its 2000 report titled "**Rebuilding America's Defenses: Strategy, Forces, and Resources for a New Century**." This document laid out the organization's vision for the future of U.S. foreign policy, arguing for a massive buildup of military power and the modernization of American defense capabilities. The report called for increased defense spending, a shift toward more agile and technologically advanced forces, and a reorganization of military bases around the world to project power more effectively. It was a blueprint for the kind of interventionist foreign policy that would later come to define the early 21st century.

A particularly controversial aspect of the **Rebuilding America's Defenses** report was its assertion that achieving PNAC's goals would be difficult without a "catastrophic and catalyzing event — like a new **Pearl Harbor**." This statement, made a year before the 9/11 attacks, has since fueled speculation and conspiracy theories about neoconservative intentions. To PNAC's critics, the suggestion that a dramatic event could spur the necessary public and political support for their agenda appeared, in retrospect, alarmingly prescient. To proponents of the movement, however, this was merely a recognition of the political reality that significant changes often require extraordinary circumstances to gain widespread acceptance.

The PNAC report also outlined specific regions of interest where U.S. intervention was deemed necessary, particularly the **Middle East**. It pointed to **Iraq** as a prime example of a regime that posed a threat to American interests, not only because of its authoritarian nature but also due to its potential to disrupt regional stability. The report argued that the U.S. should be prepared to act unilaterally if necessary, especially in cases where international cooperation or support from allies might be slow or insufficient. This emphasis on unilateral action became a defining feature of the **Bush Doctrine** and would later be used to justify the 2003 invasion of Iraq.

The influence of PNAC was not limited to think tank circles; its members occupied key positions in the **George W. Bush** administration, providing them with the platform to implement their vision. Individuals like **Dick Cheney** (Vice President), **Donald Rumsfeld** (Secretary of Defense), and **Paul Wolfowitz** (Deputy Secretary of Defense) were all connected to PNAC and played central roles in shaping U.S. foreign policy post-9/11. The transition from think tank to policy implementation was seamless, as these figures were already well-versed in the neoconservative agenda and were determined to put their ideas into practice once they gained power.

When the 9/11 attacks occurred, PNAC's vision suddenly gained traction. The sense of vulnerability and outrage felt by the American public created a political environment where calls for decisive action were met with widespread approval. The neoconservatives in the Bush administration seized the moment, using the attacks as a justification to push for the military strategies and policies they had long advocated. The public's fear of further attacks, combined with a surge of patriotism, allowed the administration to secure support for measures that might have otherwise been met with resistance.

PNAC's influence extended beyond military policy. Its emphasis on the need for a proactive, interventionist approach shaped the broader "**War on Terror**" narrative. The organization argued that the fight against terrorism required not only the elimination of immediate threats but also a strategic transformation of the Middle East. This included the promotion of democratic governments in place of authoritarian regimes, which PNAC believed would lead to long-term stability and reduce the conditions that foster extremism. The invasion of Afghanistan in 2001 was the first step in this strategy, but Iraq became the focal point and the real test of the neoconservative agenda.

The connection between PNAC's pre-9/11 recommendations and the Bush administration's post-9/11 actions is striking. The organization's call for military expansion, the targeting of Iraq, and the need for a new American strategic posture all found their way into official policy. The controversial decision to invade Iraq in 2003, despite the absence of direct evidence linking Saddam Hussein to the 9/11 attacks or proof of **Weapons of Mass Destruction (WMDs)**, reflected the neoconservative belief that reshaping the Middle East was essential to U.S. security. PNAC's blueprint for American dominance was no longer just an idea on paper; it was becoming reality, driven by a group of policymakers who were determined to reshape the world.

The Project for the New American Century may have disbanded in 2006, but its legacy remains. The vision it promoted, and the policies it influenced, continue to spark debate about the role of ideology in foreign policy and the lengths to which some will go to achieve their strategic objectives. Whether viewed as visionary or reckless, PNAC's role in the post-9/11 era offers a critical lens through which to understand the decisions that reshaped the global landscape and America's position within it.

The Influence of the Bush Administration and the Implementation of the Neocon Agenda

When **George W. Bush** took office in January 2001, the stage was set for the neoconservative agenda to move from think tank discussions into practical policy implementation. Many of the figures who had been instrumental in the Project for the New American Century (PNAC) found themselves in key positions of power within the administration. This alignment of personnel and ideology provided the Bush administration with a framework for action that had been developed and refined over years of planning and debate. The neoconservatives, who now occupied influential roles, saw an opportunity to use the levers of government to implement their vision of American dominance and global transformation.

Key PNAC figures such as **Dick Cheney**, **Donald Rumsfeld**, **Paul Wolfowitz**, and **Richard Perle** played critical roles in shaping the administration's foreign policy strategy. Vice President Cheney, in particular, was a central figure who wielded significant influence over national security decisions. As a former Secretary of Defense with deep connections to the military-industrial complex, Cheney was well-positioned to advocate for the neoconservative approach of military intervention and preemptive strikes. Similarly, Donald Rumsfeld, appointed as Secretary of Defense, shared the neoconservative belief in the necessity of a robust and assertive U.S. military presence. With Paul Wolfowitz serving as Deputy Secretary of Defense, the neoconservative trio held sway over military and foreign policy decision-making.

In the months leading up to 9/11, these policymakers were already setting the stage for an assertive foreign policy. The administration's early months saw discussions about the modernization of military forces, the expansion of defense spending, and a focus on so-called "rogue states" like **Iraq**, **Iran**, and **North Korea**. These countries were perceived as threats not only because of their potential to disrupt regional stability but also because they stood as obstacles to the neoconservative vision of spreading democracy and U.S. influence. The Bush administration's national security team was determined to address these threats, even before the catastrophic events of September 11.

The 9/11 attacks became the turning point that allowed the neoconservatives within the Bush administration to advance their agenda with unprecedented speed. In the immediate aftermath of the attacks, there was a surge of public support for decisive action, and the political climate was ripe for significant policy shifts. The Bush administration capitalized on this moment, framing the attacks as an assault not just on America but on freedom and democracy itself. This framing was critical in securing public and congressional support for the broad and ambitious "**War on Terror**."

The **War on Terror** was a strategic response that extended far beyond hunting down those responsible for the attacks. It was an opportunity for the administration to implement the neoconservative vision of transforming the Middle East through military intervention and regime change. The first target was **Afghanistan**, where the **Taliban** regime was swiftly toppled after refusing to hand over **Osama bin Laden**. The military success in Afghanistan was initially seen as a victory for the neoconservative approach, demonstrating the effectiveness of U.S. power projection and intervention. However, it was Iraq that became the central focus and the most controversial aspect of the administration's post-9/11 strategy.

Within hours of the 9/11 attacks, high-ranking officials in the Bush administration, including Rumsfeld and Wolfowitz, began discussing the possibility of targeting Iraq. Despite the fact that no evidence linked **Saddam Hussein**'s regime to the attacks, the administration was already laying the groundwork for an invasion. This fixation on Iraq was not solely a reaction to 9/11; it was the culmination of years of neoconservative planning. The PNAC's 2000 report had explicitly called for removing Saddam from power, and the post-9/11 environment provided the justification needed to put this plan into action. The administration argued that Iraq's alleged weapons of mass destruction (WMD) program posed an imminent threat to the United States and its allies, even though intelligence on this front was ambiguous at best.

In the lead-up to the 2003 invasion of Iraq, the Bush administration launched a concerted campaign to build public support. This involved not only highlighting Saddam Hussein's supposed ties to terrorism but also making the case that liberating Iraq would bring democracy to the Middle East, thereby transforming a volatile region. The neoconservative belief that establishing democratic governments would lead to stability and prosperity was central to the rationale for the invasion. They envisioned Iraq as the first domino in a series of Middle Eastern transformations, believing that success there would trigger a wave of democratization across the region.

The invasion of Iraq in March 2003 was the moment when the neoconservative vision became reality. The administration, led by Bush, Cheney, Rumsfeld, and their allies, had successfully convinced the American public and much of the international community that removing Saddam was both necessary and justified. The initial military campaign, dubbed "**Shock and Awe**," was designed to demonstrate overwhelming U.S. power and was executed with stunning efficiency. Within weeks, Saddam's regime collapsed, and the neoconservatives celebrated what they believed was the beginning of a new chapter in U.S. foreign policy — one in which America would use its military dominance to reshape the world order.

However, the neoconservative triumph was short-lived. The post-invasion period in Iraq did not unfold as the architects had planned. Instead of quickly establishing a democratic government, Iraq descended into chaos, with insurgencies, sectarian violence, and political instability undermining efforts to rebuild the country. The lack of a coherent post-war strategy and the failure to understand the complexities of Iraqi society revealed the flaws in the neoconservative approach. The emphasis on military power as the primary tool for transformation overlooked the necessity of cultural, political, and economic factors in building stable democracies.

Despite these challenges, the Bush administration continued to defend its neoconservative-driven policies. Even as Iraq became increasingly unstable, the administration insisted that the broader strategy was sound and that success was still achievable. This persistence, even in the face of mounting evidence to the contrary, highlighted the ideological rigidity of the neoconservative agenda. The commitment to reshaping the Middle East remained, even as the costs of the Iraq War — in terms of lives lost, financial expenditures, and America's global reputation — continued to escalate.

The Bush administration's implementation of the neoconservative agenda, particularly in Iraq, remains one of the most consequential and controversial aspects of U.S. foreign policy in the 21st century. While neoconservative thinkers envisioned a transformative strategy that would secure American dominance and spread democracy, the realities on the ground revealed the limitations and dangers of this approach. The legacy of these decisions continues to shape not only the Middle East but also debates about American interventionism and the role of ideology in shaping foreign policy.

The Bush Doctrine and Preemptive War

As the Bush administration pushed forward with its response to the 9/11 attacks, it articulated a new strategic framework that became known as the **Bush Doctrine**. This policy represented a dramatic shift in U.S. foreign policy, rooted deeply in the neoconservative ideology of preemption and the aggressive use of military power to achieve national security objectives. The Bush Doctrine asserted that the United States would no longer wait for threats to materialize; instead, it would take preemptive action to neutralize potential dangers before they could harm American interests. This policy, justified in the context of the "**War on Terror**," provided the rationale for the invasion of **Iraq** in 2003 and other military actions that followed.

The foundation of the Bush Doctrine was the belief that in a post-9/11 world, traditional deterrence and containment strategies were no longer sufficient. The threat posed by terrorist networks and rogue states with the potential to acquire **weapons of mass destruction (WMDs)** was seen as too urgent and unpredictable. In a speech to the **West Point Military Academy** in June 2002, President Bush articulated this shift, stating that America "must be prepared to stop rogue states and their terrorist clients before they are able to threaten or use weapons of mass destruction against the United States and our allies." This emphasis on acting unilaterally, if necessary, to defend American interests reflected a core tenet of neoconservative thought: the belief in the moral and strategic imperative of U.S. global leadership.

The Bush Doctrine also emphasized the need to spread democracy as a means of combating terrorism. The administration argued that terrorist groups thrived in authoritarian regimes and regions marked by political repression, poverty, and instability. By promoting democratic governance, the United States could create conditions less conducive to extremism. This idea was consistent with neoconservative ideology, which saw the promotion of democracy not only as a moral obligation but also as a strategic necessity for ensuring long-term global security. The Bush administration framed the invasion of Iraq as an opportunity to establish a democratic foothold in the Middle East, which they believed could catalyze a wave of democratic reform across the region.

A critical element of the Bush Doctrine was the concept of **"preventive war,"** which goes beyond traditional preemption. Preemptive war involves striking first when an imminent threat is identified, but preventive war means taking action before a threat becomes immediate. This idea was controversial because it expanded the scope of military engagement based on perceived, rather than actual, threats. Critics argued that it set a dangerous precedent for international relations, effectively allowing the United States to justify military interventions based on speculative assessments of potential dangers. Proponents, however, insisted that in an era where non-state actors like terrorist organizations could strike without warning, waiting for conclusive evidence could prove catastrophic.

The most significant application of the Bush Doctrine was the decision to invade **Iraq** in 2003. Despite the lack of direct evidence linking Iraq to the 9/11 attacks, the Bush administration argued that Saddam Hussein's regime posed an imminent threat due to its alleged WMD programs and ties to terrorist groups. In his speech to the **United Nations** in September 2002, President Bush made the case that Iraq's failure to comply with international disarmament obligations constituted a clear and present danger. The administration stressed the need for immediate action, suggesting that without intervention, Saddam could supply WMDs to terrorists, leading to catastrophic attacks similar to or worse than 9/11.

The Bush administration also relied heavily on the idea that removing Saddam would set off a domino effect, leading to democratization and stability throughout the Middle East. This argument aligned with the broader neoconservative belief that U.S. military intervention could reshape the geopolitical landscape in ways favorable to American interests. By toppling a dictator and establishing a democratic government in Iraq, the administration claimed that it could provide a model for other countries in the region, such as **Syria** and **Iran**, encouraging them to pursue political reforms. This idealistic vision, while compelling to some, was met with skepticism by others who warned that imposing democracy through military means was unlikely to succeed and could lead to unintended consequences.

To build public support for the war, the Bush administration launched an extensive media campaign, highlighting the dangers posed by Saddam's regime and framing the invasion as a necessary and justifiable act of self-defense. High-ranking officials, including Vice President Cheney, Secretary of Defense Rumsfeld, and Secretary of State **Colin Powell**, delivered speeches and made appearances in the media, emphasizing the urgency of addressing the threat Iraq allegedly posed. Powell's presentation to the **UN Security Council** in February 2003 was a pivotal moment; he presented intelligence purportedly showing Iraq's ongoing WMD activities, though much of this evidence would later be discredited. Nevertheless, the campaign was effective in garnering support, both domestically and among key international allies.

The Bush Doctrine's emphasis on unilateralism and preemptive action strained America's relationships with some of its traditional allies. While the United Kingdom, under **Prime Minister Tony Blair**, supported the invasion of Iraq, other major powers such as **France**, **Germany**, and **Russia** expressed strong opposition. The failure to secure a broad coalition through the UN led the Bush administration to form a **"Coalition of the Willing,"** composed of countries that supported the U.S. effort. This approach highlighted the administration's willingness to bypass international institutions and act independently when it believed American security was at stake.

The decision to invade Iraq, framed through the lens of the Bush Doctrine, marked a defining moment in U.S. foreign policy. It reflected the neoconservative belief that the United States should use its unmatched military power to reshape the world order, acting as a force for democracy and security. In the short term, the rapid overthrow of Saddam Hussein's regime seemed to validate the doctrine's principles, demonstrating the effectiveness of swift, decisive military action. However, the subsequent chaos and prolonged insurgency in Iraq revealed the limitations and dangers of the Bush Doctrine, as the administration struggled to achieve stability in the face of sectarian violence and widespread unrest.

In the years that followed, the Bush Doctrine's emphasis on preemptive war and unilateral action would be scrutinized, criticized, and debated intensely. The war's financial and human costs, along with the intelligence failures that led to the false claims about Iraq's WMD capabilities, challenged the notion that American military intervention could be a reliable instrument for spreading democracy and security. The legacy of the Bush Doctrine thus became intertwined with the broader debate over the role of neoconservatism in shaping U.S. foreign policy and the consequences of using military power to achieve ideological objectives.

The Aftermath of Iraq and the Legacy of the Neocon Agenda

The invasion of **Iraq** in 2003, executed under the Bush Doctrine and driven by neoconservative ideology, initially seemed to be a swift and decisive military victory. Within weeks, **Baghdad** fell, and Saddam Hussein's regime crumbled. The Bush administration celebrated this as a triumph of American power and a validation of their approach to global threats. However, as the initial euphoria faded, the challenges of the post-invasion period became glaringly apparent. The occupation of Iraq quickly descended into chaos, revealing the deep flaws in the neoconservative strategy and raising questions about the true legacy of the Bush Doctrine.

The failure to secure and stabilize Iraq after the fall of Saddam's government highlighted a critical miscalculation by the

Bush administration and its neoconservative architects. Despite their confidence in the effectiveness of U.S. military power, they had not adequately planned for the complexities of postwar reconstruction. The administration's expectation that Iraqis would greet American troops as liberators and quickly establish a democratic government proved overly simplistic and detached from the realities on the ground. Instead, the absence of a coherent post-invasion strategy left a power vacuum that was swiftly filled by insurgents, sectarian militias, and foreign fighters.

The decision to disband the **Iraqi Army** and purge members of the **Ba'ath Party** from the government, led by **Coalition Provisional Authority** head **Paul Bremer**, only exacerbated the chaos. These actions, intended to remove the remnants of Saddam's power structure, instead alienated and radicalized a significant segment of Iraq's population. Tens of thousands of trained and armed former soldiers, suddenly unemployed and with no stake in the new Iraq, turned against the occupation forces. Many joined the ranks of insurgent groups, fueling a violent resistance that the U.S. military struggled to contain. The country plunged into a brutal cycle of insurgency and counterinsurgency, with coalition forces caught in the middle of a growing sectarian civil war.

The rise of **al-Qaeda in Iraq (AQI)**, led by **Abu Musab al-Zarqawi**, was one of the most alarming consequences of the power vacuum. AQI capitalized on the chaos to launch attacks against U.S. troops and Iraqi civilians, with the goal of igniting sectarian tensions between Iraq's **Sunni** and **Shia** populations. The group's brutal tactics and indiscriminate violence led to widespread destabilization and further complicated the U.S. mission. The emergence of AQI, which would eventually evolve into the **Islamic State (ISIS)**, underscored how the U.S. invasion had not only failed to eliminate terrorism but had, in many ways, created the conditions for its growth. The invasion and occupation had transformed Iraq into a breeding ground for jihadist groups, contradicting the Bush administration's justification for the war as a means of combating terrorism.

As violence escalated, the Bush administration's vision of Iraq as a beacon of democracy in the Middle East became increasingly untenable. The neoconservative promise that democracy would flourish once a dictator was removed clashed with the sectarian and ethnic divisions that defined Iraqi society. The U.S.-backed government struggled to establish legitimacy and authority, and the attempts to organize democratic elections, while initially successful in their logistical execution, did little to address the underlying social and political rifts. Iraq's new leaders often lacked the support of the broader population, leading to widespread disillusionment and the perception that the new government was merely a puppet of the American occupiers.

The economic and human costs of the war became increasingly evident as the occupation dragged on. The U.S. military suffered thousands of casualties, and the toll on Iraqi civilians was catastrophic, with hundreds of thousands killed and millions displaced. The financial burden of the war, running into the trillions of dollars, strained the U.S. economy and led to debates about the long-term consequences of such an expansive military venture. The costs far exceeded initial estimates, and the prolonged nature of the conflict revealed the inadequacy of the administration's planning and understanding of the region's complexities.

The failure to stabilize Iraq and the subsequent rise of ISIS also had significant geopolitical repercussions. The war weakened America's standing on the international stage, as allies and rivals alike questioned the legitimacy and competence of U.S.

foreign policy. Countries that had opposed the invasion, such as **France** and **Germany**, were vindicated in their skepticism, while regional powers like **Iran** and **Syria** exploited the chaos to expand their influence. Iran, in particular, saw the removal of its longtime enemy, Saddam Hussein, as an opportunity to increase its sway over Iraq through its support for Shia militias and political parties, further complicating the American mission.

Domestically, the war and its aftermath led to a deepening division within the United States. As the situation in Iraq deteriorated, the American public's support for the war waned, and the credibility of the Bush administration came under intense scrutiny. The failure to find WMDs, which had been the central justification for the invasion, eroded trust in the government's intelligence and motives. Accusations of misleading the public and manipulating intelligence reports became common, fueling widespread anti-war protests and contributing to a polarized political climate. The war became a central issue in the 2004 and 2006 elections, with politicians on both sides of the aisle grappling with its implications.

By the time George W. Bush left office in 2009, the neoconservative vision that had shaped his administration's foreign policy lay in tatters. The promise of a democratic and stable Iraq had given way to a reality of violence, sectarianism, and instability. The Bush Doctrine's emphasis on preemptive war and unilateral action, once hailed as a bold strategy for a new era, was increasingly viewed as a reckless and costly experiment that had backfired. The neoconservative agenda, which aimed to establish American dominance and transform the Middle East, instead left the U.S. mired in an unwinnable conflict and struggling to repair its reputation.

In the years that followed, the legacy of the Iraq War and the neoconservative agenda continued to influence U.S. foreign policy. The Obama administration, inheriting the situation in Iraq, faced the difficult task of extricating American forces while dealing with the consequences of the power vacuum that remained. The rise of ISIS in the wake of the U.S. withdrawal further highlighted the long-term destabilization caused by the invasion and raised questions about the effectiveness of military intervention as a tool for nation-building and democracy promotion.

The neoconservative experiment in Iraq ultimately serves as a cautionary tale about the limits of military power and the dangers of ideology-driven foreign policy. While the architects of the Bush Doctrine believed that American strength could reshape the world, the realities of Iraq exposed the complexities and unintended consequences of such interventions. The aftermath of the Iraq War remains a pivotal chapter in understanding the neoconservative influence on U.S. policy, illustrating how even the most powerful nation can face setbacks when ideology collides with the complex realities of geopolitics and war.

Chapter 10: The Pentagon Attack and Flight 93

The Pentagon Attack - Official Account

On the morning of September 11, 2001, just minutes after the North and South Towers of the World Trade Center had been struck by hijacked airplanes, American Airlines Flight 77 was reportedly taken over by five terrorists and redirected toward Washington, D.C. The official narrative, as outlined by the **9/11 Commission Report**, describes how the Boeing 757, en route from Dulles International Airport in Washington, D.C., to Los Angeles, was hijacked at approximately 8:51 a.m. The flight's transponder was turned off, making it difficult for air traffic control to track the plane. The hijackers maneuvered the aircraft, heading toward the nation's capital, while passengers were forced to the back of the plane.

At 9:37 a.m., Flight 77 crashed into the western side of the Pentagon, the headquarters of the United States Department of Defense. The impact and subsequent explosion caused severe damage to the building, resulting in the collapse of a section of the Pentagon's outer ring. The official report stated that 125 military personnel and civilians inside the building, along with the 59 passengers and crew members on the flight, lost their lives. The attack on the Pentagon was seen as a direct assault on America's military nerve center, underscoring the audacity and precision of the terrorists' coordinated attacks.

The official account detailed the precise location of the impact. Flight 77 struck the Pentagon's west side, an area that had recently been reinforced as part of an ongoing renovation project designed to upgrade the building's structural integrity. The crash caused an intense fire, and the subsequent collapse of the impacted section highlighted the devastating effect of the attack. Emergency responders arrived swiftly, attempting to rescue survivors and extinguish the flames, but the scene was chaotic, with smoke billowing from the gaping hole in the iconic structure.

Initial reports on the day of the attack indicated confusion and uncertainty about what exactly had struck the Pentagon. Early news coverage speculated that it could have been a truck bomb or even a smaller aircraft. However, as more information became available, the narrative coalesced around the explanation that American Airlines Flight 77 had been deliberately flown into the building by the hijackers. The **Federal Aviation Administration (FAA)** and **NORAD** were scrutinized for their inability to intercept the hijacked plane despite the time gap between the hijacking and the impact. The official explanation cited communication issues, delays in relaying information between agencies, and the unprecedented nature of the attack as reasons for the delayed response.

The government swiftly released reports detailing the events leading up to the crash, emphasizing the speed and precision with which the hijackers operated. According to the official timeline, after the hijackers seized control of Flight 77, they turned the aircraft back toward Washington, D.C., flying it low and fast. The trajectory and speed were critical in evading radar detection and complicating any attempts by military jets to intercept the plane. The crash at the Pentagon, therefore, was presented as an inevitable outcome of a well-coordinated and highly organized assault that had outmaneuvered the nation's defenses.

The aftermath of the attack on the Pentagon was chaotic but also deeply symbolic. Media coverage and official statements highlighted the devastation inflicted on America's military command center. Images of the burning building, shrouded in smoke, were broadcast worldwide, reinforcing the idea that the country was under siege. Rescue efforts began immediately, with emergency personnel working to control the fires and evacuate wounded survivors. The Pentagon Memorial, established years later, would come to honor the victims of this attack, memorializing the lives lost on the flight and within the walls of the building.

Official statements in the days and weeks following the attack reinforced the severity of what had occurred. Secretary of Defense **Donald Rumsfeld** described the assault as a "tragic and devastating loss," while President George W. Bush used it to underscore the gravity of the threat posed by international terrorism. The attack on the Pentagon became a focal point for rallying support for the War on Terror, with government officials and the media framing it as a direct attack on the heart of America's military and defense capabilities.

Despite the clarity and detail provided in the official narrative, some aspects of the Pentagon attack have been points of contention for skeptics and conspiracy theorists. Nevertheless, the account presented by the **9/11 Commission** remains the most widely accepted explanation. It underscores the sheer coordination and scale of the 9/11 attacks, emphasizing that the hijackers' strategy extended beyond symbolic targets like the World Trade Center to include America's military infrastructure.

As such, the Pentagon attack is presented not only as an act of terrorism but also as a declaration of war, a moment that propelled the U.S. into an era of military engagement and domestic security reforms.

In summary, the official account of the Pentagon attack portrays a calculated and expertly executed assault on a symbol of American military power. The timeline and details provided in government reports and the 9/11 Commission's findings form a narrative that has shaped public understanding and perception of the events of that tragic day. While the account has faced scrutiny and skepticism from various quarters, it remains a central element of the broader story of 9/11—a day when terrorists targeted not only civilians but also the core of American defense.

Controversies and Anomalies Surrounding the Pentagon Crash

While the official account of the Pentagon attack paints a clear picture of the events of September 11, 2001, skeptics and researchers have raised numerous questions and pointed to anomalies that challenge this version. These controversies have become central to the debate surrounding the 9/11 attacks, with the Pentagon crash serving as a focal point for those who argue that there are inconsistencies and gaps in the official narrative.

One of the most frequently cited anomalies is the lack of clear video footage showing American Airlines Flight 77 hitting the Pentagon. The Pentagon, one of the most secure buildings in the world, is surrounded by surveillance cameras, yet the footage released to the public is limited and inconclusive. In the aftermath of the attack, the FBI quickly confiscated video recordings from nearby locations, including a gas station and a hotel. Despite requests for transparency, only a few frames of footage showing a blurry object approaching the Pentagon were released. Critics argue that if a commercial airliner truly struck the building, clearer footage should exist. This has fueled speculation that the government might be hiding evidence or manipulating information to fit the official story.

Another point of controversy revolves around the physical damage observed at the crash site. Skeptics have noted that the initial hole in the Pentagon's outer wall appeared too small to have been caused by a Boeing 757. They argue that the dimensions of the hole, which measured approximately 16 to 18 feet in diameter, did not match the wingspan or the height of a commercial jet. Additionally, photos taken before the collapse of the outer section show relatively intact windows and minimal damage surrounding the impact zone, raising further questions about whether a large aircraft could have caused such localized destruction. Some theorists have suggested that the damage might have been caused by a smaller, missile-like object rather than a commercial airliner.

Eyewitness testimony also presents a mixed picture of what happened at the Pentagon. While some witnesses reported seeing a large commercial aircraft flying low and crashing into the building, others describe seeing a smaller, less identifiable object. Some accounts even mention the absence of a plane altogether. These conflicting testimonies have led skeptics to question the reliability of the official narrative. The **9/11 Commission Report** largely focuses on a select number of eyewitnesses who corroborate the account of a commercial airliner, but critics argue that the exclusion of contradictory testimonies points to a selective framing of events.

Furthermore, skeptics often highlight the lack of visible aircraft debris consistent with a Boeing 757 at the Pentagon crash site. Unlike the World Trade Center crashes, where large pieces of fuselage and aircraft parts were visible in the wreckage, the Pentagon's crash site appeared remarkably clean. Photos taken shortly after the attack show little evidence of large wings, engines, or tail sections. The official explanation suggests that the intense fire, fueled by jet fuel, incinerated much of the plane, but skeptics argue that even in high-impact crashes, parts of the aircraft—particularly the engines and landing gear—should have remained relatively intact. The apparent absence of these large components has led some to question whether a Boeing 757 was truly involved.

The swift and coordinated response of emergency and military personnel at the Pentagon also raises suspicions for some theorists. Within minutes of the attack, the crash site was surrounded by officials, and debris was quickly removed and the area secured. Some critics argue that this rapid response was intended to control the narrative and suppress potential evidence that might contradict the official account. They point to how little time investigators had to thoroughly examine the scene before clean-up operations began, suggesting that crucial evidence might have been overlooked or deliberately concealed.

Finally, the issue of the Pentagon's recently reinforced structure has also become a point of debate. The section of the building that was struck had undergone renovations aimed at strengthening its structural integrity, a project that was completed just weeks before the attack. Skeptics question whether this was merely a coincidence or if the attackers deliberately targeted this area, knowing it would minimize casualties and damage. The fact that the renovations included blast-resistant windows and reinforced walls has led some to speculate that the attackers possessed insider knowledge, aiming for a spot that would not completely destroy the building.

In summary, the controversies and anomalies surrounding the Pentagon attack are numerous and have become a cornerstone of the broader 9/11 truth movement. Questions about the lack of clear video evidence, the size and nature of the impact hole, the absence of visible aircraft debris, and conflicting eye-witness testimonies all contribute to skepticism about the official account. Whether these anomalies are the result of genuine inconsistencies or the product of selective evidence and misinterpretation remains a matter of debate. However, these points have undoubtedly fueled ongoing speculation and investigation, ensuring that the Pentagon attack remains one of the most contested aspects of the events of 9/11.

The Heroic Narrative of Flight 93

While the attack on the Pentagon is shrouded in controversy and debate, the story of United Airlines Flight 93 has emerged as one of heroism and sacrifice. The official narrative presents a gripping and emotional account of ordinary passengers banding together to prevent further destruction and loss of life. According to the **9/11 Commission Report**, Flight 93 was hijacked by four terrorists at approximately 9:28 a.m., just minutes after the attacks on the World Trade Center and the Pentagon. Unlike the other hijacked planes, however, the passengers and crew aboard Flight 93 fought back, ultimately preventing the terrorists from reaching their intended target.

The timeline of events, as pieced together from phone calls made by passengers, paints a vivid picture of courage and resilience. After the hijackers seized control of the cockpit, passengers began calling their loved ones to report the situation and say their goodbyes. Through these conversations, they learned of the other attacks already unfolding that morning. Realizing that their hijacking was part of a larger plot, the passengers decided to take action. Led by several brave individuals, they hatched a plan to storm the cockpit and overpower the terrorists.

The phrase "Let's roll," reportedly spoken by passenger **Todd Beamer**, has become synonymous with the bravery shown that day. Beamer and other passengers used seatback phones and cell phones to coordinate with their loved ones, who relayed information about the attacks in New York and Washington, D.C. Understanding that they were likely headed for a significant target, the passengers knew they had to act. The recordings from the cockpit voice recorder captured the sounds of the struggle as the passengers tried to force their way into the cockpit, where the hijackers had locked themselves.

At 10:03 a.m., Flight 93 crashed into a field near Shanksville, Pennsylvania, killing all 44 people on board, including the four hijackers. The official report suggests that the passengers' actions directly caused the plane to crash before it could reach its target, which authorities speculate may have been either the White House or the U.S. Capitol. The story of Flight 93 became a symbol of unity, courage, and the indomitable spirit of Americans in the face of terror.

In the days and weeks following the crash, the media and government officials hailed the passengers as heroes. The site of the crash in Shanksville quickly became a place of mourning and remembrance, and a national memorial was later established to honor those who lost their lives. The narrative of Flight 93 was used to rally public support and bolster the nation's resolve to fight terrorism. President George W. Bush and other leaders frequently referenced the heroism displayed by the passengers as a testament to the strength and bravery of ordinary citizens.

The story also served a strategic purpose, emphasizing a message of hope and resilience amid the broader tragedy of 9/11. While the attacks on the World Trade Center and the Pentagon highlighted the vulnerabilities of the United States, the actions of the passengers aboard Flight 93 demonstrated that Americans were not merely passive victims but capable of heroism even in the face of overwhelming odds. The narrative of Flight

93 became an integral part of the post-9/11 identity, symbolizing the collective spirit and unity of the nation.

Despite the powerful imagery and heroism associated with Flight 93, there are elements of the official account that have drawn scrutiny. Some skeptics argue that the plane may have been shot down by the military to prevent it from reaching its target. They point to statements made by officials on the day of the attacks, including Vice President Dick Cheney's reported order authorizing the military to shoot down hijacked planes. Although the government has maintained that Flight 93 crashed because of the passengers' struggle with the hijackers, some conspiracy theorists claim that fighter jets may have intercepted the plane.

The crash site itself has also been a point of contention. Unlike typical airplane crashes, where large debris fields and wreckage are expected, the Flight 93 crash site was described as a relatively small impact crater, with limited visible debris. Photos and videos from the scene show scattered fragments, but some skeptics argue that the lack of large, identifiable aircraft parts raises questions about the official account. They suggest that if the plane had been shot down, this could explain the smaller debris field and the lack of visible wreckage.

Regardless of these debates, the story of Flight 93 has remained a powerful symbol in the narrative of 9/11. The government and media have continually emphasized the heroism of the passengers, using their actions as an example of the selflessness and bravery that define the American spirit. The **Flight 93 National Memorial**, built at the crash site, stands as a tribute to the courage displayed on that day and serves as a reminder of the sacrifices made to prevent further loss of life.

In the broader context of the 9/11 attacks, Flight 93 represents a turning point where ordinary citizens took control in the face of terror. Whether or not every detail of the official story is accurate, the heroism attributed to the passengers has had a lasting impact on how the events of that day are remembered and commemorated. The narrative of Flight 93 serves as a reminder that even in the darkest moments, acts of courage can emerge, offering hope and unity in the face of tragedy.

The Discrepancies in the Flight Data Recorder and Black Box Information

One of the critical pieces of evidence in any plane crash investigation is the flight data recorder (FDR) and cockpit voice recorder (CVR), commonly referred to as the "black boxes." These devices are designed to withstand catastrophic events, providing crucial information about the final moments of a flight. In the case of United Airlines Flight 93, both black boxes were recovered, and their contents have been instrumental in shaping the official narrative. However, the information retrieved has also raised significant questions and controversies that some argue undermine the government's account.

The official story, supported by the recordings from the cockpit voice recorder, depicts a struggle between the hijackers and the passengers, culminating in the plane crashing into a field in Shanksville, Pennsylvania. The CVR records voices and sounds from the cockpit, and it captured the chaotic and desperate struggle as passengers attempted to breach the cockpit door. This recording has been cited as compelling evidence that the passengers were able to overcome the hijackers, preventing the plane from reaching its intended target. The FBI and the **9/11 Commission** have stated that the final moments of the recording indicate a struggle for control, with the hijackers ultimately deciding to crash the plane.

However, some researchers and skeptics have pointed to inconsistencies in the CVR and FDR data that cast doubt on this version of events. One of the most debated issues is the fact that the cockpit voice recording was not fully released to the public. Only a select few, including the victims' families and members of the 9/11 Commission, were allowed to listen to the recording in its entirety, and even then, they were restricted from taking notes or discussing the content in detail. The public release consisted of a transcript and a brief, edited segment of the audio, prompting critics to question why the full recording remains inaccessible. For conspiracy theorists, the lack of transparency suggests that the government might be hiding something or selectively framing the narrative.

Another point of contention is the flight data recorder itself, which logs vital information such as altitude, speed, and heading. Skeptics argue that some of the FDR data doesn't match the official narrative. For instance, the final altitude readings reportedly show the plane descending at an unusually rapid rate, leading some to speculate that this could be consistent with an external event—such as a missile strike—rather than a controlled descent by the hijackers. While the government maintains that the rapid descent was the result of the struggle between passengers and hijackers, theorists question whether all relevant data from the FDR has been disclosed.

Moreover, the exact timing of events as presented in the flight recorder data has been scrutinized. According to the official timeline, the passengers began their counterattack at approximately 9:57 a.m., and the struggle for control lasted until the plane crashed at 10:03 a.m. However, some independent researchers claim that there are inconsistencies in the timing of certain cockpit noises and events recorded on the CVR. For example, they argue that the recorded sequence of events, such as the sounds of the cockpit door being breached, don't align perfectly with the timing of the crash, suggesting either a misrepresentation or manipulation of the data.

Skeptics also highlight that, despite the black boxes' durability and the critical information they provide, the full extent of what they recorded remains largely classified. Unlike other plane crashes where FDR and CVR data are released or detailed reports are made public, much of the information related to Flight 93's black boxes remains restricted. The government has defended this decision by citing national security concerns and the sensitive nature of the recordings. However, conspiracy theorists interpret this as a sign that the recordings might contain information that contradicts the official account or reveals alternative explanations for the crash.

In addition to the black box data, another area of controversy involves the recording quality and integrity of the CVR. Some have raised questions about whether the recording might have been edited or tampered with before being presented to the public and the families of the victims. These allegations are often based on comparisons to previous air disasters where CVR data was fully disclosed and analyzed without similar restrictions. Critics argue that the limited release of information surrounding Flight 93, coupled with the inconsistencies noted by independent analysts, suggests that the government might be controlling the narrative to prevent scrutiny or alternative interpretations of the event.

Theories that Flight 93 was potentially shot down by the military are often bolstered by these discrepancies in the black box information. Proponents of this view point to the possibility that if the military intercepted the plane, the CVR might contain audio evidence of such an event, like unusual cockpit noises or pilot communications indicating the approach of military aircraft. They argue that the selective release of the recording is an attempt to withhold information that would point to a shoot-down scenario, thus protecting the official story that emphasizes passenger heroism.

Ultimately, the questions surrounding the black boxes of Flight 93 are a significant part of the broader debate over what truly happened on that tragic day. While the official narrative celebrates the courage of the passengers who fought back, skeptics argue that the inconsistencies and lack of transparency surrounding the flight data cast doubt on the veracity of this account. The refusal to release the full recordings or detailed data from the FDR and CVR feeds into a broader pattern of secrecy and controlled information, further fueling suspicions that key elements of the events remain undisclosed. Whether these inconsistencies are the result of genuine gaps in the investigation or the deliberate withholding of evidence, they have become central to the ongoing debates about the true story of Flight 93 and its role in the events of September 11, 2001.

The Aftermath and Legacy of Flight 93

In the aftermath of September 11, the story of Flight 93 became a powerful symbol of courage and defiance. The government and media portrayed the passengers as heroes who, upon realizing the gravity of their situation, chose to act rather than allow the hijackers to strike another significant target. This narrative served not only to honor the memory of those who perished but also to rally a nation still reeling from the shock and horror of the attacks.

Shortly after the events of 9/11, officials and media outlets began to emphasize the heroism of the passengers. Government leaders, including President George W. Bush, highlighted the selfless actions taken by those aboard Flight 93 as an example of the American spirit. "They were ordinary citizens who found themselves in the most extraordinary circumstances, and they made the ultimate sacrifice for their country," Bush said in one of his speeches. The imagery of everyday Americans banding together, united against terrorism, resonated deeply with the public and helped foster a sense of unity during a time of fear and uncertainty.

The crash site in Shanksville, Pennsylvania, quickly became a focal point of national mourning. Within days, it was visited by families of the victims, first responders, and government officials. The field, initially a scene of devastation, transformed into a site of reflection and remembrance. In 2002, a temporary memorial was established, drawing thousands of visitors each year who came to pay their respects. Over time, this temporary tribute evolved into a national effort to create a permanent memorial, ensuring that the courage displayed on that day would be honored for generations to come.

In 2015, the **Flight 93 National Memorial** was formally dedicated, featuring a wall of names for each of the passengers and crew members. The memorial's design, with its open-air chapel and Tower of Voices, was intended to create a space of quiet contemplation where visitors could reflect on the events of that day and the bravery shown by those on board. The narrative of Flight 93 as a story of sacrifice and unity was enshrined not only in this physical space but also in the public consciousness, reinforcing the passengers' legacy as heroes who prevented further loss of life.

However, alongside this official narrative, alternative theories and debates have persisted. Critics and conspiracy theorists argue that the government's emphasis on the heroism of Flight 93 serves to obscure unanswered questions and controversial details. For instance, they point to the initial confusion surrounding the crash and the delayed release of information as evidence that the full story might still be hidden. Some claim that the emphasis on heroism diverts attention from the possibility that the military may have shot down the plane to prevent it from reaching its target, thereby avoiding a politically damaging admission.

Others argue that the rapid establishment of the Flight 93 narrative as one of unity and sacrifice was part of a broader effort to build support for the government's response to 9/11. By highlighting the heroism of everyday Americans, the Bush administration and other officials sought to foster a sense of patriotism and resolve, which helped justify the subsequent wars in Afghanistan and Iraq. The image of selfless, courageous passengers became a powerful tool for mobilizing public opinion, reinforcing the idea that Americans had to stand together in the fight against terrorism.

Despite these debates, the legacy of Flight 93 remains a crucial part of the national memory of 9/11. The story has been immortalized in documentaries, books, and films, including the 2006 movie **"United 93,"** which sought to portray the events with realism and respect. The film, like other portrayals, emphasized the bravery and humanity of the passengers, contributing to a collective memory that reinforces their role as symbols of American resilience.

The enduring impact of the Flight 93 story also extends into the broader context of 9/11 commemorations. The passengers and crew are remembered each year alongside the victims of the World Trade Center and the Pentagon attacks, ensuring that their actions are honored not just as part of a tragic event but as a powerful testament to the American spirit. The Flight 93 National Memorial hosts annual ceremonies, attended by survivors, families of the victims, and national leaders, who come to pay tribute to the courage and sacrifice demonstrated that day.

Nevertheless, the legacy of Flight 93 also remains a focal point for those who challenge the official 9/11 narrative. Skeptics argue that the heroic story serves as a distraction, preventing the public from critically examining the anomalies surrounding the crash. They point to the restricted access to the cockpit voice recordings and the continued classification of certain details as evidence that the truth may still be concealed.

These ongoing debates have kept Flight 93 in the spotlight, not only as a symbol of heroism but also as a central figure in the broader controversy surrounding the events of September 11.

For many, however, the story of Flight 93 transcends these debates. It represents a moment when ordinary people, faced with extraordinary circumstances, made a choice that would define their legacy and shape the nation's response. Whether or not every aspect of the official account is accepted, the bravery and sacrifice attributed to the passengers have left an indelible mark on American history. The crash site in Shanksville stands as a solemn reminder of that sacrifice, a place where visitors can connect with a story of courage that continues to resonate.

The narrative of Flight 93, like many elements of 9/11, serves both as a source of inspiration and as a point of contention. Its legacy reflects the complex ways in which tragic events are remembered, interpreted, and sometimes contested. But regardless of the debates, the passengers' courage and the unity they symbolize remain powerful reminders of resilience in the face of terror, providing a source of strength and reflection for those who visit the memorial and those who carry their story forward.

Chapter 11: First Responders and Eyewitnesses

Eyewitness Accounts of the World Trade Center Attacks

On the morning of September 11, 2001, New York City was just beginning its daily rhythm when the unimaginable unfolded. The first plane, American Airlines Flight 11, struck the North Tower of the World Trade Center at 8:46 AM. The initial impact was startling enough, but what followed in the minutes and hours afterward was a scene of unprecedented chaos and horror. Eyewitnesses who found themselves near the site recall a range of reactions—from confusion and disbelief to sheer panic.

People on the streets of Manhattan described an eerie sense of confusion as they watched the North Tower burn. Office workers, commuters, and tourists, caught up in the moment, stood in shock as the smoke billowed out of the skyscraper. Many initially thought it was an accident, a freak incident involving a small plane or perhaps an explosion within the building itself. The idea that a commercial airliner had deliberately flown into the tower was beyond imagination for most. "We just saw a huge ball of fire," one witness recounted, "and everyone was just standing there, staring at it, not understanding what had happened."

Fifteen minutes later, at 9:03 AM, United Airlines Flight 175 slammed into the South Tower, shattering any remaining illusions of an accident. The impact was captured live by news cameras and witnessed by thousands on the streets below. In the immediate aftermath, the city erupted into chaos. The crowd's collective shock turned to terror as the realization dawned: this was a coordinated attack. People screamed, some cried, and others ran frantically, trying to find safety as debris rained down from the towers. The air was filled with smoke, ash, and the echoing sounds of sirens as emergency responders rushed to the scene.

Amid the chaos, those who were closer to the towers offered chilling details of their experiences. Some described seeing the planes approaching and thought they were flying unusually low. One witness reported, "It looked like the plane was swerving, like it was aiming for the tower." Others spoke of the deafening explosion that followed each impact and the wave of heat and debris that pushed outward. "I felt the ground shake," said another observer. "It was like nothing I'd ever felt before, like the entire city shuddered."

Accounts from individuals inside the buildings provide further insight into those terrifying moments. Survivors in the North Tower described feeling the violent tremor from the impact and the fear that gripped them as they attempted to flee down stairwells filled with smoke and dust. Many of them spoke of a sense of disbelief, their minds struggling to comprehend the reality of what had just happened. Those in the South Tower, alerted by the first impact, faced an agonizing decision about whether to evacuate or remain. For some, the choice to leave saved their lives; for others, the message to stay put proved fatal when the second plane hit.

As the drama unfolded on the ground, the city's emergency response systems were overwhelmed. Eyewitnesses spoke of seeing firefighters, police officers, and paramedics rushing toward the buildings, often against the tide of civilians fleeing the area. This contrast between those running for safety and those heading into danger became a defining image of that day. The bravery of the first responders was evident, even as people watching from nearby could sense the mounting danger. "They went in without hesitation," one observer recalled. "They knew it was bad, but they kept going."

However, not all accounts fit neatly into the official narrative. Some eyewitnesses reported hearing explosions within the towers before and after the planes struck. A few described seeing flashes or bursts of light coming from lower floors as they tried to make sense of the chaos around them. These testimonies, often inconsistent or difficult to verify, have been cited by some as evidence of a more complex event than initially portrayed. The question of whether additional explosions occurred, and if so, what might have caused them, remains a point of controversy.

In the hours following the attacks, as the towers collapsed and the dust settled, eyewitnesses continued to struggle to process what they had seen. Some spoke of the surreal nature of the scene—one moment, the towers were burning; the next, they were gone. For many, the sight of the buildings collapsing seemed like a scene from a movie. "It didn't look real," one witness said. "It was like the world had come to an end."

These firsthand accounts from the streets of New York City offer a raw, unfiltered glimpse into the confusion, horror, and disbelief that marked that day. They provide a human dimension to the events, capturing the immediate, visceral reaction of people who witnessed one of the most significant tragedies in modern history. At the same time, the variations and discrepancies in their testimonies have fueled ongoing debates and alternative theories, illustrating the complex nature of memory and perception in the face of such an overwhelming event.

Testimonies from Firefighters and Police at Ground Zero

In the minutes following the first impact at the North Tower, New York City's firefighters and police officers mobilized with remarkable speed and courage. As thousands of civilians fled the area, these first responders rushed toward the burning towers, determined to save lives despite the immense risks. Their testimonies offer a powerful and haunting perspective on the events of that day, shedding light on the chaos, heroism, and horror they encountered at Ground Zero.

For firefighters from the FDNY, the scene at the World Trade Center was like nothing they had ever faced before. Many of them had responded to high-rise fires, but nothing could have prepared them for the scale and intensity of what they saw on September 11. "It was like walking into a war zone," one firefighter recalled. "The smoke, the heat, the falling debris—it was everywhere." As they entered the North Tower, many were struck by the sheer scale of the destruction. The building's lobby, usually a bustling hub of activity, was now filled with smoke, shattered glass, and terrified civilians. Firefighters and police officers worked together to organize evacuations, guiding people toward the stairwells and ensuring as many as possible could escape.

Inside the towers, first responders faced a harrowing situation. As they ascended the stairwells, they were met by panicked office workers and survivors covered in dust, some injured and others in shock. The stairwells were filled with smoke, and visibility was poor, making the evacuation efforts all the more challenging. Despite the uncertainty and danger, these brave individuals pressed on, climbing floor by floor to reach those trapped above. Many firefighters reported hearing explosions, loud enough to shake the building and cause panic among those still inside. "There were these loud bangs, like something else was going off in the building," a firefighter said. "We couldn't tell what was happening, but it felt like things were getting worse by the second."

These reports of explosions became a controversial point in the aftermath of 9/11. Several first responders recalled hearing what sounded like secondary explosions, distinct from the initial impacts of the planes. These testimonies have fueled debates and conspiracy theories suggesting that there may have been additional explosive devices planted in the towers. One firefighter explained, "It wasn't just the sound of things collapsing; it felt like controlled detonations. We heard multiple blasts—booms—that didn't match up with the structural damage we were seeing." Such accounts have been scrutinized, with some arguing they were simply the result of chaotic conditions or the collapse of internal infrastructure. Nevertheless, the persistence of these stories has kept questions alive about the true nature of the disaster.

The bravery of the police officers who responded that day is equally compelling. NYPD officers were among the first to arrive at the scene, assisting firefighters and organizing the evacuation. Some officers worked to secure a perimeter, trying to keep civilians out of harm's way while others rushed into the towers to help evacuate those inside. Many officers reported similar experiences of chaos and confusion, compounded by the mounting fear that the situation was escalating beyond their control. One officer described the moment when the South Tower collapsed: "We heard this rumbling, and everything went dark. We had no idea what had happened—just that we had to run."

In the aftermath of the collapse, the conditions at Ground Zero became even more perilous. Firefighters and police officers were engulfed in a dense cloud of debris, forcing them to navigate through a thick haze of dust and smoke. Some described the scene as apocalyptic, with visibility reduced to almost nothing and the air filled with a choking, acrid smell. Despite these conditions, first responders continued their efforts, searching for survivors among the wreckage. Their courage and determination were evident as they pushed forward, even as the collapse of the towers made the task of rescue and recovery increasingly dangerous.

One of the most striking aspects of these testimonies is the selflessness displayed by the first responders. In the face of a catastrophic event, they prioritized the safety of others, often at great personal risk. Many firefighters and police officers died when the towers collapsed, trapped under tons of debris while attempting to save those still inside. Their heroism is a testament to their commitment and bravery, and their stories have become an integral part of the narrative of 9/11.

However, their testimonies also serve as a reminder of the unanswered questions surrounding the attacks. The reports of explosions heard by many responders, both before and after the towers collapsed, remain a point of contention. Were these simply the sounds of the buildings failing under stress, or was there something more to it? Official reports have largely dismissed these claims as misinterpretations of the chaotic events, but some firefighters and police officers remain unconvinced. "I know what I heard," one firefighter stated firmly. "And it wasn't just the building coming down. There was more going on."

The bravery of the first responders who ran toward danger rather than away from it is a story of heroism and sacrifice. Their actions saved countless lives, and their accounts provide a raw, unfiltered view of the chaos that unfolded that day. Yet, the variations in their testimonies and the lingering questions they raise highlight the complexity of the events of September 11, demonstrating how different people can experience the same tragedy in profoundly different ways. As the nation continues to honor their sacrifices, the voices of these firefighters and police officers remain essential to understanding the full story of what happened on that fateful day.

The Pentagon Attack — Accounts from Military Personnel and Civilians

As New York reeled from the devastation unfolding at the World Trade Center, another catastrophic event occurred hundreds of miles away. At 9:37 AM, American Airlines Flight 77 crashed into the western side of the Pentagon, the heart of the United States Department of Defense. The attack sent shockwaves not only through the military establishment but also across the nation. The Pentagon, one of the most heavily guarded and fortified buildings in the world, was now a target. Eyewitness accounts from military personnel, office workers, and civilians nearby paint a vivid picture of the confusion and disbelief that surrounded the attack, as well as the immediate response that followed.

In the moments leading up to the crash, several eyewitnesses observed the approach of Flight 77. Many reported seeing a large commercial airliner flying at an unusually low altitude, its trajectory aiming directly for the Pentagon. John Bowman, an office worker in a nearby building, described watching the plane as it appeared to "swoop down out of nowhere." He recalled, "It was so low, you could feel it vibrating the ground before it even hit. People were yelling and pointing. No one could believe what they were seeing." Similar observations were made by drivers on the nearby highway, who reported seeing the plane flying almost at street level as it approached its target. For many, the sight was surreal—something they could only later process as an intentional attack.

Military personnel inside the Pentagon also recounted their experiences as the plane approached. For those on the side of the building struck by the aircraft, the impact was sudden and devastating. One staff member, who had just left his office moments before, described feeling a tremendous explosion that shook the entire structure. "I was just a few corridors away when it happened," he said. "The walls buckled, and everything shook. You could feel the heat immediately, and then smoke started filling the hallway." In the confusion, military and civilian staff scrambled to evacuate the building, many unsure of what exactly had transpired. Some thought it was an internal explosion, while others believed they were under missile attack.

Outside the Pentagon, civilians who witnessed the crash were in a state of shock. A nearby taxi driver described seeing the plane approach at a speed that seemed too fast for a controlled descent. "It was like it was falling from the sky," he explained. "And then there was this explosion. You could feel the blast wave. Everything just went silent for a moment, and then the screams started." For some witnesses, the experience was not just a visual and auditory shock but a physical one—an assault on the senses that left them disoriented. The smell of burning jet fuel and the sight of black smoke billowing from the side of the Pentagon added to the growing sense of horror and confusion.

Despite the chaos, emergency response teams and military personnel quickly mobilized to secure the area and begin rescue operations. The Pentagon's security and fire response units were among the first on the scene, working alongside civilian firefighters and medical teams to assess the damage and evacuate survivors. Witnesses described the scene as a "war zone," with debris scattered across the lawn, the building's walls shattered, and flames erupting from the gaping hole left by the impact. "It was like nothing I'd ever seen before," said a firefighter who responded to the scene. "You expect the Pentagon to be this fortress, and then suddenly, it's this massive, burning wreck."

However, the aftermath of the attack also raised questions that continue to fuel debates and alternative theories. Some witnesses claimed to have seen a smaller aircraft or missile rather than a large commercial jet. These accounts, while in the minority, have been used by conspiracy theorists to suggest that the official narrative might not align with the true events. One civilian observer, who was on a nearby hill at the time of the crash, claimed that the plane he saw "looked too small for a passenger jet." Others pointed to the lack of extensive aircraft debris at the crash site as evidence that something else might have struck the building. "I expected to see more wreckage," said another witness. "It just didn't add up in my mind."

The Pentagon attack has been extensively investigated; and official reports have explained the discrepancies in eyewitness testimonies as the result of confusion during a highly chaotic event. Investigators have noted that the speed and angle of the aircraft, combined with the trauma of witnessing such a sudden and violent impact, likely contributed to differing perceptions of what happened. The damage to the building and the subsequent fire also made it difficult for people on the scene to identify specific debris, as much of the wreckage was either incinerated or buried within the structure itself.

Nonetheless, these alternative accounts have remained part of the broader conversation surrounding 9/11. The debate over what precisely hit the Pentagon exemplifies the complexities of collective memory and the way in which trauma can shape, alter, and even fragment eyewitness recollections. What one person saw and understood in the moment may differ vastly from another's experience, particularly in a situation of such extreme stress.

For those inside the Pentagon who survived the attack, the events of that day left lasting scars—both physical and emotional. Many military personnel and staff have spoken of the trauma and the sense of vulnerability they felt as they watched their workplace, a symbol of American military power, come under direct assault. The attack on the Pentagon was not just a strike against a building; it was a blow to the nation's sense of security, a moment that redefined the concept of homeland defense.

The testimonies of those who were at the Pentagon on September 11 offer a powerful perspective on the events of that day. While the majority of accounts align with the official explanation, the variations and anomalies continue to be points of contention, feeding a broader narrative of suspicion and inquiry that persists in the public consciousness.

Flight 93 – The Heroic Struggle and the Mystery of its Crash

While the World Trade Center and Pentagon attacks unfolded, another tragedy was simultaneously playing out in the skies over Pennsylvania. United Airlines Flight 93, bound for San Francisco from Newark, became the stage for one of the most heroic stories of September 11. The official narrative describes how passengers, upon learning of the other hijackings via phone calls, organized an effort to retake control of the aircraft. This heroic struggle ultimately led to the plane's crash into a field near Shanksville, Pennsylvania. Yet, despite the powerful and inspiring accounts of bravery, questions have arisen regarding the details of the crash and what truly happened in the skies above Pennsylvania that morning.

According to official reports, Flight 93 was hijacked by four terrorists who aimed to strike another high-profile target, believed to be either the White House or the Capitol. Once the hijackers seized control, the passengers began making calls to their loved ones, using the plane's onboard phones and personal cell phones. Through these calls, they learned of the attacks on the World Trade Center and the Pentagon, realizing the full gravity of their situation. It was then that a group of passengers and crew members, led by individuals such as Todd Beamer, Mark Bingham, Tom Burnett, and Jeremy Glick, decided to take action. Knowing their lives were at risk but determined to prevent further loss, they formulated a plan to storm the cockpit and overpower the hijackers.

The recordings and phone transcripts from Flight 93 are both chilling and inspiring, revealing the courage of the passengers who understood their role in trying to stop another catastrophic attack. Beamer's famous words, "Let's roll," became a rallying cry, embodying the resolve and bravery of those on board. The official narrative states that during the ensuing struggle, the plane's control was compromised, and it ultimately crashed into an empty field, preventing further devastation in Washington, D.C. The site of the crash is now a memorial, honoring the passengers and crew members who are credited with saving countless lives through their heroic actions.

Despite this compelling and heroic story, alternative theories and lingering questions persist about the crash of Flight 93. The most significant of these is whether the plane was actually shot down by military aircraft, a decision made to prevent it from reaching its intended target. Some critics point to the scattered debris field, which extends several miles from the primary crash site, as evidence supporting the possibility of a mid-air explosion rather than a single, intact impact. Witnesses in the area reported seeing debris falling from the sky, and some claimed to have heard the sound of fighter jets in the vicinity before the crash occurred.

The official explanation for the debris spread is that it was caused by the high-speed impact and the disintegration of the aircraft upon crashing. Investigators concluded that the plane hit the ground at an extremely steep angle, essentially nose-diving into the earth at high speed. This, they argue, created a forceful explosion that sent fragments flying over a wide area. However, skeptics argue that the spread of debris is inconsistent with this explanation, suggesting that it indicates a different sequence of events, possibly involving military intervention. The question of whether Flight 93 was brought down by passenger action or by an official order remains a source of debate among conspiracy theorists and researchers alike.

Another point of contention lies in the lack of clear visual evidence or black box recordings from the final moments before the crash. Although the cockpit voice recorder was recovered, some critics argue that its contents, while dramatic, do not conclusively prove that the passengers breached the cockpit. The recording captures the sounds of a struggle, screams, and a final cry to "pull it down" before the crash. Official investigators concluded that the passengers were seconds away from reclaiming the plane when it went down, likely because the hijackers, realizing their mission would fail, chose to crash it deliberately. Yet, some theorists argue that the exact sequence of events is still unclear, and without direct video evidence, the full truth remains elusive.

Further adding to the mystery is the timeline and response of the U.S. military. On the morning of September 11, the North American Aerospace Defense Command (NORAD) scrambled fighter jets in response to the hijackings, but they were unable to intercept the first three flights in time. By the time Flight 93 was recognized as a potential threat, the military had begun to mobilize more aggressively. The delay in NORAD's response to the earlier hijackings has been a point of criticism, but it also raises questions about what actions were taken once Flight 93 was identified as a target. In the aftermath, government officials maintained that the military did not shoot down Flight 93, emphasizing the passengers' heroism. However, skeptics remain unconvinced, pointing to the confusion and conflicting reports from that day as evidence that something may have been concealed.

Eyewitness accounts from civilians on the ground provide further complexity to the story. Some residents near Shanksville reported seeing a plane flying at an unusually low altitude, followed by a plume of smoke. Others claimed they heard explosions before the crash or saw smaller aircraft in the vicinity, possibly military jets. These accounts have fueled speculation that the military was prepared to shoot down Flight 93 if necessary and may have done so once it became clear the hijackers would not relinquish control. While official reports have largely dismissed these accounts as mistaken interpretations in the midst of chaos, they continue to be referenced by those questioning the full narrative.

Despite the controversies and unanswered questions, the story of Flight 93 remains a powerful symbol of courage and sacrifice. The passengers' willingness to confront the hijackers and their selfless determination to protect others exemplify the resilience and heroism that emerged on September 11. The debates surrounding the crash—whether it was the result of their valiant struggle or a last-minute military decision—do not diminish their bravery. Instead, they highlight the complex and often fragmented nature of truth in moments of crisis, where multiple perspectives and interpretations converge.

As we look back at the events of Flight 93, the narrative remains a blend of heroism, tragedy, and mystery. Whether one accepts the official version or questions the details, there is no denying the profound impact of the passengers' actions. They faced unimaginable circumstances and chose to fight, embodying a spirit of resilience that continues to inspire. However, the questions that linger about their final moments serve as a reminder that, even in the face of such extraordinary bravery, the full truth of that day's events may forever remain just out of reach.

The Legacy of Flight 93 – Memorials, Myths, and Continued Controversies

The story of Flight 93 and its passengers has become an enduring symbol of courage, unity, and sacrifice. The crash site in Shanksville, Pennsylvania, is now home to the Flight 93 National Memorial, a place where people from across the country and around the world come to honor the lives lost on that fateful day. However, while the memorial pays tribute to the heroism of the passengers and crew, the controversies and unanswered questions surrounding Flight 93 continue to shape its legacy, giving rise to both admiration and skepticism.

The memorial site, designed with solemn reverence, includes a long walkway that traces the flight's path and a wall of names commemorating the 40 passengers and crew members who perished. At the heart of the site stands the Tower of Voices, a tall structure containing wind chimes that produce a haunting sound meant to echo the voices of the fallen. It's a place that invites reflection and offers a space for the public to grapple with the events of that day. For many visitors, the memorial is a powerful reminder of the bravery exhibited by ordinary citizens who, when confronted with a life-or-death situation, chose to fight back. It represents not just a tragic loss but also a testament to the human spirit's capacity for courage and resilience.

Yet, even as the memorial stands as a symbol of unity and heroism, alternative narratives and skepticism persist, challenging the mainstream account of what transpired aboard Flight 93. In the years following 9/11, conspiracy theories surrounding the plane's crash have multiplied, casting doubt on the official version of events and introducing the idea that the government may have obscured the truth. Some theorists argue that the very existence of the memorial itself, with its somber design and focus on heroism, is part of an effort to solidify a particular narrative in the public consciousness, one that diverts attention from lingering questions about what really happened.

One of the most persistent controversies revolves around the timing and nature of the crash. Skeptics point to inconsistencies in the timeline and the reported communications between the FAA, NORAD, and the military. Some believe that the U.S. government, faced with an imminent threat to Washington, D.C., may have ordered the military to shoot down Flight 93, preventing it from reaching its target. While officials have repeatedly denied this scenario, these suspicions have been fueled by early reports and eyewitness accounts that mention seeing military aircraft in the vicinity before the crash. Furthermore, some conspiracy theorists argue that the lack of video evidence and the fragmented nature of the debris field suggest a more complex sequence of events than the official narrative describes.

The release of the 9/11 Commission Report sought to clarify these events, offering a comprehensive analysis of the day's timeline and the heroic actions taken by the passengers. The report concluded that the plane was not shot down but rather crashed as a direct result of the passengers' struggle with the hijackers. The cockpit voice recorder, which captured the intense moments before impact, supports this version, highlighting the bravery of those who fought to reclaim the plane. Nevertheless, the absence of physical evidence visible to the public, combined with the secrecy surrounding certain military communications, leaves room for speculation.

In addition to questions about the crash itself, some critics focus on the passengers' phone calls made during the flight.

While most people accept these calls as genuine, a subset of skeptics claims that the technology available at the time would not have allowed for successful cell phone communication from the altitude and speed of Flight 93. This argument, however, has been largely debunked by telecommunications experts who explain that, while unlikely, such calls were indeed possible under specific conditions. Despite these explanations, the persistence of these doubts shows how deeply some individuals distrust official accounts, reflecting a broader sense of skepticism toward government transparency and truthfulness.

Despite the ongoing controversies, the legacy of Flight 93 remains overwhelmingly one of courage and unity. In the aftermath of 9/11, the story of the passengers' bravery became a powerful rallying point for a grieving nation. The phrase "Let's roll," spoken by Todd Beamer during the final moments of the flight, became a national slogan, symbolizing the resilience and resolve that Americans sought to embody in response to the attacks. The story of Flight 93 transcended the immediate tragedy, becoming a part of American mythology—a narrative of ordinary people rising to extraordinary circumstances.

The memorial in Shanksville serves not only as a place of remembrance but also as a focal point for this legacy. For family members of the victims, it is a sacred space, offering a sense of closure and a place to honor their loved ones. For visitors, it's an opportunity to reflect on the broader implications of 9/11 and the personal sacrifices made that day. Yet, as the memorial helps cement the narrative of heroism, it also becomes a site where the complex interplay between history, memory, and myth unfolds. For those who question the official account, the memorial's emphasis on heroism, while genuine, seems to overshadow the more uncomfortable questions that remain unanswered.

In the years since 9/11, the debates over Flight 93's crash and the broader events of that day have become emblematic of a divided approach to understanding history and truth. For many, accepting the story of the passengers' heroism is essential to honoring their sacrifice and maintaining a sense of unity. For others, the inconsistencies and lack of transparency signal a deeper issue—one that suggests the need for a more critical look at the information provided by authorities.

Ultimately, the legacy of Flight 93 is a reflection of both the power and the fragility of collective memory. The heroism of the passengers is undeniable, and their actions have rightfully earned them a place in the annals of American history. However, the questions and controversies that linger serve as a reminder that even the most inspiring narratives can be layered with complexity and ambiguity. As the years go on, the story of Flight 93 will continue to inspire, but it will also remain a focal point for those seeking to uncover the full truth of what happened on that fateful day.

Chapter 12: The Anthrax Attacks

The Timeline of the Anthrax Attacks

In the weeks following the September 11 attacks, the United States faced yet another wave of terror—this time, in the form of anthrax-laced letters that sowed panic and fear across the country. The anthrax attacks, sometimes referred to as "Amerithrax," began on September 18, 2001, just one week after the devastation of 9/11. Letters containing anthrax spores were mailed to major media outlets and government offices, triggering a sense of heightened vulnerability in an already traumatized nation.

The first wave of letters targeted media organizations, including ABC, CBS, NBC, and the New York Post, as well as the Florida-based tabloid publisher American Media Inc. The initial victims of the attacks were employees who handled these letters, leading to several cases of anthrax infection. In some cases, people inhaled the spores, resulting in pulmonary anthrax, a deadly form of the disease. At this stage, the public knew little about the unfolding crisis, but health officials and law enforcement were beginning to piece together the puzzle, realizing they were dealing with a new, invisible threat.

On October 9, 2001, a second wave of anthrax letters was sent, this time targeting political figures. Two of these letters reached the offices of Democratic Senators Tom Daschle and Patrick Leahy. These letters, like the earlier ones sent to media organizations, contained threatening messages and a fine white powder identified as anthrax spores. The targeting of high-profile political figures intensified the panic, as it became evident that these attacks were not random but rather strategic attempts to disrupt the nation's leadership and incite fear within the government.

The anthrax letters were quickly linked to five deaths and 17 non-fatal infections. Robert Stevens, a photo editor for American Media Inc., was the first known casualty, succumbing to inhalation anthrax on October 5, 2001. His death marked the beginning of a public health crisis that would see a scramble to contain the spread of the spores and prevent further casualties. Hospitals and clinics in cities affected by the letters were overwhelmed with people fearing exposure, leading to a nationwide effort by the Centers for Disease Control and Prevention (CDC) to manage the situation. Decontamination procedures were put in place, including the fumigation of buildings, and postal workers were given antibiotics to prevent further infections.

As the nation grappled with these terrifying events, the anthrax attacks became a major focus of law enforcement and intelligence agencies. The FBI launched an investigation known as "Amerithrax" to track down the source of the letters and identify the perpetrator. Simultaneously, the CDC and other public health organizations raced to contain the spread of the disease, distributing antibiotics like ciprofloxacin (Cipro) to those potentially exposed to anthrax spores. The rapid response to these incidents highlighted both the nation's preparedness for bioterrorism and its vulnerability to such attacks.

The anthrax letters intensified an already high state of alert. In the immediate aftermath of 9/11, many Americans felt a renewed sense of patriotism and solidarity, but the anthrax attacks reignited fear and uncertainty. Who was behind this new wave of terror? Was it linked to Al-Qaeda or other foreign enemies? Could the attacks be part of a coordinated effort to destabilize the United States further? The absence of clear answers and the spread of misinformation created a climate of paranoia. The media, eager to keep pace with the rapid developments, often fueled speculation and fear, as reports surfaced of potential new targets and additional suspicious packages.

By the end of October 2001, with no immediate resolution or arrests, the anthrax attacks had taken on a life of their own. The government continued to warn the public about the potential for further biological threats, urging vigilance and encouraging Americans to report any suspicious packages or activity. As the investigation progressed, questions arose about the source of the anthrax spores and the sophisticated nature of the attack. While authorities initially suspected foreign terrorists, evidence increasingly pointed to the possibility that the attack was domestic in origin.

The timeline of the anthrax attacks—from the first letters mailed in mid-September to the final confirmed infection in October—illustrates how these events compounded the fear and uncertainty of a post-9/11 world. The attacks were not just a random act of terror; they were strategically timed to maximize psychological impact, hitting the nation when it was already reeling from the shock of the World Trade Center and Pentagon attacks. In this climate of heightened anxiety, the anthrax letters deepened the sense of vulnerability, transforming public spaces like mailrooms and government offices into potential danger zones.

The anthrax attacks marked a critical turning point in the nation's post-9/11 narrative. They underscored the United States' vulnerability not only to large-scale terrorist attacks but also to small-scale, insidious threats capable of spreading chaos and fear. The timeline of events reveals the calculated nature of the attacks and sets the stage for a complex investigation that would challenge the nation's ability to respond to a new kind of enemy—one that remained invisible and elusive, lurking in the seemingly innocuous envelopes that arrived in mailboxes across America.

The Early Suspicions and Investigation

In the immediate aftermath of the anthrax attacks, the nation's attention was fixated on finding those responsible. Still reeling from the shock of 9/11, the American public and government officials were quick to connect the two events. With a heightened sense of vulnerability and a widespread belief that more attacks could be imminent, suspicions naturally turned to foreign terrorists. The idea that these anthrax-laced letters were a coordinated follow-up by Al-Qaeda or a rogue state like Iraq took root almost instantly.

Government officials and media outlets fueled these early suspicions. High-profile figures, including Vice President Dick Cheney and Secretary of State Colin Powell, publicly suggested that Iraq's suspected biological weapons program might be involved. The media echoed these claims, reporting extensively on the possibility that Saddam Hussein's regime had a hand in the anthrax attacks. Speculation ran rampant as some pundits proposed that the anthrax attacks could be part of a broader plot involving multiple terrorist cells aiming to cripple the United States further. This narrative quickly gained traction, and fear spread throughout the country, prompting a surge in anxiety over biological warfare.

The FBI, alongside the Centers for Disease Control and Prevention (CDC) and other agencies, launched an intensive investigation codenamed "Amerithrax" to track down the source of the attacks. In the initial phase of the investigation, authorities worked under the assumption that the anthrax was foreign-made. They scoured intelligence databases for links between the spores found in the letters and known bioweapons programs in Iraq and other hostile nations. Investigators sought to piece together any connections between the anthrax attacks and the perpetrators of 9/11, believing that the timing and delivery method might point to a larger, coordinated assault.

As the investigation intensified, authorities worked to identify where the spores were processed and how they ended up in the U.S. mail system. The CDC, in collaboration with state health departments, analyzed the biological makeup of the anthrax spores to determine their origin. The process was painstaking, requiring sophisticated laboratory testing and collaboration with experts in biological warfare. Early analysis suggested that the spores had been professionally refined, indicating that the anthrax was not something an amateur could have produced in a basement lab. This revelation further heightened fears that a sophisticated network was behind the attack—one with access to advanced biological weapons technology.

The media played a crucial role during this period, amplifying the government's suspicions and feeding the narrative of foreign involvement. Major news networks ran continuous coverage, often speculating about the connections between Iraq, Al-Qaeda, and the anthrax letters. Some pundits framed the anthrax attacks as a possible justification for military action against Iraq, with narratives suggesting that if Saddam Hussein was indeed behind the attacks, he posed an immediate threat to the United States. Such reports added to the sense of urgency, with journalists and experts debating whether the U.S. should act pre-emptively to prevent further biological or chemical attacks.

At the same time, misinformation and rumors spread quickly. Reports of suspicious packages and false alarms inundated emergency services across the country, creating a chaotic atmosphere. Postal workers, fearing for their safety, demanded better protections as many post offices were shut down for decontamination. Public health officials faced a wave of panic from citizens who believed they had been exposed to anthrax. Pharmacies reported spikes in sales of antibiotics, particularly Cipro, which had been identified as an effective treatment for anthrax exposure. This sense of fear, heightened by an unclear and developing situation, placed immense pressure on investigators to find answers swiftly.

The initial framing of the anthrax attacks as a continuation of 9/11 not only influenced the public's perception but also shaped the direction of the investigation. With a foreign threat in mind, authorities pursued potential links to overseas terrorist networks, focusing on known operatives who might have had access to or knowledge of biological weapons. Intelligence agencies, including the CIA, ramped up efforts to infiltrate and surveil suspected terrorist cells in the hope of uncovering evidence that would tie them to the anthrax attacks. For a time, this direction seemed logical, given the timing of the attacks and the rising fear of further acts of terror.

However, as the weeks went by, no concrete evidence emerged linking foreign terrorists to the anthrax letters. Investigators began to face the reality that their initial assumptions might be misguided. Despite the intense focus on foreign threats, the evidence remained elusive. No intercepted communications, captured operatives, or seized documents provided a definitive link between Al-Qaeda or Iraq and the anthrax attacks. The absence of proof began to sow doubt, both within law enforcement circles and among independent experts who closely followed the case.

As the early phase of the investigation wound down, a critical question loomed: If it wasn't foreign terrorists, then who was behind the attacks? The shift in focus would soon move from the Middle East to much closer to home, where new theories would emerge that challenged the very foundation of the government's initial assumptions. The search for the source of the anthrax would become more complex and controversial as the investigation pivoted toward the possibility of a domestic origin.

The Shift Toward a Domestic Suspect

As the Amerithrax investigation continued, it became increasingly clear that the initial focus on foreign terrorists was yielding no concrete results. Despite the enormous resources deployed and the intense scrutiny of known terrorist groups and hostile states, investigators were unable to find any direct link between the anthrax-laced letters and foreign entities such as Al-Qaeda or Iraq. This failure to confirm early suspicions marked a turning point in the investigation and forced authorities to confront a new, more unsettling possibility: that the perpetrator could be someone within the United States.

By late 2001 and early 2002, the FBI and other agencies began considering the idea that the anthrax attacks might not have been orchestrated by international terrorists, but rather by a domestic actor with access to sophisticated biological materials. This shift was partly driven by the emerging scientific evidence about the nature of the anthrax spores used in the attacks. Analysis by scientists at the CDC and other labs revealed that the spores were highly refined, of a purity and quality suggesting they had been processed using advanced methods. This level of expertise pointed to someone with specific knowledge of bioweapons, potentially someone connected to a U.S. lab or military program.

The anthrax strain itself—identified as the "Ames strain"—was another clue that pointed investigators in a domestic direction. The Ames strain was a type of anthrax commonly used in U.S. biodefense research. It was not widely available outside a small number of highly secure facilities in the United States. This information raised alarming questions: How did this strain, usually restricted to research labs, end up in the hands of a perpetrator capable of weaponizing it and sending it through the mail? The possibility that someone within the U.S. biodefense community might be involved began to take shape as a leading theory.

The FBI, realizing the implications of this new direction, started focusing its investigation on scientists and workers with access to U.S. biodefense laboratories. They began questioning individuals who had worked in these facilities, particularly those who had access to anthrax samples. The shift toward a domestic suspect also necessitated cooperation with the Department of Defense and other government agencies that oversaw bioweapons research. Investigators had to navigate the complex and highly secretive world of U.S. biodefense, which was protected by layers of security and bureaucracy. The challenge was not just identifying who had the technical capability but also discerning who might have had the motivation to carry out such an attack.

As the FBI dug deeper, they discovered that access to the Ames strain was more widespread than initially thought. While only a limited number of facilities officially held samples, the strain had been distributed over the years to various labs for research purposes. The network of people who could potentially have accessed the strain expanded, creating a complicated web of suspects. The realization that the perpetrator might have been a trusted figure within the scientific community—or even a government employee—was deeply unsettling and led to a new phase of intense scrutiny.

Among those questioned was Dr. Steven Hatfill, a scientist who had worked with the U.S. Army's biodefense program at Fort Detrick, Maryland. Hatfill became a person of interest due to his background and his access to anthrax samples during his time in the program. Despite a lack of definitive evidence, his name was leaked to the media, and he quickly became the subject of intense public and press speculation. Hatfill's life was turned upside down as the FBI publicly announced him as a "person of interest." The media frenzy that followed highlighted the high-stakes nature of the investigation and the FBI's determination to find a culprit, but it also raised concerns about the agency's methods and the potential for wrongful targeting.

While Hatfill's involvement became a focal point for the FBI and the media, critics argued that the government was too quick to pin blame on him without sufficient evidence. Civil liberties advocates raised alarms about the ethics of the investigation, noting that Hatfill's rights were being trampled as he faced constant surveillance, searches of his property, and relentless public scrutiny. The intense focus on Hatfill illustrated the pressure the FBI was under to show progress in the case, but it also demonstrated the difficulties of investigating an attack that required both a sophisticated understanding of bioweapons and insider access.

As the investigation continued, the scientific community itself became increasingly divided over the evidence. Some experts argued that while the Ames strain pointed to a domestic source, it was still possible that foreign actors had acquired it through espionage or other means. Others believed that the focus on a domestic suspect was correct and that the FBI needed to narrow its search to those with direct access to the labs handling the Ames strain. This debate illustrated the complexities of the investigation and the uncertainty surrounding the origins of the attacks.

In shifting focus toward a domestic suspect, the FBI encountered new challenges. The idea that the anthrax attacks might have been an inside job, possibly carried out by someone working within the U.S. government or military, raised troubling implications. Such a revelation would mean that the nation's own security apparatus had been infiltrated or corrupted. It also highlighted the risks associated with the U.S. biodefense program, which had been ramped up in the 1990s in response to perceived threats but now appeared vulnerable to exploitation by those within its own ranks.

By early 2002, the Amerithrax investigation had evolved from a hunt for foreign terrorists to a search for a potential domestic bioterrorist. This shift was a turning point, marking a significant departure from the post-9/11 narrative that had initially framed the attacks as part of a larger global war on terror. It also underscored the complexity of dealing with bioterrorism, which, unlike traditional forms of terrorism, required specialized knowledge and access to sophisticated materials—resources that were more likely to be found within the United States than abroad.

The Emerging Evidence and the Case Against Bruce Ivins

As the investigation progressed and the focus increasingly turned inward, the FBI and its partners in the scientific community continued to search for a suspect with both the motive and capability to carry out the anthrax attacks. The case against Steven Hatfill, initially publicized and widely speculated upon, had begun to lose momentum as no concrete evidence linked him directly to the crime. Under growing pressure to solve the case, the FBI turned its attention to another scientist within the U.S. biodefense program: Dr. Bruce Ivins.

Bruce Ivins was a microbiologist who had worked for years at the United States Army Medical Research Institute of Infectious Diseases (USAMRIID) at Fort Detrick, Maryland. Fort Detrick was one of the few facilities with access to the Ames strain of anthrax, the same strain used in the attacks. Ivins had dedicated much of his career to studying anthrax and developing vaccines to protect against its use as a bioweapon. On the surface, Ivins seemed an unlikely suspect—a respected scientist committed to preventing bioterrorism. However, as investigators delved deeper into his background, they uncovered information that raised serious concerns.

The first piece of evidence that drew attention to Ivins was his proximity to and expertise with the Ames strain. As a senior researcher at Fort Detrick, he had not only access to the strain but also the technical capability to refine and weaponize it. The spores used in the attacks were sophisticated, indicating that they had been processed to achieve a high level of purity. This level of refinement was consistent with work conducted at facilities like USAMRIID, and Ivins, with his years of experience and hands-on work with anthrax, had the skills necessary to produce such spores. Investigators began to scrutinize his laboratory records and work habits closely, searching for discrepancies that might suggest his involvement.

The investigation revealed that Ivins had spent an unusual amount of time in the lab during the period leading up to the attacks. His work logs showed that he had been present late at night and on weekends, far beyond the hours typically required for his duties. When questioned about this, Ivins claimed he was working on experiments related to the anthrax vaccine, but the FBI found inconsistencies in his explanations. The timing of his late-night lab sessions coincided suspiciously with the preparation and mailing of the anthrax letters, leading investigators to consider whether these sessions might have been used to create the weaponized spores.

Further evidence against Ivins emerged from his behavior and correspondence. The FBI obtained emails that he had sent in the years prior to the attacks, which hinted at growing paranoia and erratic thoughts. In some messages, he expressed fears of persecution, frustrations with his colleagues, and a sense of isolation. Investigators also uncovered communications that suggested Ivins held strong views about the importance of biodefense programs and felt that the government and public were not taking the threat of bioterrorism seriously enough. This raised the possibility that he might have viewed the anthrax attacks as a way to draw attention to these issues and secure more funding for his research and other biodefense efforts.

The idea that Ivins might have had a motive beyond simple malice began to take shape. Some experts proposed that he could have been driven by a misguided sense of duty or a desire to highlight the very real threat of bioterrorism in a way that would compel the government to act. In the wake of 9/11, funding and attention to biodefense were increasing, and a bioterror attack would undoubtedly bolster that trend. If Ivins, in his own distorted view, believed that orchestrating such an attack would save lives in the long run by preparing the nation for future threats, his actions might have seemed justified to him. This theory fit the profile of someone deeply embedded in the biodefense community and convinced of the importance of his work.

In addition to examining Ivins's motives, investigators also analyzed physical evidence linked to the letters. Forensic experts were able to trace the type of envelopes used back to a batch sold at a specific post office not far from Ivins's home. The postmarks on the letters, indicating they were sent from New Jersey, matched the timeframe of when Ivins was known to have traveled through that area. While these connections were circumstantial, they added to the mounting case against him, suggesting that he had both the opportunity and access needed to carry out the attacks.

As the FBI built its case, they faced the challenge of turning this web of circumstantial evidence into something more concrete. Forensic science played a crucial role in this effort. Genetic analysis of the anthrax spores revealed markers that matched samples held at Fort Detrick, further linking the crime scene to Ivins's workplace. Although the Ames strain was not exclusive to Fort Detrick, the genetic fingerprint was consistent with the specific batch stored there, reinforcing the theory that the spores had been sourced from Ivins's lab.

The FBI's focus on Ivins intensified, and he was placed under surveillance. Agents interviewed colleagues, friends, and family, painting a picture of a man who was increasingly isolated and, according to some, mentally unstable. Ivins's behavior became more erratic as the investigation closed in. He expressed fear of being blamed for the attacks, and his emails revealed a deepening sense of paranoia. To some, his behavior appeared to be that of a man under intense pressure, possibly guilty, and aware that he was the primary target of the investigation.

Despite the accumulating evidence, the case against Ivins was not without controversy. Critics argued that the FBI's focus on Ivins resembled the flawed pursuit of Steven Hatfill. Some scientists who had worked with Ivins defended his character, stating that he was a dedicated researcher who would never commit such an act. Others within the scientific community questioned whether the genetic evidence and circumstantial connections were strong enough to prove his guilt beyond a reasonable doubt. This debate underscored the difficulties of building a case based largely on scientific analysis and circumstantial evidence in the absence of a confession or definitive proof.

As investigators continued to build their case, Ivins's situation became increasingly precarious. The pressure mounted, and his behavior grew more erratic. The stage was set for a dramatic conclusion to the Amerithrax investigation—one that would leave lingering questions about the true origins of the attack and whether justice had indeed been served.

The Tragic End and Lingering Questions

As the FBI intensified its scrutiny of Bruce Ivins, the situation took a tragic turn. Ivins, already under tremendous stress, felt the walls closing in. In July 2008, just as the FBI was preparing to file charges that would have likely led to his arrest, Ivins died by suicide. He overdosed on a combination of prescription medication, leaving behind a trail of unanswered questions and a sense of unresolved justice. The FBI quickly announced that Ivins's death effectively closed the case, declaring him the sole perpetrator of the anthrax attacks. However, the circumstances surrounding his death and the strength of the evidence against him left many skeptical and unconvinced.

The FBI presented its case against Ivins in a press conference shortly after his death. They outlined the key elements of their investigation: Ivins's access to the Ames strain, his late-night work hours, his erratic behavior, and his motives. The agency cited genetic analysis linking the anthrax spores used in the attacks to Ivins's lab at Fort Detrick, and they emphasized his history of mental health issues as evidence that he was capable of carrying out such a crime. However, without a trial or opportunity for cross-examination, the FBI's narrative remained untested, and many saw the explanation as incomplete or even convenient.

Critics pointed out several flaws and inconsistencies in the FBI's case. First, they noted that despite the genetic link to Fort

Detrick, there was no definitive proof that Ivins himself had prepared or mailed the anthrax letters. The lab was used by numerous personnel, and the FBI could not definitively place Ivins at the scene when the letters were mailed. While the FBI had evidence of Ivins's frequent late-night lab sessions, they could not prove that these sessions were directly related to preparing the anthrax spores. Furthermore, the agency's reliance on circumstantial evidence—such as Ivins's travels near the location of the mailings—did not conclusively prove his involvement.

Some of Ivins's colleagues and friends defended him, asserting that he was a man who had dedicated his life to preventing bioterrorism, not perpetrating it. They described him as a brilliant but deeply troubled scientist, someone who had struggled with mental health issues but who, in their view, was unlikely to commit such a heinous act. To them, the FBI's portrayal of Ivins was a distortion, driven by the need to find a scapegoat after years of fruitless investigation. They argued that Ivins's suicide, while tragic, was a result of the intense pressure he faced during the investigation, not an admission of guilt.

The FBI's handling of the case also drew criticism from legal experts and civil liberties advocates, who accused the agency of pressuring Ivins and violating his rights. In the years leading up to his death, Ivins had been under constant surveillance. His home and workplace were searched repeatedly, and his communications were monitored. The FBI's public campaign, which effectively labeled him as the prime suspect before charges were even filed, raised concerns about due process and the presumption of innocence. These actions echoed the controversial treatment of Steven Hatfill, the previous person of interest who was eventually exonerated and awarded a settlement for the wrongful targeting.

In response to the FBI's announcement that Ivins was the perpetrator, independent experts and analysts called for a more thorough review of the evidence. Some argued that the genetic analysis, while compelling, did not conclusively prove Ivins's guilt, as the Ames strain had been widely distributed to other labs over the years. They questioned whether the FBI had fully investigated all possible avenues, including the potential involvement of other individuals within the biodefense community or the possibility that the strain could have been obtained through espionage. The speed with which the case was closed after Ivins's death fueled speculation that the FBI, under pressure to provide closure to the public, was eager to find a suspect—any suspect—who fit the narrative.

The Department of Justice stood by the FBI's conclusions, asserting that Ivins's death was a tragic but decisive end to the investigation. However, in the years following the closure of the case, several reports and independent reviews emerged that cast doubt on the FBI's findings. The National Academy of Sciences (NAS), which had been commissioned by the FBI to review the scientific evidence, released a report in 2011 that raised concerns about the strength of the genetic evidence linking the anthrax spores to Ivins's lab. The NAS found that while the genetic markers were consistent with those found at Fort Detrick, they could not conclusively rule out other sources. This report reignited debate over whether the FBI had acted too hastily in naming Ivins the sole perpetrator.

Additionally, questions were raised about Ivins's mental state and whether he was capable of such a complex crime. Some experts believed that while Ivins's behavior was troubling, it was not sufficient to establish a motive or capability for launching such an attack. Ivins's work colleagues pointed out that preparing weaponized anthrax of the quality used in the attacks required not only technical skill but also specific equipment and knowledge of aerosol delivery systems, elements that Ivins's lab work did not necessarily provide him with. Others noted that while Ivins had expressed frustration and paranoia in his emails, these were not uncommon traits among scientists working under pressure, especially in a high-security, high-stakes environment like Fort Detrick.

The unresolved nature of the anthrax attacks, despite the FBI's claims of closure, left many Americans with lingering doubts. The attacks themselves had a profound impact on the national psyche, occurring so soon after the trauma of 9/11 and further reinforcing the sense of vulnerability. The FBI's assertion that a lone scientist had carried out the attacks did not satisfy all the questions surrounding the case. If Ivins had indeed acted alone, why had no one in his circle or his workplace detected his activities sooner? And if he had not, who else could have been involved, and why were they not brought to justice?

The mystery of the anthrax attacks remains one of the most controversial chapters in the post-9/11 era. For some, Ivins's death is a convenient end to an investigation that struggled to find answers for too long, while others view it as a tragedy that robbed the public of a chance to learn the full truth. The story of Bruce Ivins is a reminder of the dangers of jumping to conclusions in the face of uncertainty and the need for due process, even in cases involving national security.

In the end, the case against Bruce Ivins left more questions than answers. It exposed the limitations of forensic science in criminal investigations and highlighted the pressures facing law enforcement agencies under intense public and political scrutiny. Whether Ivins was truly the perpetrator, a scapegoat, or a man driven to the brink by the weight of suspicion may never be definitively known. What remains is the troubling legacy of the anthrax attacks and the reminder that, even in the most technologically advanced nations, justice can sometimes elude us, leaving only shadows and speculation in its wake.

Chapter 13: The War on Terror and the Invasion of

The Shift from Afghanistan to Iraq

In the immediate aftermath of September 11, 2001, the Bush administration's response was swift and decisive. The primary objective was clear: to dismantle the al-Qaeda network responsible for the attacks and to overthrow the Taliban regime in Afghanistan, which had provided a safe haven for Osama bin Laden and his followers. Operation Enduring Freedom was launched on October 7, 2001, marking the beginning of the United States' military campaign in Afghanistan. This move had overwhelming support from both Congress and the American public, who viewed it as a necessary response to the horrific events of 9/11.

The war in Afghanistan initially seemed successful. U.S. forces, alongside the Northern Alliance, quickly ousted the Taliban from power and disrupted al-Qaeda's operations. However, despite this early success, the Bush administration's focus soon began to shift. By early 2002, public statements by high-ranking officials, including President George W. Bush, Vice President Dick Cheney, and Secretary of Defense Donald Rumsfeld, began to emphasize Iraq as a growing threat. Saddam Hussein's regime, they argued, was not only oppressive but potentially dangerous to global security. The administration started to link Iraq's government to terrorism and weapons of mass destruction (WMDs), suggesting that the regime might be willing to provide such weapons to terrorist groups like al-Qaeda.

The transition in focus from Afghanistan to Iraq puzzled many observers at the time. Iraq had not been directly implicated in the 9/11 attacks, and there was little evidence to suggest that Saddam Hussein had any operational ties to al-Qaeda. The shift raised questions about the administration's motives and intentions. However, Bush and his key advisors framed Iraq as a critical front in the newly declared "War on Terror." They argued that, to prevent another catastrophic attack on American soil, the U.S. needed to be proactive, targeting not only the terrorists themselves but also the regimes that might support them.

In his State of the Union address in January 2002, President Bush referred to Iraq, along with Iran and North Korea, as part of an "Axis of Evil." This phrase marked a significant rhetorical escalation, casting Saddam Hussein's Iraq as a central player in the global threat to U.S. security. It also indicated a strategic pivot. The Bush administration began to portray the threat from Iraq as an urgent matter, even as the war in Afghanistan continued. This rhetoric, paired with increasingly alarming statements about Iraq's potential to develop and use WMDs, laid the groundwork for building a case for military intervention.

Behind the scenes, this shift was driven by influential figures within the administration who had long advocated for regime change in Iraq. Vice President Dick Cheney, Secretary of Defense Donald Rumsfeld, and Deputy Secretary of Defense Paul Wolfowitz were key proponents of a more aggressive policy toward Iraq. They argued that toppling Saddam Hussein would not only eliminate a dictator they had long viewed as hostile but also serve as a demonstration of American power and resolve. They believed that removing Saddam would create a ripple effect, encouraging democratic movements across the Middle East and reasserting U.S. dominance in a region of strategic importance.

To justify the shift in focus, the administration needed to create a narrative that linked Iraq to the broader threat of terrorism. This effort was not without its challenges, as intelligence linking Saddam Hussein's regime to al-Qaeda was tenuous at best. Previous assessments by intelligence agencies had largely dismissed any significant connection between the secular Ba'athist government of Iraq and the fundamentalist Islamic extremists of al-Qaeda. However, the Bush administration selectively highlighted intelligence reports that suggested otherwise, emphasizing any possible links, no matter how dubious or circumstantial.

Throughout 2002, the administration's public messaging intensified. President Bush and his advisors repeatedly warned that Saddam's regime was not only in possession of WMDs but was actively seeking to expand its arsenal. They claimed that Iraq's weapons capabilities posed a direct threat to the United States and its allies, arguing that if Saddam acquired nuclear, chemical, or biological weapons, he could potentially share them with terrorist organizations. The specter of a "smoking gun" in the form of a mushroom cloud was invoked, amplifying public fear and urgency. These statements aimed to create a sense of imminent danger, making the case that America could not afford to wait for an attack to happen.

By mid-2002, the shift from Afghanistan to Iraq was nearly complete. Afghanistan remained a theater of ongoing military operations, but it was clear that Iraq had become the administration's primary focus. In Congress, debates about Iraq's potential threat began to overshadow discussions about stabilizing Afghanistan. The media also started to shift its attention, with news outlets increasingly echoing the administration's warnings about Iraq's supposed WMD program and its links to terrorism.

This shift was not without its critics. Some within the intelligence community expressed skepticism about the administration's focus on Iraq, arguing that the evidence for Saddam's involvement in terrorism or possession of WMDs was weak. Lawmakers and international allies, including several key members of NATO, also questioned the wisdom of diverting resources from the ongoing effort in Afghanistan. Critics warned that launching another military campaign would stretch U.S. forces thin and risk further destabilizing the Middle East. However, these concerns were often overshadowed by the administration's relentless push to portray Iraq as the next critical front in the War on Terror.

Ultimately, the shift from Afghanistan to Iraq laid the groundwork for the events that would follow in 2003. The Bush administration's focus on Iraq's perceived threat transformed the public narrative, building a case for intervention that would eventually lead to the invasion of Iraq. The decision to shift attention and resources from Afghanistan to Iraq marked a pivotal moment in the post-9/11 era, one that would have far-reaching consequences for U.S. foreign policy and global security in the years to come.

The Role of Intelligence and WMD Claims

The Bush administration's push to invade Iraq hinged on a single, compelling narrative: that Saddam Hussein possessed weapons of mass destruction (WMDs) and was prepared to use them, either directly or through terrorist proxies like al-Qaeda. The American public, still reeling from the shock of 9/11, was particularly sensitive to the idea of another catastrophic attack. The administration's strategy relied on a combination of selective intelligence, high-profile briefings, and media amplification to convince the nation and its allies that Iraq represented an imminent and unavoidable threat.

At the heart of the administration's case was the assertion that Iraq possessed chemical, biological, and possibly nuclear weapons. In support of this claim, the administration pointed to intelligence reports that suggested Saddam had not only retained but also expanded his WMD programs, in defiance of United Nations sanctions and inspections. The most publicized of these pieces of intelligence was the claim that Iraq had attempted to purchase uranium from Niger—a claim that would later prove to be unfounded and controversial.

Secretary of State Colin Powell's address to the United Nations on February 5, 2003, became the centerpiece of the administration's efforts to make the case for war. Powell, a respected military leader and diplomat, presented what was described as "solid" evidence that Iraq was continuing its WMD programs. Using satellite images, intercepted communications, and testimony from Iraqi defectors, Powell argued that Iraq had mobile biological weapons labs and hidden stockpiles of chemical weapons. His presentation was designed to be the ultimate proof, aimed not only at the American public but also at the international community, where support for an invasion remained uncertain.

However, many of the intelligence claims presented by Powell and others in the administration were based on questionable sources. One of the most notorious was an Iraqi defector codenamed "Curveball," who claimed to have direct knowledge of Iraq's mobile biological weapons labs. While his testimony was a cornerstone of the administration's argument, it later came to light that his credibility had been seriously doubted by several intelligence agencies, including the CIA. Despite these doubts, his claims were selectively highlighted and amplified to fit the administration's narrative. Other pieces of evidence, like the aluminum tubes allegedly intended for uranium enrichment, were similarly disputed by experts within the intelligence community. Many analysts believed the tubes were more likely intended for conventional rocket use, yet this detail was downplayed or ignored in favor of a more alarming interpretation.

The administration's reliance on cherry-picked intelligence and questionable sources was not without internal controversy. Within the CIA, there were analysts who expressed skepticism about the strength of the evidence against Iraq. These dissenting voices raised concerns that the intelligence was being manipulated or "fixed" around a pre-determined policy goal: regime change. Some CIA officials privately worried that the administration was exaggerating the threat, while others felt pressure to align their assessments with the preferred narrative. Similarly, the State Department's Bureau of Intelligence and Research (INR) consistently expressed doubts about Iraq's alleged nuclear program, but their assessments were often overshadowed by the more hawkish interpretations from the Pentagon's Office of Special Plans, an office that some critics accused of cherry-picking intelligence that supported a pro-war agenda.

Despite these internal debates, the Bush administration continued to present a united front to the public. Top officials, including Vice President Dick Cheney and National Security Advisor Condoleezza Rice, repeatedly warned that the next terrorist attack might come in the form of a "mushroom cloud." Cheney, in particular, was vocal in asserting that Saddam had reconstituted his nuclear weapons program and was actively seeking nuclear material. His public statements often went further than the intelligence reports themselves, creating a sense of urgency and fear that another attack was not just possible, but likely, if the U.S. did not act.

In addition to claims about WMDs, the administration also sought to establish a link between Saddam Hussein's regime and al-Qaeda. This was a crucial aspect of their case, as it tied Iraq directly to the 9/11 attacks in the minds of the American public. The Bush administration claimed that Iraq had provided training, support, and safe harbor for al-Qaeda operatives. Yet, many within the intelligence community and the military were skeptical of these assertions. Historically, Saddam's secular Ba'athist regime and al-Qaeda's fundamentalist ideology were fundamentally at odds, making any significant collaboration unlikely. Nevertheless, the administration highlighted a few tenuous connections, such as a supposed meeting between an Iraqi intelligence officer and 9/11 hijacker Mohamed Atta in Prague—a meeting that was later discredited.

The intelligence supporting the WMD claims and the alleged ties to al-Qaeda was far from conclusive, but it was presented with absolute certainty. President Bush's 2003 State of the Union address underscored this approach when he declared that "the British government has learned that Saddam Hussein recently sought significant quantities of uranium from Africa." This statement, despite later being proven false, was part of a larger effort to build a sense of inevitability about military action. The administration's strategy was clear: to shape public perception and build a coalition of allies by emphasizing the threat posed by Saddam's regime, regardless of the gaps and uncertainties in the intelligence.

Despite significant international opposition and growing skepticism from some lawmakers and analysts, the intelligence narrative was effective in mobilizing support for the invasion. In October 2002, Congress passed the Iraq Resolution, authorizing the use of military force against Iraq. The vote was influenced heavily by the administration's presentation of intelligence, which framed the decision as a matter of national security and an extension of the fight against terrorism. Many lawmakers later expressed regret, citing that they felt misled by the intelligence presented to them.

The use of intelligence to build the case for the Iraq war remains one of the most controversial aspects of the conflict. The administration's selective approach, prioritizing reports that supported their agenda while ignoring or downplaying contradictory evidence, would later be criticized as a manipulation of the intelligence process. As the war unfolded and no WMDs were found, these criticisms grew louder, leading to a broader debate about the integrity of the decision-making process that led the United States into war.

The Role of the PNAC and the Drive for Regime Change

To fully understand the Bush administration's push for war in Iraq, one must look beyond the immediate aftermath of 9/11 and examine the ideological roots that had been taking shape long before the attacks. Central to this ideological framework was the Project for the New American Century (PNAC), a neo-conservative think tank founded in 1997. PNAC's mission was to promote American global leadership through a combination of military strength, economic dominance, and the spread of democratic ideals. Many of its members would later hold influential positions within the Bush administration, and their vision played a critical role in shaping U.S. foreign policy after 9/11.

PNAC's core belief was that the United States, as the world's preeminent superpower, had a unique opportunity—and responsibility—to reshape the international order in its image. The organization argued that American leadership, backed by military force, was essential for maintaining global stability and protecting U.S. interests. A key component of PNAC's vision was the need to overthrow hostile regimes, particularly in the Middle East, that posed threats to American dominance and the stability of global markets. Among these, Saddam Hussein's Iraq was a primary target.

In a 1998 open letter to then-President Bill Clinton, PNAC members, including Donald Rumsfeld, Paul Wolfowitz, and Richard Perle, urged the U.S. government to adopt a policy of regime change in Iraq. They argued that Saddam's continued defiance of UN sanctions and his pursuit of weapons of mass destruction posed a significant threat that could not be ignored. They pushed for military action, claiming that only by removing Saddam from power could the United States secure its interests and promote democracy in the region. While Clinton's administration did not act on these recommendations, the seeds of a future conflict were already being planted.

When George W. Bush assumed the presidency in 2001, many PNAC signatories found themselves in key positions of power. Donald Rumsfeld became Secretary of Defense, Paul Wolfowitz was appointed Deputy Secretary of Defense, and Dick Cheney, a long-time advocate of American military dominance, was Vice President. With these individuals holding critical roles in the administration, the ideas championed by PNAC quickly began to influence U.S. policy. The neoconservative vision of a more assertive and interventionist America aligned perfectly with their long-standing belief that Saddam Hussein needed to be removed from power.

9/11 provided the catalyst that PNAC and its supporters within the Bush administration needed to implement their agenda. The terrorist attacks were seen as a justification for a broader campaign to reshape the Middle East, using military force if necessary. The administration's shift in focus from Afghanistan to Iraq was not merely a response to a perceived threat; it was also an opportunity to advance the neoconservative objective of regime change. The attacks allowed the Bush administration to frame the invasion of Iraq as part of the larger

War on Terror, giving them the political and public support needed to pursue their goals.

In September 2000, just a year before the 9/11 attacks, PNAC published a report titled *Rebuilding America's Defenses: Strategy, Forces, and Resources for a New Century*. The report outlined a blueprint for maintaining American global hegemony in the 21st century, emphasizing the need for a significant military presence in the Middle East. Notably, the report argued that the United States would need to increase defense spending, expand its military capabilities, and be willing to use preemptive force to protect its interests. However, the report also acknowledged that such transformative changes would be difficult to achieve absent "some catastrophic and catalyzing event—like a new Pearl Harbor."

The attacks on September 11, 2001, became the event that PNAC had suggested would be necessary to mobilize public support for an expanded and aggressive military agenda. In the aftermath of the attacks, the Bush administration quickly adopted a strategy that mirrored the recommendations laid out by PNAC. The idea of preemption, or striking first to neutralize potential threats before they materialized, became a central tenet of the administration's national security doctrine. This shift allowed the administration to frame the invasion of Iraq as a necessary and preventive measure, even though Iraq had not been directly linked to the 9/11 attacks.

The influence of PNAC and its vision for American military dominance became increasingly apparent as the administration built its case for war. Key figures like Rumsfeld, Wolfowitz, and Cheney were at the forefront of the effort to present Iraq as an imminent threat. They emphasized the dangers posed by Saddam Hussein's regime, using the specter of WMDs and terrorism to justify the need for preemptive action. For these officials, removing Saddam was not only about neutralizing a dictator but also about setting the stage for a broader transformation of the Middle East. They believed that by overthrowing Saddam and establishing a democratic government in Iraq, the United States could trigger a wave of democratic reforms throughout the region.

Despite skepticism from some intelligence agencies and international allies, the administration remained committed to its goal of regime change. The belief in the transformative power of military intervention was so deeply ingrained among neoconservatives that they viewed any opposition as short-sighted or even unpatriotic. Critics who questioned the administration's focus on Iraq, including high-ranking military officers and intelligence analysts, were often marginalized or dismissed. The neoconservative agenda had become the driving force behind U.S. foreign policy, and its proponents were determined to see it through.

The administration's fixation on Iraq also had economic and strategic motivations, which aligned with PNAC's vision of maintaining American global hegemony. Iraq, with its vast oil reserves and strategic location in the Middle East, represented a key asset for U.S. interests. By toppling Saddam's regime, the administration aimed to secure a foothold in the region, ensuring access to resources and the ability to project power. PNAC and its allies in the Bush administration believed that a U.S.-friendly government in Iraq would serve as a stabilizing force and a counterbalance to Iran's influence, furthering America's long-term strategic goals.

In retrospect, the role of PNAC and the neoconservative ideology in the lead-up to the Iraq War reveals the extent to which long-standing policy goals were merged with the post-9/11 security narrative. The administration's case for war, built on selective intelligence and a relentless public relations campaign, was not solely about countering terrorism; it was also about fulfilling an ideological vision that had been in the making for years. The decision to invade Iraq was shaped as much by the desire to reshape the Middle East as it was by any immediate threat Saddam Hussein may have posed. The PNAC vision of a new American century, backed by military force and strategic dominance, had found its moment, and the Iraq War became its defining expression.

The "Weapons of Mass Destruction" Narrative

As the Bush administration pushed forward with its plan for regime change in Iraq, the narrative of Weapons of Mass Destruction (WMDs) became the central justification for war. The idea was simple yet powerful: Saddam Hussein, an already despised dictator, possessed chemical, biological, and possibly nuclear weapons that could threaten American lives and global security. The administration presented this as an immediate and pressing danger, one that necessitated swift military intervention.

The use of the WMD narrative was not accidental; it was a strategic decision that capitalized on the fear and uncertainty created by the events of 9/11. The Bush administration understood that in the post-9/11 climate, the American public and its representatives in Congress were more inclined to support preemptive action if it meant preventing another catastrophic attack. By framing Iraq as a direct and imminent threat, the administration could rally support for its broader geopolitical goals under the guise of national security.

However, the evidence supporting the claim that Iraq possessed WMDs was thin, and in many cases, highly dubious. Intelligence reports were often based on outdated information, hearsay, or sources with questionable credibility. One such source was an Iraqi defector codenamed "Curveball," whose claims about Iraq's mobile biological weapons labs were later discredited. Despite the questionable nature of this information, it was used to build a compelling case for war. The administration selectively presented intelligence that aligned with its objectives, downplaying or ignoring reports that contradicted the narrative. For example, while some intelligence agencies expressed doubts about Iraq's ability to produce nuclear weapons, this skepticism was minimized in public statements.

The administration's efforts to bolster the WMD narrative also involved enlisting allies to present a united front. In a now-infamous presentation before the United Nations in February 2003, Secretary of State Colin Powell laid out what was described as irrefutable evidence of Iraq's WMD programs. Using satellite images, intercepted communications, and the testimony of defectors, Powell claimed that Iraq had hidden stockpiles of chemical and biological weapons, mobile labs, and the capability to produce nuclear weapons. The presentation was designed to be a turning point, convincing the international community that military intervention was not only justified but necessary.

Despite the strong rhetoric, many UN member states and international observers remained unconvinced. The evidence presented was largely circumstantial, and several countries, including France, Germany, and Russia, called for continued inspections and diplomacy rather than immediate military action. The UN's own weapons inspectors, led by Hans Blix, had not found any conclusive proof of WMDs despite conducting thorough searches throughout Iraq. Blix reported that while Iraq's cooperation was inconsistent, there was still no evidence to suggest that Saddam's regime had active WMD programs. These findings raised significant doubts, but the Bush administration persisted, arguing that Saddam was simply adept at hiding his weapons and that further delay would be too risky.

The administration also faced skepticism at home. In the U.S., some intelligence officials and analysts questioned the reliability of the WMD evidence being presented to the public and to Congress. The CIA, for example, had not fully endorsed some of the more sensational claims, such as Iraq's alleged attempts to purchase uranium from Niger—a claim that later became a focal point of controversy when it was included in President Bush's 2003 State of the Union address. This episode, often referred to as the "yellowcake scandal," demonstrated how intelligence was manipulated or exaggerated to fit the preordained narrative of war.

To counter these doubts and maintain public support, the Bush administration engaged in a full-scale media campaign. They coordinated with sympathetic media outlets to amplify the WMD threat and to frame the war as a just and necessary response to an imminent danger. High-ranking officials, including Vice President Dick Cheney, National Security Advisor Condoleezza Rice, and Secretary of Defense Donald Rumsfeld, made repeated appearances on television, emphasizing the risks of inaction. Cheney, in particular, warned of a "mushroom cloud" as the ultimate consequence if the U.S. failed to act against Iraq's nuclear ambitions. Such statements played on the fears of an already anxious public, linking the threat posed by Iraq directly to the trauma of 9/11.

In Congress, the administration's WMD narrative had the desired effect. In October 2002, lawmakers voted overwhelmingly to authorize the use of military force in Iraq. Many members of Congress, both Democrats and Republicans, expressed reservations about the decision but felt compelled to act based on the information presented to them. The Bush administration's messaging had created a sense of urgency; to vote against the war resolution, in the eyes of many politicians, was to appear unpatriotic or indifferent to national security. The pressure to conform to the administration's line was immense, and dissenting voices were often marginalized or labeled as un-American.

As the U.S. prepared for war, the WMD narrative became the foundation upon which the invasion was justified. It provided a seemingly clear and compelling rationale: removing Saddam Hussein was not just a matter of regime change; it was an act of self-defense. The administration's ability to control and shape the narrative demonstrated the power of fear-based messaging and the manipulation of intelligence. It showcased how easily public sentiment and international consensus could be swayed when confronted with the specter of an invisible, catastrophic threat.

Ultimately, the absence of WMDs in Iraq—despite extensive searches following the invasion—would become one of the most controversial aspects of the war. It raised critical questions about the credibility of intelligence, the motives of those who advocated for war, and the extent to which the public had been misled. For now, however, the WMD narrative had done its job: it had provided the Bush administration with the political and public support necessary to launch a full-scale invasion of Iraq, setting the stage for a conflict that would have far-reaching consequences for both the region and the world.

The Aftermath and the Unraveling of the WMD Myth

The initial phase of the Iraq invasion, launched in March 2003, proceeded with swift military success. Baghdad fell within weeks, and images of the statue of Saddam Hussein being toppled symbolized what appeared to be a decisive victory. However, as U.S. forces took control of Iraq, the anticipated discovery of Weapons of Mass Destruction—promised as the central justification for the war—never materialized. This absence set off a chain of events that gradually unraveled the narrative that had driven the United States and its allies into conflict.

As coalition troops scoured suspected WMD sites throughout Iraq, they found none of the chemical, biological, or nuclear weapons that had been portrayed as imminent threats. U.S. military units, accompanied by specialized weapons inspectors, meticulously searched facilities identified in pre-war intelligence reports. Yet, time and again, these missions came up empty-handed, finding either abandoned infrastructure or benign civilian installations. The absence of evidence sparked confusion and, eventually, suspicion. The Bush administration initially downplayed these findings, claiming that the weapons were likely hidden or that Saddam's regime had destroyed them just before the invasion. But as weeks turned into months, and still no WMDs were uncovered, the administration's credibility began to suffer.

In the United States, public sentiment shifted from patriotic support for the war effort to skepticism and frustration. Critics who had previously been sidelined or labeled as unpatriotic for questioning the WMD narrative now found a receptive audience. Media outlets that had initially echoed the administration's rhetoric started to investigate the pre-war intelligence claims more critically. High-profile journalists and news organizations began to expose the gaps, contradictions, and manipulation within the intelligence used to justify the war. Reports emerged that intelligence analysts who expressed doubts about the existence of WMDs were marginalized or pressured to alter their assessments to align with the administration's narrative.

In July 2003, the controversy reached a boiling point when former U.S. ambassador Joseph Wilson publicly challenged the administration's claims about Iraq's attempts to purchase uranium from Niger—a key element used to build the case for war. Wilson's New York Times op-ed, "What I Didn't Find in Africa," detailed his investigation into the alleged uranium deal and his conclusion that there was no credible evidence to support it.

His piece directly contradicted the administration's narrative, drawing significant attention and controversy. The Bush administration's response was swift and severe, culminating in the exposure of Wilson's wife, Valerie Plame, as a covert CIA operative—a move widely seen as an act of retaliation. The subsequent investigation and media firestorm highlighted the lengths to which the administration would go to protect its narrative and discredit its critics.

Internationally, the absence of WMDs became a source of diplomatic embarrassment for the United States and its allies. Countries that had supported the invasion, such as the United Kingdom, faced intense scrutiny from their own citizens and political opposition. In the UK, the Blair government was accused of exaggerating intelligence to justify its support for the war, leading to a series of inquiries and investigations. The most prominent of these was the Hutton Inquiry, which examined the death of Dr. David Kelly, a British weapons expert who had expressed doubts about the government's WMD claims and had faced intense media and political pressure as a result. The inquiry revealed how intelligence had been "sexed up" to fit a predetermined policy, further eroding public trust.

The final blow to the WMD narrative came with the comprehensive report by the Iraq Survey Group (ISG) in 2004. The ISG, led by weapons inspector Charles Duelfer, conducted an exhaustive search for WMDs and concluded that Iraq had no active WMD programs at the time of the U.S. invasion. The report stated that while Saddam Hussein may have intended to revive these programs in the future, his regime was essentially disarmed and incapable of producing WMDs in the short term. The Duelfer Report, while thorough, confirmed what had become increasingly apparent: the central justification for the war was unfounded.

The fallout from this revelation had significant implications for the Bush administration and its foreign policy agenda. Domestically, it led to a decline in public trust and a surge in anti-war sentiment. Critics accused the administration of either gross incompetence or deliberate deceit. The phrase "Bush lied, people died" became a rallying cry for anti-war activists, and protests against the war grew in size and intensity. Politicians who had previously supported the invasion found themselves facing backlash from their constituents and scrambled to distance themselves from the decision. The midterm elections of 2006 saw significant gains for the Democratic Party, largely attributed to voter dissatisfaction with the ongoing conflict in Iraq and the failure to find the promised WMDs.

Within the intelligence community, the failure to locate WMDs led to widespread internal reviews and reforms. The CIA and other agencies faced intense criticism for their role in the pre-war intelligence assessments. The Senate Intelligence Committee's investigation into pre-war intelligence on Iraq found that the Bush administration had selectively used intelligence to support its policy objectives and that there were "serious flaws" in how the information was presented to the public. The intelligence failures prompted calls for greater oversight and accountability, leading to changes in how intelligence was gathered, analyzed, and communicated.

For the Bush administration, the legacy of the WMD narrative continued to cast a long shadow. While the administration attempted to shift the focus of the Iraq war's justification toward spreading democracy and fighting terrorism, the initial promise of disarming a rogue state with dangerous weapons was never forgotten. The failure to find WMDs remains a pivotal moment in modern American history, symbolizing the consequences of intelligence manipulation, the dangers of unchecked political power, and the long-term costs of war based on questionable premises.

The unraveling of the WMD myth is a powerful reminder of how narratives can be constructed, sold, and dismantled. It underscores the need for critical scrutiny of government claims, especially when the stakes involve war, global security, and the loss of countless lives. For those who had questioned the official narrative from the start, the absence of WMDs served as vindication, but it also highlighted the tragic reality of a conflict initiated under false pretenses—a reality that the world would continue to grapple with for years to come.

Chapter 14: Suppressing Dissent: Whistleblowers an

The Culture of Silence and Intimidation

In the aftermath of September 11, 2001, the United States was gripped by a sense of fear and urgency. The attack's unprecedented scale and impact created an environment where dissent was not only discouraged but actively suppressed. The government's narrative was swiftly formed and widely disseminated, framing the attacks as an act of war that demanded an equally forceful response. In this atmosphere, questioning or challenging the official version of events became synonymous with disloyalty, and the silencing of skeptics and whistleblowers became a priority.

The swift passage of the USA PATRIOT Act in October 2001 symbolized the government's expanding powers in the name of national security. The Act, designed to prevent further attacks, granted broad authority to federal agencies, including expanded surveillance capabilities and the ability to detain individuals suspected of terrorism-related activities without the usual due process protections. The fear of future attacks and the desire for security led to widespread public support for these measures, but they also created a chilling effect on freedom of speech. Government employees, journalists, and citizens who dared to question or criticize the administration's actions risked being labeled as unpatriotic or even as potential security threats.

Within federal agencies, the culture of silence became deeply entrenched. Intelligence agencies like the FBI, CIA, and NSA, already shrouded in secrecy, became even more opaque. Employees were reminded that their loyalty was to the agency and, by extension, to the government's narrative. Those who had information that contradicted or raised doubts about the official story faced an unspoken pressure to keep quiet. The fear of retaliation was not unfounded; individuals who spoke out risked being demoted, losing their security clearances, or even losing their jobs altogether. For many, the choice was clear: remain silent or face the consequences.

This culture extended beyond government employees to journalists and media outlets. The Bush administration skillfully manipulated the media, emphasizing the importance of national unity and the need to support the war on terror. This appeal to patriotism was effective in stifling critical coverage, as major news organizations were wary of appearing unpatriotic or of alienating viewers who supported the government's response. In a time when the country was still reeling from the trauma of the attacks, questioning the official narrative was portrayed as an affront to the victims and the heroes who responded on that fateful day.

Journalists who tried to dig deeper into the events of 9/11 or the government's actions afterward often encountered resistance, both from their editors and from the government itself. Media outlets, under pressure to maintain access to key political figures and military officials, self-censored or downplayed stories that deviated from the accepted line. For example, investigations into intelligence failures, suspicious financial transactions leading up to the attacks, or the connections between government officials and defense contractors were frequently dismissed as fringe topics or conspiracy theories. Reporters who pushed these stories were sometimes reassigned, pressured to abandon their investigations, or faced with a lack of institutional support.

The chilling effect of this culture was felt throughout the country. Civil liberties organizations like the American Civil Liberties Union (ACLU) warned of the dangers posed by the expanded surveillance powers granted under the PATRIOT Act. Activists and critics who organized protests or spoke out against government policies risked being monitored by federal agencies. In some cases, peaceful demonstrations were infiltrated by law enforcement, and participants found themselves under scrutiny, even if their activities were legally protected under the First Amendment.

The message was clear: dissent would not be tolerated. In the immediate aftermath of 9/11, this atmosphere of intimidation served to reinforce the government's narrative and to stifle any challenges. By creating an environment where questioning the official story was associated with disloyalty and potential criminality, the administration effectively suppressed the voices of skeptics and whistleblowers. The culture of silence and intimidation became a powerful tool, ensuring that the official version of events would dominate public discourse, while those who might have spoken out were left with the difficult choice of risking their careers and personal safety or remaining complicit through their silence.

High-Profile Whistleblowers and Their Stories

Despite the intense pressure to conform and the risks associated with speaking out, some individuals chose to come forward with information that contradicted the official narrative of 9/11. These whistleblowers often faced severe consequences for their actions, but their stories became crucial for those questioning the events of that day. They revealed a pattern of suppressed evidence, ignored warnings, and systematic obfuscation within the government's response, providing a glimpse into a hidden side of the 9/11 story.

One of the most prominent whistleblowers was Sibel Edmonds, a former FBI translator who gained attention for her claims about intelligence failures and corruption within the agency. Edmonds, who worked in the FBI's language division, was responsible for translating and analyzing intercepted communications related to terrorism. During her time at the bureau, she encountered numerous instances of crucial information being deliberately overlooked or mishandled. She alleged that FBI translators were pressured to alter translations and that some personnel had close connections to foreign interests, creating conflicts of interest.

Edmonds also claimed that the FBI possessed significant intelligence before 9/11 indicating an impending attack involving airplanes, yet these warnings were not acted upon. When she attempted to report her concerns, she was met with resistance and intimidation. Instead of investigating her claims, the FBI dismissed her and labeled her a troublemaker. She was subsequently fired, and the Justice Department invoked the rarely used "state secrets" privilege to gag her, effectively preventing her from revealing further details about her findings. Despite the gag order, Edmonds persisted in bringing attention to her case, eventually founding the National Security Whistleblowers Coalition to support others who faced similar challenges.

Another key figure was William Binney, a former high-ranking official at the National Security Agency (NSA). Binney, who had worked at the NSA for over 30 years, was one of the architects of the agency's data collection programs. In the wake of 9/11, Binney and his colleagues developed a program called "ThinThread," which was designed to efficiently gather intelligence while protecting the privacy of U.S. citizens through encryption and minimization techniques. However, the NSA chose to abandon ThinThread in favor of a more invasive and costly program called "Trailblazer." This new program bypassed legal safeguards, leading to widespread surveillance of American citizens.

Binney, along with fellow NSA colleagues, raised concerns about the legality and ethics of the NSA's actions, arguing that the agency was violating constitutional rights. When his warnings were ignored, he retired and became an outspoken critic of the NSA's mass surveillance practices. Binney's revelations highlighted how the government had not only ignored opportunities to prevent the 9/11 attacks but also exploited the tragedy as a pretext for expanding its surveillance capabilities. In retaliation, the FBI raided his home, confiscated his computers, and intimidated him with threats of prosecution.

Coleen Rowley, another whistleblower, was an FBI agent who tried to alert her superiors about missed opportunities to apprehend terrorists before the 9/11 attacks. Based in the Minneapolis office, Rowley and her team arrested Zacarias Moussaoui, a suspicious flight student who would later be identified as a potential co-conspirator in the 9/11 plot. Despite their repeated requests for a search warrant, FBI headquarters dismissed their concerns and refused to take action. In the aftermath of the attacks, Rowley wrote a detailed memo outlining how internal bureaucracy and negligence prevented crucial information from reaching those who could have stopped the attacks. Her testimony before the Senate Judiciary Committee and her courage in speaking out earned her Time magazine's co-"Person of the

Year" title in 2002. However, her career suffered, as she faced hostility from her colleagues and superiors.

These whistleblowers, along with others like Thomas Drake and Mark Rossini, highlighted a pattern of suppressed intelligence and ignored warnings within federal agencies. Their stories provided crucial insights into how opportunities to prevent the attacks were missed, not due to a lack of information but because of a failure—or refusal—by authorities to act. They also underscored the lengths to which the government would go to silence those who dared to speak out.

By revealing these insider accounts, whistleblowers challenged the official story, exposing the contradictions and omissions that were otherwise obscured. The government's aggressive response to these individuals—firing them, prosecuting them, and using legal tools to silence them—demonstrated the seriousness with which it sought to control the narrative surrounding 9/11. These stories became rallying points for skeptics and independent researchers, who saw in these whistleblowers' experiences proof that the truth about 9/11 had been manipulated, if not outright concealed.

For whistleblowers like Edmonds, Binney, and Rowley, the decision to speak out was not made lightly. They knew the consequences they would face, yet they felt compelled by a sense of duty to reveal what they knew. In an environment where silence and compliance were rewarded, their courage and persistence provided crucial evidence for those questioning the official narrative and fighting for greater transparency. Despite their struggles, these whistleblowers laid the groundwork for a broader movement seeking to expose the truth about what happened on September 11, 2001.

The Discrediting and Marginalization of Skeptics

One of the most effective strategies used to suppress dissent and silence critics of the official 9/11 narrative was the systematic discrediting and marginalization of those who dared to question the government's account. In a society where the trauma of the attacks was still raw, the public's desire for unity made any alternative explanations or criticism seem unpatriotic. The government and mainstream media capitalized on this sentiment, portraying skeptics as conspiracy theorists, extremists, or individuals seeking to profit from tragedy. This tactic served to isolate and discredit those who raised legitimate questions or presented evidence that contradicted the established story.

From the earliest days after the attacks, anyone challenging the official narrative was labeled a "truther"—a term that quickly took on a negative connotation. By categorizing skeptics under this umbrella, the media and government officials painted them as fringe elements with dubious credibility. The term became synonymous with irrationality and paranoia, making it easier to dismiss any concerns they raised. Instead of engaging with the evidence or addressing the questions, the authorities used this label to discredit the messenger, ensuring that the message itself would be ignored or ridiculed.

Mainstream media outlets played a crucial role in this campaign to marginalize critics. Journalists who raised questions about discrepancies in the 9/11 Commission Report, the collapse of Building 7, or the government's knowledge of the hijackers before the attacks were often met with skepticism or outright hostility from their editors and peers. Investigative reports that deviated from the official narrative were either buried or framed in a way that suggested they were the work of extremists. News programs frequently featured "experts" who ridiculed conspiracy theories, reinforcing the notion that anyone questioning the official story was not to be taken seriously.

The 9/11 Commission itself, which was tasked with investigating the events of that day, also contributed to the marginalization of skeptics. Though billed as an independent and comprehensive investigation, the commission was plagued by conflicts of interest and was heavily influenced by political pressure. Many of its members had close ties to the very institutions they were supposed to be investigating, and the commission's executive director, Philip Zelikow, had a longstanding relationship with key members of the Bush administration. Critics argued that the commission was designed to reinforce the official narrative rather than uncover the truth. However, when skeptics voiced these concerns, they were dismissed as paranoid or as politically motivated individuals attempting to undermine the government.

The media and government also used psychological tactics to discourage dissent. By framing skeptics as dangerous or subversive, authorities created an environment where people felt uncomfortable associating with or even listening to alternative viewpoints. This approach played on the public's fear and sense of duty to support the nation during a time of crisis. Anyone who questioned the government's actions risked being seen as un-American or as undermining the sacrifices made by first responders, military personnel, and the victims of the attacks. The government skillfully manipulated public sentiment, turning patriotism into a tool for silencing criticism.

High-profile individuals who spoke out against the official narrative also faced intense backlash. Filmmakers, authors, and public figures who dared to question the events of 9/11 were often vilified. For example, when former Governor Jesse Ventura openly criticized the government's account of 9/11 and highlighted the inconsistencies in the official narrative, he was labeled a conspiracy theorist and marginalized in the media. Ventura's experiences were emblematic of a broader pattern:

prominent voices who challenged the government's version of events were swiftly discredited, and their motives were called into question.

In some cases, even members of the 9/11 victims' families who sought transparency were targeted. Known as the "Jersey Girls," a group of widows whose husbands perished in the World Trade Center became vocal advocates for an independent investigation into the attacks. While they initially received support for their efforts to hold the government accountable, they were eventually criticized and smeared as opportunists by some media outlets and political figures. Rather than acknowledging their right to seek the truth about the deaths of their loved ones, critics framed their activism as politically motivated or as an attempt to exploit the tragedy for personal gain.

The systematic marginalization of skeptics extended beyond public figures to the broader public as well. Social media platforms and online forums became battlegrounds where alternative explanations of 9/11 were mocked and dismissed. Skeptics who attempted to share their findings online faced harassment, deplatforming, or outright bans. Government agencies, particularly the Department of Homeland Security, monitored these spaces for signs of dissent, and some individuals found themselves under scrutiny simply for expressing doubts about the official story. This climate of hostility made it difficult for independent researchers and concerned citizens to connect, share information, or organize, further isolating those who questioned the government's account.

By branding skeptics as irrational or dangerous, the government and media effectively neutralized the impact of alternative explanations and discouraged the public from exploring them. Instead of fostering a healthy debate about one of the most significant events in modern history, authorities shut down conversation, reinforcing the idea that the official narrative was not only accurate but also beyond reproach. This campaign to discredit and marginalize critics served to stifle legitimate questions and prevent the public from examining the deeper issues surrounding 9/11, ensuring that the dominant story remained unchallenged and unquestioned.

The Legal and Legislative Clampdown on Dissent

Beyond the media and public relations strategies used to discredit skeptics, the U.S. government employed legal and legislative measures to suppress dissent and control the narrative surrounding 9/11. These measures were aimed not only at silencing whistleblowers and critics but also at creating an atmosphere of fear and compliance that discouraged others from questioning the official account. By passing sweeping laws and enacting policies that expanded surveillance and curtailed civil liberties, the government effectively limited the space for open debate and investigative journalism, making it increasingly difficult for alternative viewpoints to gain traction.

One of the most significant legislative tools used to clamp down on dissent was the USA PATRIOT Act, passed in the immediate aftermath of the attacks. Sold to the public as a necessary measure to combat terrorism and protect national security, the PATRIOT Act granted unprecedented powers to law enforcement and intelligence agencies, allowing them to monitor citizens without traditional judicial oversight. The act expanded surveillance capabilities, enabling the government to wiretap phones, track online activity, and access financial records with minimal checks and balances. Although these measures were justified as essential for preventing future attacks, they also created an environment where critics and whistleblowers risked government surveillance and harassment simply for speaking out.

Journalists and activists who dared to investigate or question the official narrative of 9/11 often found themselves under scrutiny. The expanded powers granted by the PATRIOT Act allowed federal agencies to surveil individuals and organizations critical of government policies under the guise of national security. The line between legitimate anti-terrorism measures and the suppression of dissent blurred, and investigative journalists who delved into controversial areas of the 9/11 story reported increased intimidation tactics. For example, journalists experienced invasive background checks, were placed on watchlists, or found their sources threatened. The chilling effect was clear: any attempt to uncover discrepancies in the official narrative came with the risk of personal and professional consequences.

Whistleblowers, particularly those within the intelligence community, faced even harsher repercussions. The government's use of the Espionage Act to prosecute whistleblowers became a key strategy in silencing those who revealed inconvenient truths. This century-old law, initially intended to punish spies and traitors, was repurposed to target government employees who disclosed information to the media or the public. By labeling whistleblowers as criminals, the government not only discredited their testimonies but also deterred others from coming forward with critical information. This approach was evident in cases like that of Thomas Drake, an NSA whistleblower who exposed government waste and illegal surveillance practices. Drake was charged under the Espionage Act and faced the possibility of decades in prison, despite the fact that his disclosures involved public interest issues rather than classified secrets that posed a security risk.

Additionally, the government's aggressive use of "state secrets" privilege further hindered the ability of whistleblowers and skeptics to bring their cases to light. By invoking this privilege, the government could prevent critical information from being disclosed in court, effectively shutting down lawsuits and investigations that might have revealed mismanagement, negligence, or even complicity in the events leading up to and following 9/11. This legal strategy was not only used to protect intelligence operations but also as a shield to prevent any judicial scrutiny of potential wrongdoing. Sibel Edmonds, for example, was gagged using this privilege, which restricted her from sharing her knowledge of pre-9/11 intelligence failures and internal FBI corruption. This tactic sent a clear message: challenging the official story or attempting to hold powerful institutions accountable could result in legal silencing and professional ruin.

The implementation of no-fly lists and other forms of travel restrictions also became a method of controlling and punishing dissent. Under these policies, individuals who were critical of the government or who engaged in activism related to 9/11 truth-seeking often found themselves banned from air travel without explanation or recourse. This effectively limited their ability to participate in conferences, rallies, or media events, isolating them from their networks and supporters. These restrictions were often justified under the broad and vague concept of "national security," but they also served as a means to curtail the activities of those who posed a threat to the dominant narrative. Activists and skeptics reported being targeted, with some claiming they were harassed or questioned when attempting to board flights. This form of intimidation was aimed at discouraging others from joining or supporting the movement, reinforcing the notion that dissent would come with serious consequences.

In addition to these measures, the government also utilized the Foreign Intelligence Surveillance Act (FISA) courts, which operated in secret, to authorize the surveillance of individuals suspected of being involved in activities deemed hostile or subversive. Critics argued that FISA courts lacked transparency and operated without the due process guarantees typical of the U.S. judicial system. This meant that people could be surveilled based on vague or unsubstantiated claims, with no opportunity to challenge the legality of these actions. The use of these secret courts further eroded public trust in the government's intentions, suggesting that those in power were more interested in controlling information and silencing opposition than in ensuring national security.

These legal and legislative actions created a climate where dissent was not only discouraged but actively punished. By expanding surveillance, prosecuting whistleblowers, and limiting the ability of journalists and activists to operate freely, the government ensured that the official narrative of 9/11 remained dominant. At the same time, these measures instilled fear, preventing others from engaging in critical analysis or questioning the broader implications of the event. The message was clear: those who challenged the status quo risked not just their reputations but also their freedom.

In this environment, it became increasingly difficult for any counter-narrative to gain traction. The combination of legal intimidation, media manipulation, and legislative overreach created an effective barrier to open discussion and investigation. The government's control over the flow of information and its readiness to clamp down on dissent ensured that the version of events presented to the public would remain largely unchallenged, protecting the interests and actions of those in power while undermining the pursuit of truth.

The Impact on Freedom of Speech and Civil Liberties

The events of 9/11 not only reshaped America's political landscape but also had a profound impact on fundamental freedoms, particularly freedom of speech and civil liberties. In the name of security and patriotism, the government implemented policies and fostered a culture that stifled dissent and limited the ability of citizens, journalists, and activists to freely express their views or investigate the official narrative of the attacks.

This environment of fear and self-censorship created a chilling effect that still echoes today, as questioning authority or raising concerns about government policies has become increasingly fraught with consequences.

In the immediate aftermath of 9/11, the mood of the country shifted dramatically. The trauma and shock experienced by Americans gave rise to a heightened sense of nationalism and unity, which was leveraged by the government to push through controversial legislation like the USA PATRIOT Act. While the act was promoted as a necessary tool to prevent further attacks, it fundamentally altered the balance between national security and civil liberties. Surveillance powers were expanded, allowing the government to monitor citizens in ways that would have previously been considered unconstitutional. The right to privacy, a cornerstone of American freedom, was significantly eroded, with little transparency or oversight to protect against abuse.

This erosion of civil liberties also had a direct impact on freedom of speech. As the government expanded its surveillance capabilities, those who spoke out against the official 9/11 narrative or criticized U.S. foreign policy found themselves at greater risk of being monitored, investigated, or labeled as unpatriotic. The atmosphere of fear that permeated the country discouraged open debate and critical inquiry, as individuals who questioned the government's actions or sought to investigate inconsistencies in the official account of the attacks faced not only public backlash but also the possibility of government retribution. In this environment, even those who believed in the right to question authority found themselves weighing the potential consequences of doing so.

Journalists, in particular, faced increased pressure to conform to the official narrative. Media outlets, many of which were closely linked to corporate interests aligned with the government's post-9/11 policies, often chose to suppress stories that challenged the dominant viewpoint. Investigative journalists who sought to report on alternative explanations for the attacks or expose flaws in government policies encountered roadblocks, ranging from lack of support from their editors to threats of legal action. The combination of corporate influence and government pressure created a media environment where self-censorship became a norm. Journalists and media organizations that valued their credibility and funding were less likely to publish stories that deviated from the accepted narrative, fearing both economic repercussions and reputational damage.

Activists and whistleblowers also found their freedom of speech curtailed in the post-9/11 world. As the government expanded its surveillance state, those who attempted to organize protests or speak out against the government's actions were often targeted. Activist groups that critiqued the War on Terror, the invasion of Iraq, or the expansion of surveillance powers found themselves under intense scrutiny. Organizers were placed on watchlists, and their communications were monitored, making it difficult to coordinate efforts without risking government intervention. The labeling of dissenting voices as "threats to national security" not only justified increased surveillance but also discouraged others from joining such movements out of fear of being targeted themselves.

Whistleblowers faced even more severe consequences. Individuals who came forward with evidence contradicting the official story of 9/11 or exposing government wrongdoing were met with harsh retaliation. The government's use of the Espionage Act to prosecute whistleblowers served as a stark warning to those who might have considered coming forward. By criminalizing the act of revealing classified information, even when it was in the public interest, the government sent a message that dissent would not be tolerated. Edward Snowden and Chelsea

Manning are prominent examples of whistleblowers who faced severe punishment for revealing the truth about government surveillance and misconduct, illustrating how the government's stance on whistleblowing had shifted toward viewing it as an act of treason.

The result of these combined efforts was a chilling effect on public discourse. The fear of surveillance, legal repercussions, and public backlash led many to self-censor, avoiding topics that might be considered controversial or critical of the government. Academic institutions, once seen as bastions of free thought and open debate, also felt the impact. Professors who explored alternative explanations for 9/11 or who criticized the government's foreign policy were sometimes ostracized, losing funding opportunities or being pressured to change their research focus. This atmosphere of suppression extended beyond politics and journalism, infiltrating spaces traditionally associated with intellectual freedom.

Despite these challenges, some individuals and organizations continued to fight for freedom of speech and the protection of civil liberties. Civil rights groups such as the American Civil Liberties Union (ACLU) and advocacy organizations like the Electronic Frontier Foundation (EFF) took on legal battles to challenge the government's expansion of surveillance and its attempts to silence dissenting voices. These organizations argued that the erosion of civil liberties under the guise of national security was an unacceptable compromise and that a democracy must protect the right to question, debate, and criticize even in times of crisis. While their efforts did achieve some victories, the broader trend toward limiting free speech and expanding surveillance powers continued.

The suppression of dissent after 9/11 has had long-lasting consequences. The precedent set during that time paved the way for subsequent administrations to expand surveillance and clamp down on dissent, citing the ongoing threat of terrorism as justification. The impact on American society has been profound, as the lines between security and civil liberties remain blurred. For many, the post-9/11 world represents a shift toward a more authoritarian approach to governance, where dissent is no longer seen as a democratic right but as a risk to national security.

In conclusion, the aftermath of 9/11 saw a significant curtailing of freedom of speech and civil liberties in the United States. Through expanded surveillance, legal intimidation, and the creation of a culture that equated dissent with disloyalty, the government ensured that the official narrative remained unchallenged. The impact of these measures continues to be felt today, as Americans navigate an environment where the right to speak freely is increasingly compromised in the name of national security. The consequences of this shift serve as a reminder of the importance of safeguarding civil liberties, even in times of crisis, to maintain a truly free and open society.

Chapter 15: 9/11 Families Seeking Truth

The Initial Shock and Grief of 9/11 Families

On the morning of September 11, 2001, the world watched in horror as two planes crashed into the Twin Towers of the World Trade Center, another struck the Pentagon, and a fourth went down in a field in Pennsylvania. For the families of those on board the planes, as well as the thousands of people working in the towers, that day was a nightmare unlike any other. Shock and disbelief gripped the nation, but none felt it as deeply as those who lost loved ones in the attacks. The morning that began like any other was transformed into a day of unimaginable tragedy, leaving families struggling to comprehend the reality that their loved ones were gone.

In the hours and days following the attacks, families experienced an overwhelming mix of emotions: fear, confusion, anger, and, most of all, grief. Many spent hours frantically calling hospitals and emergency services, holding onto hope that their loved ones might be among the survivors. For some, the agonizing wait turned into the painful confirmation of loss as officials contacted them to deliver the heartbreaking news. For others, the absence of information became a lingering torment, as they clung to the possibility that their family members might still be alive, trapped but safe, somewhere within the debris. The uncertainty was almost as unbearable as the loss itself.

In the immediate aftermath, the media coverage was relentless, broadcasting images of destruction and chaos that only deepened the pain for families who watched helplessly as the events unfolded. The nation rallied around these grieving families, and an outpouring of support came from across the globe. Vigils, memorials, and tributes were organized, and the families found themselves caught between the public's collective mourning and their own private grief. In a time when they needed solace, they were often thrust into the spotlight, becoming symbols of the nation's sorrow. While the public attention provided some comfort, it also made it difficult for many families to process their emotions away from the gaze of the world.

During these early days, the overwhelming message of unity and patriotism provided some solace. The country came together in a display of solidarity, and for many families, the sense of shared grief was a source of strength. Political leaders, including President George W. Bush, promised justice and retribution for those responsible. The families, in their grief and desire for answers, often took comfort in these assurances. The official narrative that emerged—that the attacks were orchestrated by al-Qaeda terrorists led by Osama bin Laden—was widely accepted in those initial weeks, providing a sense of clarity amid the chaos. In the face of such tragedy, many families felt a need to believe that the government was doing everything possible to bring those responsible to justice and to protect the country from future attacks.

However, even as the narrative took shape, the personal stories of loss were varied and deeply individual. Some families found solace in their faith, leaning on spiritual communities for support. Religious services became a way to gather, mourn, and make sense of the incomprehensible. Others turned to grief counseling and support groups, seeking solace in shared experiences with those who understood the depth of their pain. For parents who lost children, children who lost parents, and spouses suddenly left alone, the shock of 9/11 was compounded by the challenge of moving forward without the people who had been central to their lives.

Memorials and remembrance became central to the process of grieving. Families participated in ceremonies and events dedicated to their loved ones, finding some measure of peace in knowing that their loss was not forgotten. The city of New York, as well as other locations directly impacted, became sites of pilgrimage and reflection. The impromptu memorials that sprang up near Ground Zero, where people left flowers, photographs, and mementos, were poignant reminders of the individual lives lost amid the overwhelming scale of the tragedy. These acts of remembrance helped to anchor the grief in something tangible, offering a way for families and friends to keep the memories of their loved ones alive.

Yet, the trauma for many families extended beyond the initial shock. As rescue and recovery efforts continued, the search for remains became a central focus. For months, recovery workers sifted through the rubble at Ground Zero, hoping to find identifiable remains that could be returned to families for proper burial. Some families received phone calls weeks or even months later, informing them that parts of their loved ones had been identified. These moments brought both relief and a resurgence of grief, as they provided a painful reminder of the magnitude of the loss. For others, the lack of remains or the return of only partial remains left them grappling with unresolved feelings, unable to fully close the chapter.

For the 9/11 families, the initial shock and grief were only the beginning of a long and painful journey. The profound loss they experienced was accompanied by the struggle to understand the incomprehensible. Even as they participated in memorials and sought solace in community and faith, the question of "why" lingered. It was a question that, for many, would ultimately lead them down a path of seeking deeper answers and challenging the official explanations they had initially accepted in their state of grief.

The Rise of Doubts Among Family Members

As the dust settled and the initial shock of 9/11 gave way to grief, some family members of the victims began to scrutinize the official narrative. In the early days, the overwhelming sorrow and the sense of national unity made it difficult for many to question the story being presented by the government and media. The narrative was simple: 19 hijackers, coordinated by al-Qaeda, had carried out the deadliest terrorist attack in American history. The government's response was swift, framing it as a war on terror that demanded immediate and unwavering support. However, as months turned into years, some families started to notice inconsistencies, contradictions, and gaps in the official account, prompting them to ask uncomfortable questions.

Many of these doubts began with the 9/11 Commission itself, which was established in late 2002 after months of pressure from victims' families. Initially, the government had resisted calls for an independent investigation, arguing that it was too soon and that resources were needed elsewhere. This hesitation raised suspicions among some family members. Why, they wondered, would their own government resist a full and transparent investigation into the deaths of their loved ones? After all, wasn't it in the nation's best interest to understand exactly how such a catastrophic failure could have occurred?

As the commission began its work, it became clear that the families were not content to sit on the sidelines. Groups like the 9/11 Family Steering Committee formed, made up of relatives who were determined to hold the government accountable and uncover the truth. They demanded that the commission pursue specific lines of inquiry and subpoena witnesses who could provide critical testimony. Yet, as the process unfolded, some family members grew increasingly disillusioned. They saw firsthand how certain questions were dismissed or glossed over. Key witnesses, such as then-National Security Advisor Condoleezza Rice, initially refused to testify publicly, only relenting after intense pressure from the families. Even then, many felt that her testimony was evasive and unsatisfactory.

Among the most troubling aspects for the families were the persistent gaps in the timeline of events leading up to the attacks. Many wondered how it was possible for such a well-coordinated plot to go undetected, given the vast resources and intelligence capabilities of the U.S. government. The commission's report ultimately cited "intelligence failures" and communication breakdowns, but for some families, these explanations felt insufficient. They began to suspect that the government was either hiding something or, worse, had allowed the attacks to happen for political reasons. The reluctance of certain government officials to engage fully with the commission only fueled these suspicions.

The families' doubts were also heightened by the discovery of inconsistencies in the official accounts of the day itself. Survivors and first responders reported explosions and other anomalies that did not align with the government's explanation of the buildings' collapse. Some family members began to explore alternative theories, turning to independent researchers and experts for more information. They found comfort in knowing that others were also questioning the official version of events. Together, they began to form a movement dedicated to seeking the truth, feeling that they owed it to their lost loved ones to uncover what really happened.

The growing sense of unease among some 9/11 families was not without consequences. For many, it meant becoming estranged from others who still fully believed in the government's account. Within families and communities, the debate over what really happened on September 11 led to division. Some family members were labeled as conspiracy theorists, their grief dismissed as misdirected anger. But for those who doubted, the stakes were too high to remain silent. They believed that their loved ones had been victims of a crime far more complex than the government was willing to admit. To honor their memories, they felt a responsibility to pursue the truth, even if it meant standing apart from the mainstream narrative.

This search for truth led some families to uncover evidence that was previously ignored or dismissed. The families pushed for the declassification of documents and sought access to information that could shed light on the events of that day. They raised questions about the identities of the hijackers, some of whom were later reported alive and living in other countries. They challenged the lack of air defense response and pointed out the troubling coincidence of military drills simulating hijackings occurring on the same day. These questions formed the foundation of a growing movement of 9/11 families and supporters who were determined to hold those in power accountable.

Ultimately, the rise of doubts among family members marked a turning point in the story of 9/11. What began as a simple desire for closure evolved into a quest for truth, as they demanded answers to the uncomfortable and often disturbing questions that emerged. For these families, the pain of losing their loved ones was compounded by the fear that justice had not been served and that those responsible—whether through negligence, malice, or worse—had not been held accountable. The families' pursuit of answers would continue to challenge the official narrative, turning their grief into a force for truth and transparency.

The 9/11 Families Unite for Justice

As doubts about the official story of 9/11 grew among certain family members, many of them realized that their individual efforts would be stronger if they came together as a united front. In the months and years following the attacks, several groups formed, composed of family members who shared a common goal: to uncover the truth about what happened on September 11 and to hold those responsible accountable. These groups, including the 9/11 Family Steering Committee and Families of September 11, became powerful voices advocating for transparency and accountability in the face of governmental resistance.

The journey toward unity was not always straightforward. In the immediate aftermath of the attacks, most families were focused on coping with their grief and finding ways to memorialize their loved ones. But as the government's official explanation solidified, and as the 9/11 Commission's work progressed, some families felt increasingly frustrated by the lack of clarity and the dismissive attitude toward crucial questions. These frustrations led to informal gatherings and meetings, where family members exchanged stories, shared their doubts, and discussed their concerns about the investigation. Over time, these informal groups became more organized, forming alliances that would prove vital in their quest for justice.

The 9/11 Family Steering Committee emerged as one of the most vocal and influential groups. Comprised of widows, parents, children, and siblings of those who died in the attacks, the committee represented a cross-section of those who had suffered the most profound losses. These family members were not content to simply accept the government's version of events; they demanded a thorough and independent investigation, something that the Bush administration initially resisted. The committee's persistence eventually forced the government's hand, leading to the formation of the 9/11 Commission. However, the families' involvement did not end there. They closely monitored the commission's progress, submitted hundreds of questions, and continued to apply pressure to ensure that their concerns were addressed.

The families' commitment to uncovering the truth went beyond their own personal losses. Many felt that they had a responsibility not only to their loved ones but also to the American public and the global community. They believed that a complete and honest investigation was essential to prevent future tragedies. The family groups became advocates not just for transparency in the case of 9/11 but also for broader governmental accountability. They saw their work as part of a larger struggle to ensure that the institutions designed to protect the public were held to the highest standards.

However, working together as a united front was not without its challenges. Within the broader 9/11 family community, there were differing opinions on how to approach the quest for truth. Some family members wanted to focus solely on memorializing their loved ones and supporting the government's efforts to combat terrorism. Others, however, were deeply skeptical of the official story and wanted to challenge the government more directly. This divergence led to the formation of different groups, each with its own focus and approach. Despite these differences, there was a shared understanding among all the families that they had been forever changed by the events of September 11, and they had a right to demand answers.

The collaboration among the families also extended beyond U.S. borders. As the global impact of 9/11 became clear, family members reached out to others around the world who had experienced similar losses due to terrorism or state violence. This international network of support helped strengthen their resolve and provided a broader perspective on the fight for truth and accountability. The families learned from one another's experiences and began to see their own struggle as part of a larger, international effort to confront and expose governmental misconduct, cover-ups, and human rights abuses.

Through their unity, the 9/11 families built a movement that could not be easily ignored. Their persistent lobbying, media outreach, and public events kept the issue of 9/11 transparency in the spotlight, even as the government and mainstream media tried to move on from the tragedy. The families used their collective voice to challenge the official narrative, demand the release of classified documents, and call for further investigation into unresolved questions. Their courage and determination transformed them from grieving individuals into activists and advocates for justice.

This unified effort did not always yield immediate results. The families often faced stonewalling and dismissive responses from officials. Yet, their persistence was undeniable. They understood that their strength lay in their unity, and by standing together, they could amplify their voices and keep pressure on the institutions that had, in their view, failed them. They organized press conferences, rallied supporters, and mobilized public opinion, ensuring that their message reached a wide audience. Their efforts inspired not only other 9/11 families but also members of the public who had begun to harbor doubts about the official story. The 9/11 families' fight for justice became a beacon for those questioning the government's version of events.

The determination of the 9/11 families to seek justice high-lighted the power of unity in the face of tragedy. By coming together, they were able to turn their grief into a force for change, demanding accountability and transparency. Their efforts underscored the importance of collective action, showing that even in the wake of the most profound loss, individuals could find strength in solidarity. They understood that while they could not bring back their loved ones, they could honor their memory by fighting for the truth and ensuring that the lessons of 9/11 were not forgotten.

The Fight for an Independent Investigation

The 9/11 families' push for truth led them to confront the harsh reality that the government's investigation was neither as independent nor as thorough as they believed it needed to be. From the outset, many family members viewed the Bush administration's reluctance to form a commission as deeply suspicious. Months after the attacks, as grieving families began to demand answers, the administration repeatedly resisted calls for an independent investigation, citing national security concerns and the ongoing war on terror as reasons to delay. This resistance only deepened the families' determination to pursue a comprehensive and impartial inquiry into the events of that day.

The families' persistence led to the creation of the 9/11 Commission in late 2002, but the battle was far from over. They soon realized that the commission itself was hampered by political pressures and compromises that threatened its integrity. The commission's initial head, Henry Kissinger, was a controversial choice due to his past as Secretary of State and his connections to various foreign governments. His appointment was met with immediate outcry from the families, who feared that his involvement would turn the investigation into a mere formality. After persistent pressure from the families, Kissinger stepped down, and the commission was restructured, but doubts about its impartiality lingered.

Another concern for the families was the limited budget and resources allocated to the commission. In stark contrast to the extensive funds allocated to investigating the Clinton-Lewinsky scandal, the initial budget for the 9/11 Commission was only $3 million—an amount that seemed insufficient to investigate the most significant attack on American soil since Pearl Harbor. Families and advocates argued that this reflected a lack of seriousness on the government's part, and they campaigned for more funding, eventually securing an increase. Still, the families felt that the commission was constrained by financial and political limitations, casting doubt on whether it could truly get to the bottom of what happened.

Throughout the commission's work, the 9/11 families remained actively involved, often serving as watchdogs to ensure that their concerns were addressed. They provided lists of questions, called for the inclusion of specific witnesses, and demanded transparency at every step. One of their primary demands was for key government officials to testify publicly and under oath. Initially, the Bush administration resisted these requests, offering to have President George W. Bush and Vice President Dick Cheney meet with the commission privately and off the record. The families viewed this as unacceptable and launched a public campaign demanding that these high-ranking officials testify in a transparent manner. Although Bush and Cheney eventually did meet with the commission, it was done in a private, unsworn session, reinforcing the families' concerns that crucial information was being withheld.

The families also pressured the commission to address the numerous intelligence failures leading up to 9/11. They questioned why intelligence agencies like the CIA and FBI had not acted on the warnings they had received about potential terrorist attacks involving airplanes. The commission's report ultimately cited bureaucratic issues and a lack of communication as primary factors, but for many families, these explanations seemed insufficient. They felt that there were still too many unanswered questions about why these warnings had not been acted upon and why critical information had not been shared. The families pushed for deeper investigation into possible motives behind these intelligence failures, but they were often met with resistance.

Another critical point of contention was the commission's handling of the collapse of the Twin Towers and World Trade Center Building 7. Families demanded a thorough investigation into the engineering and structural details behind the buildings' collapses, especially given the conflicting accounts from engineers and architects who had analyzed the footage. They asked the commission to consider alternative theories, including the possibility of controlled demolition, which had gained traction among some experts. However, the commission largely dismissed these theories, focusing instead on the idea that the impact of the planes and subsequent fires caused the buildings to fall. The families argued that this dismissal showed a lack of willingness to fully explore all possibilities, leading them to question the commission's objectivity.

Despite these challenges, the families persisted. They attended hearings, organized protests, and kept the media spotlight on the commission's proceedings, ensuring that their voices remained central to the investigation. They understood that their involvement was crucial for maintaining the integrity of the inquiry, and they refused to be sidelined or ignored. The families' presence served as a constant reminder that the commission's work had real consequences and that the truth mattered not just for them but for the nation as a whole.

Ultimately, the 9/11 families' fight for an independent investigation highlighted the power of citizen advocacy in holding government accountable. While the commission's final report did answer some questions, many families felt it left much unresolved. Their efforts revealed the complexities of navigating the intersection of grief, justice, and politics, as they continued to seek transparency in an environment where it often seemed elusive. Despite their frustrations, the families' determination ensured that the push for a thorough investigation could not be easily dismissed. Their struggle for truth, and the resistance they encountered, would inspire future generations of activists questioning official narratives and demanding accountability.

Legal Battles and the Pursuit of Accountability

As the 9/11 families continued their quest for truth and justice, many found that seeking answers through official channels, like the 9/11 Commission, was not enough. Dissatisfied with the commission's findings and frustrated by the government's continued secrecy, some family members turned to the courts in an attempt to hold responsible parties accountable. These legal battles became a significant aspect of the families' fight, representing both a path to potential justice and a demonstration of the obstacles facing those challenging powerful institutions.

One of the most prominent lawsuits filed by the families was against Saudi Arabia, a country that had long been suspected of having connections to the 9/11 attackers. With 15 of the 19 hijackers being Saudi nationals, and reports suggesting financial ties between Saudi officials and the hijackers, many families felt that Saudi Arabia played a role in the attacks. For years, however, the U.S. government shielded Saudi Arabia from lawsuits by invoking sovereign immunity. This legal doctrine protects foreign governments from being sued in American courts, leaving the families without recourse. Undeterred, they lobbied

Congress, pushing for the passage of the Justice Against Sponsors of Terrorism Act (JASTA), which would allow them to sue foreign governments for acts of terrorism on U.S. soil.

In 2016, after years of relentless advocacy by the families, JASTA was passed by Congress, despite a veto from President Obama. This was a significant victory for the 9/11 families, demonstrating the power of their unity and determination. However, the passage of JASTA was just the beginning. The families still faced an uphill battle in court as they attempted to prove Saudi involvement. The legal process was long and complex, with the Saudi government and its allies deploying an army of lawyers to fight the claims. Despite these challenges, the families remained steadfast, viewing the lawsuit not only as a means to achieve justice but also as a way to uncover information that had long been hidden. For them, the courtroom became another battleground in their struggle to bring the truth to light.

In addition to lawsuits against Saudi Arabia, some families also pursued legal action against U.S. entities and government officials they believed were negligent or complicit in the attacks. These lawsuits focused on various aspects of the 9/11 tragedy, from the alleged failures of the FAA to protect U.S. airspace to accusations that intelligence agencies had ignored or suppressed critical warnings. Some families even attempted to sue members of the Bush administration, including Vice President Dick Cheney and Secretary of Defense Donald Rumsfeld, arguing that their actions—or lack thereof—contributed to the attacks. These legal efforts faced significant hurdles, with courts often dismissing the cases due to the complexities of proving negligence or intent in the context of national security.

Beyond lawsuits, the families also fought to obtain classified documents that they believed could provide more information about the attacks. Over the years, the government repeatedly refused to release certain files, citing national security concerns. These included the "28 Pages," a section of the congressional report on 9/11 that detailed possible links between Saudi officials and the hijackers. For over a decade, the families, alongside sympathetic lawmakers, pushed for the declassification of these pages. In 2016, they finally succeeded in getting them released. While the pages did not provide the smoking gun some had hoped for, they did reveal previously undisclosed connections, further fueling the families' determination to pursue their legal battles against Saudi Arabia and other entities.

The 9/11 families also faced pushback from within the legal system and the media. Critics argued that their lawsuits were based on conspiracy theories or that they risked harming U.S. foreign relations and national security interests. These accusations often came from powerful figures in government and the legal profession, creating an uphill battle for the families in the court of public opinion. Despite this, the families stood firm, maintaining that their pursuit was not about destabilizing the nation but about achieving justice for their loved ones and ensuring transparency. Their courage in confronting not only foreign governments but also their own demonstrated the extent of their resolve.

Amid these legal battles, many families faced another difficult decision: whether to accept settlement offers. Some entities and corporations, including airline companies and security firms, sought to settle with families outside of court to avoid drawn-out litigation and public scrutiny. These settlement offers were often substantial, and for some families, they represented a way to gain some sense of closure and financial stability after years of suffering. However, other families refused to settle, believing that accepting money would undermine their pursuit of accountability. They argued that settlements allowed those potentially complicit in the attacks to escape the scrutiny of a public trial. This divide showed the complexity of the families' struggle, as they balanced the desire for justice with the practical realities of legal battles and the need for personal closure.

For those families who chose to press forward, the courtroom remained a place where they could demand accountability and force powerful entities to confront their actions—or inactions—on September 11. Even as the legal process dragged on for years, with numerous setbacks and appeals, the families' determination never wavered. They continued to fight for access to evidence, for the right to have their day in court, and for the opportunity to challenge the official narrative of 9/11 through legal means. For them, the legal battles symbolized a larger fight against injustice and secrecy, and their resolve transformed the courtroom into yet another arena in their ongoing quest for the truth.

The legal battles of the 9/11 families highlighted both the strengths and limitations of the American justice system. On the one hand, they demonstrated that citizens could challenge the most powerful governments and institutions when united by a shared cause. On the other, they exposed how difficult it could be to achieve justice when those same institutions controlled the flow of information and wielded significant influence over the legal process. The families' fight, however, was about more than just the courtroom; it was about creating a legacy of accountability, ensuring that their loved ones were not forgotten, and making certain that future generations would not face the same obstacles in their search for the truth.

Chapter 16: The Architects and Engineers for 9/11

The Formation and Purpose of Architects & Engineers for 9/11 Truth (AE911Truth)

In the years following the tragic events of September 11, 2001, many individuals across various professions began to question the official explanations for the collapse of the World Trade Center buildings. Among these skeptics was Richard Gage, a licensed architect with over 20 years of experience in designing and constructing steel-framed buildings. In 2006, Gage founded Architects & Engineers for 9/11 Truth (AE911Truth), an organization dedicated to re-examining the events of 9/11 from a scientific and structural perspective. Gage's motivation stemmed from his growing concerns that the official reports, particularly those by the National Institute of Standards and Technology (NIST), failed to adequately explain the unprecedented collapse of the buildings.

AE911Truth began as a small initiative, with Gage reaching out to colleagues and other professionals in his field to gather support. Initially, the response was mixed; some were hesitant to align themselves with a movement that challenged the government's narrative. However, Gage's efforts soon gained traction as he presented a compelling case based on architectural and engineering principles. Architects, structural engineers, and demolition experts began to join the cause, united by a shared concern that the events of 9/11, particularly the way the Twin Towers and Building 7 collapsed, did not align with their professional understanding of how steel-framed buildings behave under stress. This growing community formed the foundation of AE911Truth, which aimed to provide a credible, science-based platform for professionals who questioned the official story.

The organization's mission was clear: to investigate the evidence related to the World Trade Center's destruction, educate the public and the architectural community, and advocate for a new, independent investigation into the events of 9/11. AE911Truth emphasized that its work was not driven by political ideology but by a commitment to scientific integrity and truth. The organization aimed to approach the issue from a purely technical standpoint, avoiding political rhetoric and instead focusing on structural analysis, materials science, and witness testimony. This professional, evidence-based approach was intended to differentiate AE911Truth from other groups within the 9/11 truth movement, some of which were often dismissed as conspiratorial.

At the core of AE911Truth's formation was a belief that the official explanation—fires and structural damage caused by the impact of the airplanes—was insufficient to account for the rapid, symmetrical, and complete collapses observed on September 11. Gage and his colleagues argued that such collapses, particularly that of Building 7 (which was not struck by an airplane), appeared more consistent with controlled demolition techniques than with the progressive structural failure described by NIST. AE911Truth contended that the absence of significant resistance during the collapse of these buildings, the presence of molten metal in the debris, and eyewitness accounts of explosions prior to and during the buildings' collapse all pointed to a scenario involving pre-planted explosives.

To bolster its credibility and build a strong professional community, AE911Truth launched campaigns to gather signatures from licensed architects and engineers who supported the call for a new investigation. Within a few years, the organization had gathered thousands of signatures from professionals willing to publicly state their doubts about the official 9/11 narrative. This growing list served as a powerful testament to the widespread skepticism within the architectural and engineering fields and underscored the organization's message that the anomalies observed in the World Trade Center's destruction warranted further examination. AE911Truth's website prominently displayed the names and credentials of these professionals, lending the movement legitimacy and encouraging others to step forward.

The organization's purpose extended beyond advocating for a new investigation; it also aimed to educate the public and the professional community about the evidence it had gathered. AE911Truth hosted seminars, workshops, and presentations across the country, often featuring Richard Gage and other experts explaining their findings in detail. These events were designed not only to inform but also to encourage other professionals to join the movement, creating a ripple effect that would spread AE911Truth's message far and wide. By leveraging the credibility of licensed architects and engineers, the organization aimed to create a growing body of evidence that would be difficult for authorities and the media to ignore.

AE911Truth also focused on producing educational materials, including documentaries and in-depth reports, that could be easily shared and disseminated. One of its most well-known documentaries, *9/11: Explosive Evidence – Experts Speak Out*, featured numerous professionals discussing their concerns about the official narrative and presenting the evidence that led them to conclude that the buildings' collapses were likely the result of controlled demolition. The documentary was screened across the United States and internationally, reaching a wide audience and further solidifying the organization's reputation as a credible, science-based group.

As AE911Truth grew, it faced significant challenges, including pushback from the media and professional organizations. However, the formation of the group and its rapid expansion demonstrated a crucial aspect of the post-9/11 era: the willingness of professionals to question even the most established narratives when those narratives did not align with their expertise and experience. For AE911Truth, the events of September 11 represented not only a tragedy but also a pivotal moment for the architectural and engineering communities to uphold their commitment to truth and transparency.

The Evidence Challenging the Official Story

As AE911Truth began its mission to uncover the truth behind the collapse of the World Trade Center buildings, it compiled a significant body of evidence that challenged the official narrative put forth by government agencies like the National Institute of Standards and Technology (NIST). Central to the organization's argument was the assertion that the physical evidence did not align with the explanations given. In their view, the NIST reports, which attributed the collapses to the structural damage caused by the airplanes and subsequent fires, overlooked or dismissed key anomalies that pointed toward an alternative cause.

One of the most critical pieces of evidence presented by AE911Truth concerns the collapse of World Trade Center Building 7 (WTC 7). Unlike the North and South Towers, Building 7 was not struck by an airplane, yet it collapsed in a manner that, according to AE911Truth, closely resembled a controlled demolition. The building fell symmetrically into its footprint at near free-fall acceleration, a phenomenon the group argued could not be explained by fire alone. AE911Truth highlighted that Building 7's collapse was the first instance in history of a steel-framed high-rise building coming down due solely to fires. They asserted that the collapse was too uniform and sudden, suggesting that it was more consistent with a scenario involving pre-placed explosives.

Further evidence cited by AE911Truth included eyewitness testimonies from individuals present at the scene on 9/11. These testimonies, collected from first responders, journalists, and survivors, described hearing and seeing explosions both before and during the collapses of the Twin Towers and Building 7. For example, firefighters on the ground reported hearing loud blasts and witnessing flashes of light—a sequence that many demolition experts would recognize as characteristic of controlled demolition charges. AE911Truth emphasized that these accounts were largely ignored or downplayed in official reports, yet they provided crucial insights into what might have really happened within the buildings before they collapsed.

AE911Truth also focused on the presence of molten metal found in the debris at Ground Zero. Numerous reports and photographs documented pools of molten metal beneath the rubble of the Twin Towers weeks after the collapse. This finding was perplexing to many in the architectural and engineering communities because the fires resulting from jet fuel and office materials burn at temperatures far below the melting point of steel. AE911Truth argued that the presence of molten steel was a strong indication that an incendiary material, such as thermite or its more advanced form, nanothermite, could have been used to weaken and cut through the steel beams, causing the buildings to collapse in a controlled manner.

The group also scrutinized the speed and symmetry of the collapses, particularly those of the Twin Towers. NIST's explanation was that the impact of the airplanes dislodged fire-proofing materials and weakened the structural integrity of the buildings, ultimately leading to their collapse. However, AE911Truth pointed out that the rate at which the towers fell—essentially free fall for several seconds—indicated that there was little to no resistance as the buildings came down. In a natural, gravity-driven collapse, AE911Truth argued, there would be significant resistance from the lower floors as they absorbed the falling debris, slowing down the collapse and causing it to be uneven and partial rather than the rapid, symmetrical fall observed.

Moreover, AE911Truth highlighted the discovery of small particles of what appeared to be thermitic material in the dust samples collected from the World Trade Center site. A peer-reviewed study published by scientists and researchers associated with AE911Truth claimed that these particles, which exhibited explosive properties, could be remnants of nanothermite, a high-tech explosive capable of cutting through steel with extreme precision. The group asserted that these findings were a smoking gun, contradicting the narrative that fire alone was responsible for the collapses.

The evidence presented by AE911Truth also extended to an analysis of the debris removal process. The rapid clearing of steel beams and other structural components from Ground Zero raised red flags among members of the organization. They argued that this prevented a thorough forensic investigation that could have uncovered signs of explosives or other tampering. AE911Truth pointed out that, in a crime scene of such magnitude, standard procedure would have called for preserving evidence rather than removing it at such a rapid pace. The removal of the steel, which was then shipped overseas for recycling, meant that any opportunity to conduct a comprehensive, independent analysis was lost.

To strengthen its case, AE911Truth referenced historical examples of building fires and collapses, none of which mirrored the rapid, symmetrical descent of the World Trade Center buildings. The group argued that even in cases where high-rise buildings had been engulfed in flames for hours, the structures remained standing or, at the very least, did not fall at near free-fall speeds. For AE911Truth, this provided further proof that the official story failed to align with the physical evidence and historical precedents of structural behavior under fire.

The organization's efforts to challenge the official story were not limited to presenting physical evidence. AE911Truth also focused on the lack of transparency and inconsistencies in the investigations conducted by NIST and other agencies. They pointed out that NIST's refusal to release certain computer modeling data and its dismissal of alternative hypotheses, such as controlled demolition, indicated a lack of openness in the investigative process. This, AE911Truth argued, only added to the suspicion that key details about the buildings' destruction were being intentionally obscured.

Ultimately, AE911Truth's presentation of evidence was designed to build a compelling case for reopening the investigation into 9/11. By highlighting inconsistencies, presenting physical anomalies, and relying on professional expertise, the organization aimed to demonstrate that the official narrative did not hold up under scrutiny. For AE911Truth, the questions surrounding the collapse of the World Trade Center were not mere technicalities but vital pieces of the puzzle that, if examined openly and honestly, could uncover the truth about what really happened on that fateful day.

The Science Behind Controlled Demolition

A core argument put forth by AE911Truth revolves around the parallels between the collapses of the World Trade Center buildings and controlled demolitions. The organization, composed of licensed architects and engineers, drew on their professional expertise to suggest that the visual and physical characteristics of the collapses mirrored those of buildings intentionally brought down using explosives. By diving into the science behind controlled demolition, AE911Truth aimed to provide a technically sound, evidence-based challenge to the official explanation.

One of the most striking features of the collapses, according to AE911Truth, was the speed at which the buildings fell. The Twin Towers, each over 1,300 feet tall, collapsed in roughly 10 seconds—close to free-fall speed. In a controlled demolition, explosives are placed strategically to remove the structural supports of a building simultaneously, allowing it to fall into its footprint without resistance. AE911Truth argued that the nearly free-fall acceleration observed in the World Trade Center buildings indicated a sudden and simultaneous failure of all the core supports, which is highly unusual in a natural collapse. Normally, the collapse of such massive structures would encounter significant resistance from the floors below, slowing the process. Instead, the rapid, uniform descent of the towers suggested to AE911Truth that all resistance was removed in a controlled manner.

The organization also examined the collapse of World Trade Center Building 7 (WTC 7), which they described as the most obvious case of controlled demolition. WTC 7, a 47-story skyscraper that was not directly hit by any airplane, collapsed late in the afternoon on September 11. Unlike the Twin Towers, the collapse of WTC 7 was not immediately explained by the impact of an aircraft. Instead, the official narrative attributed its fall to fires caused by debris from the nearby North Tower. However,

AE911Truth highlighted that this explanation did not account for the symmetrical and sudden nature of the collapse, which closely resembled classic controlled demolitions.

AE911Truth emphasized that in controlled demolitions, the aim is to bring a building down in such a way that it folds into its own footprint, minimizing damage to surrounding structures. This is typically achieved by placing explosives on key load-bearing points of the building's structure. In the case of WTC 7, the building fell symmetrically, and its facade remained intact as it descended straight down, features consistent with a controlled demolition rather than a collapse due to fire damage. Furthermore, AE911Truth pointed to video footage showing a visible kink forming at the roofline of WTC 7—a telltale sign of a controlled implosion where the central support columns are removed first, causing the building to fold inward.

In addition to the visual evidence, AE911Truth referenced the thermal evidence supporting their hypothesis. The presence of molten metal found in the debris piles of all three buildings raised serious questions. Photographs and reports from the cleanup crews described molten steel flowing like lava weeks after the collapse. The temperatures required to melt steel far exceed those that would be produced by jet fuel or office fires. This anomaly led AE911Truth to explore the possibility that thermite, a substance capable of reaching the necessary temperatures, could have been used to cut through the steel columns. The use of thermite, which burns at over 4,000 degrees Fahrenheit, could explain the presence of molten metal and would be consistent with the techniques used in controlled demolitions to sever critical structural components.

The group also conducted studies and experiments to test the hypothesis that nanothermite—a more advanced and potent form of thermite—might have been used in the demolition of the towers. According to AE911Truth, the presence of nanothermite was supported by the discovery of red-gray chips found in dust samples collected from the World Trade Center site. Researchers associated with AE911Truth subjected these chips to analysis and found that they exhibited properties consistent with high-energy materials used in military-grade explosives. These findings, published in peer-reviewed journals, challenged the NIST report, which made no mention of thermite or nanothermite as potential factors.

Furthermore, AE911Truth pointed out the pattern of destruction in the steel beams that were recovered from the site. Several beams showed evidence of angled cuts that appeared too precise to be the result of chaotic fires and gravity alone. In controlled demolitions, steel columns are often cut at angles to control the direction of the collapse, ensuring the building falls inward. The presence of such cuts, AE911Truth argued, was consistent with the deliberate use of incendiaries or explosives designed to sever the beams and facilitate the buildings' symmetrical falls.

The organization also cited eyewitness testimonies from firefighters and rescue personnel who reported hearing loud, sequential explosions before the buildings collapsed. These accounts, they argued, aligned with the patterns observed in controlled demolitions, where explosives are detonated in stages to ensure a coordinated and efficient collapse. For instance, many firefighters described hearing explosions not just at the impact zones, but also at the base of the buildings, suggesting that charges could have been planted throughout the structures to weaken them systematically. These observations were largely omitted or downplayed in official reports, but AE911Truth considered them critical pieces of the puzzle.

Additionally, AE911Truth pointed out that despite the NIST report's conclusions, the agency's own computer models could not replicate the way the buildings fell without manually adjusting the parameters to simulate a collapse. This led AE911Truth to argue that the official explanation lacked a solid foundation and that a controlled demolition scenario offered a more consistent and scientifically plausible explanation for the buildings' behavior on 9/11.

In making their case, AE911Truth urged for a new, independent investigation that would allow for a comprehensive examination of all the evidence, including the possibility of explosives. They argued that such an investigation would be vital for both accountability and transparency, offering a chance to resolve the contradictions and inconsistencies that they believed remained unaddressed. For AE911Truth, understanding the science behind controlled demolitions was not only key to challenging the official narrative but also essential for ensuring that the true nature of the attacks was revealed.

NIST's Investigation and Its Controversial Findings

The National Institute of Standards and Technology (NIST) was tasked with investigating the collapse of the World Trade Center buildings, and its findings have been central to the official narrative. However, AE911Truth and other skeptics have raised significant concerns about the methodology, transparency, and conclusions of the NIST report. They argue that key evidence was ignored or misrepresented and that the agency's analysis was tailored to fit a predetermined conclusion. This point delves into NIST's investigation, the controversies surrounding its findings, and AE911Truth's counterarguments.

When NIST released its final report on the collapse of the Twin Towers in 2005, the agency concluded that the buildings fell due to the impact of the planes and the subsequent fires that weakened the steel structure. The report emphasized that the jet fuel ignited fires that spread across multiple floors, compromising the structural integrity of the buildings. According to

NIST, the loss of fireproofing due to the impact and the intense heat from the fires caused the steel to soften, leading to the floors sagging and the columns buckling, ultimately resulting in a progressive collapse.

AE911Truth contends that NIST's explanation, while detailed, does not hold up under scrutiny. One of the primary criticisms is that NIST did not address the rapid and symmetrical nature of the collapse. According to AE911Truth, the agency's models failed to accurately simulate the collapse without making what they consider to be questionable adjustments. In particular, NIST's computer models required manual manipulation of certain parameters to initiate a collapse similar to what occurred on 9/11. AE911Truth has argued that these modifications were necessary because, under normal circumstances, the buildings would not have collapsed in the manner described without the use of explosives or other incendiary devices.

A major point of contention is the absence of any mention of molten steel or the potential use of thermite in NIST's report. As AE911Truth highlights, numerous eyewitnesses, including firefighters and rescue workers, reported seeing molten steel at the site in the days and weeks following the collapse. Photographs and video footage also showed streams of molten material pouring from one of the towers before it fell. AE911Truth argues that the temperatures required to produce molten steel far exceed what could be generated by jet fuel or typical office fires, suggesting the involvement of another, more powerful heat source. Despite these reports, NIST did not include or investigate the possibility of thermite or any other explosive substances in its analysis.

AE911Truth has also criticized NIST's approach to World Trade Center 7 (WTC 7), the 47-story building that collapsed in the late afternoon on September 11. In its report, NIST attributed the collapse of WTC 7 to fires ignited by debris from the North Tower. The agency stated that these fires weakened critical columns, causing the building to collapse in what they described as a progressive failure. However, AE911Truth argues that this explanation fails to account for the building's free-fall acceleration and symmetrical collapse, which closely resembled a controlled demolition. The organization points out that NIST initially denied that the building fell at free-fall speed, only to later revise its statement after facing pressure from independent researchers who provided irrefutable evidence.

The admission of free-fall acceleration became a turning point for AE911Truth. They argued that the sudden and complete failure of all structural supports, necessary for such a collapse, could not be explained by fire alone. AE911Truth has called for an independent investigation into WTC 7, contending that the evidence for controlled demolition is stronger than the case for a fire-induced collapse. They assert that NIST's unwillingness to explore or test for the presence of explosives shows a bias towards confirming a pre-established narrative rather than conducting an open and thorough investigation.

Another criticism from AE911Truth focuses on NIST's decision to withhold the full details of its computer models used to simulate the collapse of the buildings. NIST has stated that it cannot release the models due to "national security" concerns, a move that has only fueled suspicion among skeptics. AE911Truth argues that withholding such crucial information undermines transparency and prevents independent experts from verifying or challenging NIST's conclusions. To them, an open and transparent review process is essential for maintaining public trust and ensuring the credibility of the findings.

Furthermore, AE911Truth disputes NIST's claim that the fireproofing material was dislodged by the plane impacts, making the steel beams vulnerable to the fires. The organization points out that the official explanation does not sufficiently address why similar skyscrapers that have endured more intense fires or impacts did not suffer a total collapse like the Twin Towers. According to AE911Truth, NIST's selective focus on certain elements while disregarding others creates an incomplete and misleading picture.

AE911Truth also highlights the selective nature of NIST's investigation when it comes to evidence of explosions. The NIST report dismissed multiple eyewitness accounts of explosions heard in the towers before and during their collapse, attributing the sounds to non-explosive causes like structural failure or air pressure releases. AE911Truth argues that the sheer number and consistency of these testimonies, particularly from firefighters and first responders trained to recognize explosions, cannot be easily dismissed. They believe that a thorough investigation would have included testing for explosive residues and conducting interviews with these eyewitnesses in a manner that did not preemptively rule out the possibility of explosives.

In response to NIST's findings, AE911Truth has published its own reports and conducted independent studies to present alternative explanations. They call for a new, independent investigation with full transparency and access to all available data, including the structural blueprints and the details of the computer models used by NIST. AE911Truth argues that without such an investigation, the official narrative remains incomplete and leaves too many unanswered questions.

Point 4 illustrates the deep divide between the official explanation provided by NIST and the arguments put forth by AE911Truth. The controversy underscores the demand for a more open and unbiased investigation, one that considers all evidence and addresses the inconsistencies that, according to skeptics, remain unresolved.

The Call for a New Investigation and the Search for Accountability

The architects and engineers behind AE911Truth have long called for a new, independent investigation into the events of 9/11, arguing that the existing official reports are riddled with inconsistencies and omissions. For these professionals, the truth extends beyond understanding what brought down the towers; it involves holding those responsible accountable. Point 5 delves into AE911Truth's efforts to initiate a renewed inquiry, the challenges they face, and their vision for achieving justice.

The call for a new investigation is rooted in AE911Truth's belief that the official reports—primarily the 9/11 Commission Report and NIST's investigations—fail to fully explain the collapses of the Twin Towers and WTC 7. Richard Gage, the founder of AE911Truth, and his team of experts assert that the evidence points to controlled demolition, not the fire-induced progressive collapse suggested by NIST. To them, only a new, independent body with full access to all relevant data, including structural blueprints, demolition testing, and eyewitness testimonies, can provide an unbiased and accurate assessment of what transpired.

One of AE911Truth's central strategies has been to garner public support and political backing for this new investigation. The organization has organized conferences, distributed educational materials, and engaged in outreach through documentaries, podcasts, and public speaking events. Their goal is to make the case that the official story is not just incomplete but potentially misleading. They argue that unless the public is made aware of these discrepancies and rallies behind their cause, the truth about 9/11 will remain obscured.

AE911Truth has also filed petitions and lobbied members of Congress to initiate a new inquiry. They present their case not just as a matter of historical importance but as a vital issue for national security and public safety. According to them, if the real cause of the building collapses is not identified, similar vulnerabilities could be exploited again. They emphasize that if controlled demolition was indeed involved, then the implications are far-reaching, suggesting either a catastrophic failure of intelligence or, as some allege, deliberate foul play by powerful elements within or outside the government.

Despite their efforts, AE911Truth has faced significant challenges in gaining traction for their campaign. The group has often been dismissed by mainstream media and labeled as "conspiracy theorists," a term they argue is used to discredit any legitimate questioning of the official narrative. The organization counters this portrayal by emphasizing their professional credentials and scientific approach. They stress that their demands for a new investigation are not based on wild speculation but on years of empirical research, peer-reviewed studies, and the first-hand accounts of professionals who were on the scene that day.

One of the major legal efforts undertaken by AE911Truth involved submitting a petition to the U.S. Attorney's Office in New York, demanding the convening of a grand jury to investigate the possibility of explosives being used in the demolition of the World Trade Center buildings. The petition was backed by a comprehensive dossier of evidence, including the testimony of experts, analysis of structural anomalies, and reports of explosive materials found in the debris. AE911Truth argued that, under federal law, this evidence necessitated a deeper investigation into the events of 9/11. However, despite the thoroughness of their submission, the petition has not yet led to a new investigation, highlighting the uphill battle the organization faces in its quest for accountability.

AE911Truth has also worked internationally to bring attention to their cause, collaborating with professionals and activists worldwide. The group has presented its findings to governments and engineering associations in countries like Japan and Canada, urging them to reconsider the official explanations. They argue that the truth about 9/11 is not just an American issue but a global one, given how the event reshaped international policies, military engagements, and civil liberties around the world. By building an international coalition, AE911Truth aims to put pressure on the U.S. government and other involved parties to revisit and re-examine the evidence.

In addition to pursuing legal and political avenues, AE911Truth emphasizes the need for public education and awareness. They believe that grassroots support is crucial for any movement seeking truth and justice. The organization continues to release educational materials, documentaries, and expert-led panels to disseminate their findings and foster a critical perspective among the public. They highlight the stories of whistleblowers, eyewitnesses, and first responders whose accounts, they argue, have been marginalized or ignored. By giving a platform to these voices, AE911Truth hopes to build a compelling case for why a new investigation is not only justified but necessary.

At the heart of AE911Truth's mission is a fundamental belief in accountability. The group argues that if controlled demolition or any form of foul play is proven, it would signify one of the most significant betrayals in American history. They call for a thorough examination of the chain of command, the intelligence failures, and any potential actors—domestic or foreign—who may have played a role in orchestrating or covering up the events of 9/11. For AE911Truth, achieving justice means holding accountable those who were responsible, regardless of their power or position.

Point 5 highlights AE911Truth's continued efforts to advocate for a transparent and independent investigation into the events of September 11. Despite facing resistance from both governmental bodies and the mainstream media, the organization remains committed to its mission. Its members believe that only by uncovering the full truth can society move forward and prevent similar tragedies from occurring in the future. The chapter closes by emphasizing the importance of persistence in the pursuit of truth, even in the face of formidable opposition.

Chapter 17: Psychological Barriers to Accepting th

Cognitive Dissonance and Emotional Resistance
When faced with the suggestion that 9/11 could have been an inside job, many people experience a powerful emotional and psychological reaction. The notion fundamentally conflicts with their deeply ingrained beliefs about their country, government, and the world around them. This discomfort is what psychologists call "cognitive dissonance," a mental state that occurs when a person's beliefs are challenged by new information that contradicts what they've accepted as true. The emotional resistance to accepting such information is strong, as it threatens the very foundation of their understanding and identity.

Cognitive dissonance is a defense mechanism, and it works to protect the individual's sense of stability. For most Americans, the belief that the United States is a beacon of freedom and democracy is central to their identity. They trust their government to act in their best interests and to protect them from threats, both foreign and domestic. Accepting that elements within their own government could have orchestrated or allowed the attacks would shatter this trust. It would force a reevaluation not only of the events of 9/11 but of the entire political and social system they've believed in for so long. The mind, seeking to avoid this dissonance, tends to reject or downplay evidence that contradicts these beliefs, preferring instead to maintain the status quo.

For many, the emotional weight of accepting an inside job theory is too heavy to bear. Such a realization would mean acknowledging that those in power might not only be capable of deception on a massive scale but also that they may be willing to sacrifice innocent lives for their own political or financial gain. This idea is horrifying, and the emotional response it triggers can include anger, fear, sadness, or a deep sense of betrayal. The mind instinctively seeks to protect itself from these painful emotions by rejecting the idea altogether.

This process often leads to the dismissal of evidence without critical analysis. Even when confronted with compelling facts or testimonies that contradict the official narrative, individuals may find ways to rationalize or disregard this information to protect their emotional and psychological well-being. For instance, they might label alternative explanations as "conspiracy theories" or dismiss those presenting them as untrustworthy or unpatriotic. By doing so, they create a psychological buffer, insulating themselves from the discomfort of cognitive dissonance and reinforcing their existing beliefs.

Moreover, the emotional resistance is often compounded by a sense of patriotism. For many, 9/11 is not just a historical event; it is a traumatic and deeply personal moment. The attacks represented an assault on American values, a tragic loss of life, and a call to unity and resilience. To suggest that the government had any role in orchestrating or allowing such an event feels, to some, like an act of betrayal. It goes against the collective narrative of heroism, sacrifice, and national strength that emerged in the aftermath. Accepting that the very people tasked with protecting the country may have betrayed it is an emotional hurdle that many simply cannot overcome.

This emotional attachment to the official story makes it difficult for individuals to objectively analyze evidence that suggests an alternative explanation. Even when presented with scientific analyses, expert testimonies, or whistleblower accounts, the emotional weight of these revelations can be too much to process. As a result, people often find comfort in the simplicity and clarity of the official narrative, preferring it to the uncertainty and distress that would come with questioning it.

In the end, cognitive dissonance and emotional resistance are powerful psychological forces that shape public perception and response to controversial theories like the inside job hypothesis. They create a protective shield that allows individuals to maintain their worldview and emotional equilibrium, even when confronted with evidence that might suggest otherwise. Recognizing and understanding these barriers is crucial for anyone seeking to engage in meaningful discussions about 9/11 or similar events, as it highlights the deep-seated emotional and psychological factors at play.

The "Big Lie" Theory

The concept of the "Big Lie" is a psychological phenomenon that helps explain why people may find it difficult to accept the idea that 9/11 was an inside job. Originally popularized by Adolf Hitler in *Mein Kampf*, the theory suggests that if a lie is colossal and outrageous enough, people are more likely to believe it, simply because they cannot fathom that someone would have the audacity to fabricate such an enormous falsehood. The reasoning behind this is that while people may tell small lies, most would never imagine crafting an untruth so vast and consequential. This inherent disbelief in the possibility of a "Big Lie" creates a psychological barrier that makes it easier for individuals to accept official narratives rather than explore alternative explanations, no matter how compelling.

In the case of 9/11, the official story told by the U.S. government and echoed by the mainstream media presents a straightforward narrative: a group of foreign terrorists attacked the United States, and the government, despite its efforts, was unable to prevent the tragedy. For most people, this explanation seems plausible and aligns with their understanding of the world. It reinforces the notion of the U.S. as a target for its values and freedom, making it a logical target for extremists. The story, while tragic, fits into a framework that feels familiar and understandable.

However, the idea that the government itself could have been complicit in the attacks, or even played a direct role in orchestrating them, is a much larger and more shocking assertion. It challenges not only the specifics of what happened on that day but also the fundamental trust people have in their leaders and institutions. Accepting such a possibility would require a leap of imagination and a willingness to consider that those in power might lie on a grand scale—bigger than anything most people could conceive of themselves. This is precisely where the "Big Lie" theory becomes relevant. The very audacity of such a claim makes it difficult for people to process and accept, leading many to dismiss it outright as too far-fetched to be true.

Moreover, the "Big Lie" works in tandem with the psychological tendency to trust established authority figures and institutions. When the government, mainstream media, and respected officials all echo the same narrative, it reinforces the perception that their version of events must be accurate. These authorities are seen as the gatekeepers of truth and information, and for many, the idea that all of them could be complicit in perpetuating a lie of this magnitude seems inconceivable. Thus, when confronted with the possibility that 9/11 was not what it seemed, people are more likely to cling to the official story as a safeguard against the unsettling notion that those they trust could deceive them on such a grand scale.

This reluctance to question the official narrative also stems from the inherent risk involved in challenging such an all-encompassing claim. Accepting the possibility of an inside job would not only mean re-examining one's perception of the 9/11 attacks but would also lead to a domino effect, causing people to question other major events and decisions made by the government. This, in turn, could lead to a broader distrust in the system itself, a frightening and uncomfortable prospect for many. The human mind naturally seeks stability and order, and embracing the chaos that comes with questioning the "Big Lie" disrupts this sense of equilibrium.

The "Big Lie" theory is effective because it capitalizes on the public's faith in authority and the belief that deception, if it occurs, is typically small-scale and limited in scope. The idea that a lie could be so massive, involving multiple agencies, political figures, and media outlets, strains credulity. This psychological reaction is precisely what those who craft such narratives rely upon. By creating a lie that is so grand and audacious, they ensure that the majority of the public will find it easier to accept the official version of events, which appears simpler and more believable by comparison.

Understanding the impact of the "Big Lie" theory is crucial for examining why the idea of an inside job remains difficult for many to accept. It reveals how psychological manipulation can be used to create a sense of security around a false narrative, making it difficult for alternative explanations to gain traction. Recognizing this pattern allows for a deeper understanding of how information is controlled and how narratives are crafted to maintain power and influence public perception. For those seeking truth, acknowledging the existence and power of the "Big Lie" is an essential step in breaking through the psychological barriers that prevent people from questioning the status quo.

The Comfort of the Status Quo

Another powerful psychological barrier preventing people from accepting the possibility of 9/11 as an inside job is the comfort found in maintaining the status quo. For many, the official narrative provides a sense of familiarity and order in an otherwise chaotic and uncertain world. It offers a simple explanation: the United States was attacked by foreign terrorists, and the government responded heroically. This version of events fits neatly within the broader framework of American identity—one that emphasizes resilience, heroism, and the fight against external threats. It allows people to process the tragedy without fundamentally challenging their worldview or their trust in institutions.

When confronted with alternative explanations, such as the idea that elements within the government could have orchestrated or allowed the attacks, people face the discomfort of potentially having to dismantle their entire understanding of the event. This would not only mean accepting that their government might have betrayed them but also reconsidering their perception of history, patriotism, and the trustworthiness of those in power. The status quo, while imperfect, provides a sense of security and stability. Disrupting it by questioning a cornerstone event like 9/11 threatens to unravel that stability.

The psychological attachment to the status quo is rooted in a natural human desire for predictability and control. When the world makes sense, people feel safer and more secure. The official account of 9/11 offers a clear enemy, a straightforward story, and a narrative of good versus evil. It provides a sense of closure and allows people to move forward, rallying around the idea of national unity and resilience. In contrast, the inside job theory introduces ambiguity and uncertainty. It challenges the idea of a clear-cut enemy and suggests that those who are supposed to protect citizens might be capable of betrayal. For many, this is a deeply unsettling and unacceptable thought. By rejecting it, they preserve their sense of order and control.

Moreover, maintaining the status quo aligns with social conformity and the collective acceptance of a shared reality. When the majority of the population, the government, and the media all reinforce a single narrative, it becomes the dominant version of events. People find comfort in being part of the majority and aligning themselves with the commonly accepted view. Challenging this narrative means stepping outside the collective consensus and, in a sense, becoming an outsider. This can be a frightening prospect, as it may lead to social isolation or being labeled as a "conspiracy theorist." The fear of social ostracism reinforces the preference for the status quo, making it psychologically easier for people to accept the dominant narrative, even if they encounter evidence that contradicts it.

The status quo also offers an element of national identity and pride. For many Americans, 9/11 is a symbol of national strength and resilience. The official narrative frames the event as an attack on American values—freedom, democracy, and peace. The subsequent response, including the war on terror, was positioned as a defense of these values and a fight against a clear enemy. For those who identify strongly with these ideals, accepting an alternative explanation would feel like a betrayal of their national identity. It would mean acknowledging that the symbols and actions they rallied behind were, in some way, tainted or manipulated. In contrast, the official story preserves their sense of patriotism, allowing them to feel pride in their country's response and unity in the face of adversity.

Furthermore, the psychological comfort of the status quo is bolstered by the sheer scale of the deception required to pull off an inside job of this magnitude. For many, the idea that numerous government agencies, military officials, and media organizations could have coordinated such a massive cover-up seems beyond belief. Accepting such a possibility requires confronting the uncomfortable truth that those who hold power may not always have the public's best interests at heart. This realization forces individuals to question not just the events of 9/11 but also the integrity of the system as a whole. For most, this is a daunting and overwhelming task. It is far easier to accept the official account, which aligns with their existing beliefs, than to undertake the emotional and cognitive burden of unraveling a complex web of deception.

Ultimately, the comfort of the status quo is a powerful force that reinforces the acceptance of the official narrative. It provides emotional security, a sense of belonging, and a stable framework within which people can navigate the world. To challenge this status quo is to risk unsettling their entire worldview, which requires not only a willingness to confront difficult truths but also the emotional resilience to cope with the implications. For those who do question the official story, it often means enduring a lonely and challenging journey. But for many, the comfort of maintaining the status quo, even if it means turning a blind eye to potential inconsistencies or unanswered questions, is simply too compelling to resist.

Cognitive Dissonance and the Difficulty of Reconciling Conflicting Beliefs

Cognitive dissonance plays a crucial role in shaping how people respond to information that contradicts their deeply held beliefs. This psychological phenomenon occurs when a person is confronted with evidence or ideas that conflict with their existing worldview, creating an uncomfortable state of tension.

The mind naturally seeks to resolve this tension, often by dismissing or rationalizing the new information rather than altering the established belief system. This tendency is particularly relevant when it comes to the events of 9/11, as the inside job theory directly challenges fundamental assumptions about government integrity, national security, and the nature of terrorism.

When people are presented with evidence that contradicts the official narrative of 9/11—such as the controlled demolition hypothesis, inconsistencies in the Pentagon attack, or suspicious financial transactions—they experience cognitive dissonance. Accepting this information would mean acknowledging the possibility that the government, an institution they may trust and rely on for safety, could have played a role in orchestrating the attacks. This realization conflicts with the belief that the government exists to protect its citizens and uphold democratic values. As a result, people often reject the new information as a way to preserve their sense of security and maintain their trust in institutions.

The discomfort associated with cognitive dissonance can be so strong that it compels individuals to go to great lengths to rationalize or ignore evidence that does not fit their worldview. For example, they might discredit sources of alternative information by labeling them as "conspiracy theorists" or unreliable. This tactic allows them to maintain the belief that the mainstream media and government are trustworthy while dismissing information that could disrupt their sense of reality. Others might focus on small inconsistencies in the alternative explanations as a way to dismiss the entire theory, even if the overall pattern suggests something worth investigating. In this way, cognitive dissonance leads individuals to filter information selectively, accepting only that which reinforces their existing beliefs.

The more deeply ingrained a belief is, the stronger the cognitive dissonance when that belief is challenged. For many Americans, the events of 9/11 are tied to a sense of national identity and patriotism. They remember the unity and resilience displayed in the aftermath, as well as the widespread narrative of heroism that emerged. To question the official story is not just to challenge a historical fact; it is to challenge an emotional and collective experience shared by millions. For those who lived through the attacks and felt the impact firsthand, this emotional attachment makes it even harder to accept the possibility that their own government could have been complicit. The idea feels like a betrayal, not only of their trust but also of the sacrifices made by those who responded to and died in the attacks.

Moreover, the human mind has a natural tendency to avoid information that causes psychological discomfort. In situations where accepting the truth would lead to a loss of trust, safety, or identity, the mind will often resort to denial or avoidance. This is particularly evident when people are faced with information that suggests corruption, deceit, or malfeasance at the highest levels of government. Acknowledging such possibilities could lead to a loss of faith not only in the government but in the social structures that give life a sense of order and predictability. Faced with the prospect of such a profound and unsettling shift, many people choose to reject the new information outright, preferring to believe that any inconsistencies in the official narrative are either coincidences or misunderstandings rather than evidence of a deeper conspiracy.

Cognitive dissonance is also compounded by the emotional investment people have in the post-9/11 world and the subsequent war on terror. The events of September 11th were not only a national tragedy but also a rallying point for military action, policy changes, and a broader narrative about the fight against terrorism. Many people supported the wars in

Afghanistan and Iraq, believing them to be necessary responses to the attacks. To entertain the idea that 9/11 was an inside job means to also question whether these wars were justified or if they were based on false premises. This would mean acknowledging the possibility that lives were lost, resources were spent, and policies were implemented under false pretenses. The emotional and cognitive burden of accepting such a reality is immense, and for many, it is easier to maintain the belief that the official narrative is true.

To reduce cognitive dissonance, some people compartmentalize the information they receive. They may acknowledge that some aspects of the official account are questionable but stop short of accepting the entire inside job theory. This partial acceptance allows them to feel as if they are critical thinkers who are open to alternative explanations without fully embracing the idea that the government could have orchestrated such a devastating event. This middle ground, while appearing rational, still serves the same purpose: it minimizes discomfort by allowing them to remain within the boundaries of the generally accepted narrative.

In conclusion, cognitive dissonance is a powerful psychological barrier that prevents many individuals from seriously considering the possibility of 9/11 being an inside job. The emotional and cognitive strain of reconciling conflicting beliefs—between trusting one's government and acknowledging its potential for duplicity—leads people to rationalize, reject, or avoid information that challenges their worldview. By doing so, they protect themselves from the discomfort of confronting a reality that feels too threatening, choosing instead to preserve their sense of safety, trust, and national identity.

Social and Cultural Pressures to Conform to the Official Narrative

Beyond individual psychological factors, there are powerful social and cultural pressures that influence how people perceive and respond to information about 9/11. Societal norms, group identity, and the desire for acceptance all play significant roles in shaping one's willingness—or unwillingness—to question the official story. The fear of being labeled, marginalized, or ostracized often deters people from openly entertaining alternative explanations, even when they may have personal doubts about the mainstream narrative.

After 9/11, the United States entered a period of heightened patriotism and solidarity. The attacks united people under a shared sense of grief and resilience, and there was a widespread emphasis on supporting the nation and its government. This wave of unity created an environment where skepticism was not only discouraged but viewed as unpatriotic. People who questioned the government's response or the official account were quickly dismissed as conspiracy theorists, and such labeling served as a warning to others about the social consequences of dissent.

In the years following the attacks, phrases like "never forget" and symbols like the American flag became ubiquitous, reinforcing a collective memory centered around unity and heroism. The framing of 9/11 as a direct assault on freedom and democracy helped to cement the narrative that the United States was a victim, and its government and military were protectors. Accepting an alternative explanation that implicated elements of the government itself would not only challenge this narrative but also threaten the sense of community and shared purpose that many Americans found comforting in the wake of the tragedy. Consequently, people who even hinted at questioning the official account risked being labeled as unpatriotic or disrespectful to the victims and their families.

In many social contexts, questioning the mainstream narrative of 9/11 carries a stigma. Being associated with "conspiracy theories" is often seen as irrational or fringe, and people fear the reputational damage that might come with expressing doubt. This stigma serves as a powerful deterrent; individuals are more likely to conform to the accepted narrative to avoid criticism or ridicule. The social dynamics of conformity and the desire for acceptance mean that even when people privately have doubts, they may choose not to express them publicly or even explore them further. The need to fit in, especially within tight-knit communities or workplaces where loyalty to the country is highly valued, creates an environment where questioning the government becomes a social risk.

The mainstream media also plays a critical role in reinforcing social conformity. For years after the attacks, the media emphasized themes of heroism, national unity, and the fight against terrorism. Stories that deviated from these themes or questioned the official account were often sidelined or discredited. Alternative viewpoints, when they did appear, were frequently portrayed as irrational or unsubstantiated, further marginalizing those who raised them. This consistent messaging created an echo chamber effect, where individuals primarily encountered information that reinforced the official story and excluded dissenting voices. The more the mainstream media normalized the official narrative and condemned alternatives, the more difficult it became for people to entertain different perspectives without feeling isolated or ostracized.

Political leaders also played a role in discouraging dissent by framing the post-9/11 period as a time of war, where loyalty was equated with patriotism and unity was essential for national security. In the immediate aftermath, President George W. Bush and other officials called for Americans to support their government's response to the attacks. Dissent was painted as a distraction or even a potential aid to enemies of the state. This rhetoric left little room for questioning the government's actions or policies without risking accusations of disloyalty. The pressure to align with the official narrative was intense, particularly when military personnel were deployed overseas in response to the attacks. Supporting the troops became synonymous with supporting the narrative, further intertwining patriotism with conformity.

Cultural and social dynamics also contribute to the difficulty of questioning authority, especially when it pertains to events as emotionally charged as 9/11. In the United States, there is a strong cultural emphasis on respecting authority figures, including government officials, law enforcement, and the military. This respect, ingrained through various social institutions like schools, workplaces, and the media, reinforces the idea that questioning the motives or actions of these figures is inappropriate or even subversive. When such authority figures consistently reinforce the official story, deviating from it can feel like a betrayal of these cultural values.

Furthermore, social media has added another layer to the pressure to conform. Online platforms amplify group dynamics, where likes, shares, and comments can create echo chambers that reward conformity and penalize dissent. Users who express skepticism about 9/11 or suggest alternative explanations often face backlash, trolling, or ostracism from online communities. This reinforces the fear of social consequences and discourages individuals from publicly questioning the mainstream narrative, even if they privately harbor doubts.

Collectively, these social and cultural pressures make it challenging for individuals to consider alternative explanations for 9/11, regardless of the evidence presented. The fear of isolation, ridicule, or being labeled as unpatriotic creates a powerful incentive to align with the mainstream narrative, even when individuals may have questions or reservations. These dynamics help explain why, more than two decades after the attacks, the official account remains deeply ingrained in the American psyche. The pressure to conform is not only a matter of individual psychology but a broader cultural phenomenon that discourages deviation from the accepted version of events.

In summary, the social and cultural pressures surrounding 9/11 are substantial. From the immediate aftermath, which emphasized unity and patriotism, to the ongoing stigma associated with questioning the official account, people are discouraged from exploring alternative narratives. The fear of social exclusion, reputational damage, or being labeled as unpatriotic or irrational serves as a barrier, compelling many to accept the official story despite personal doubts. These forces, combined with psychological factors like cognitive dissonance, create a powerful system that reinforces conformity and suppresses dissent, making it difficult for individuals to fully investigate or accept the idea that 9/11 could have been an inside job.

Chapter 18: Rebuilding the 9/11 Truth Movement

The Early Years of the 9/11 Truth Movement

In the immediate aftermath of the September 11 attacks, the atmosphere in the United States was one of profound shock, grief, and fear. The images of the Twin Towers collapsing and the Pentagon in flames became seared into the collective memory of the world. In the midst of the chaos, the official narrative was swiftly established: a group of 19 terrorists, primarily from Saudi Arabia, had executed a meticulously planned attack under the direction of al-Qaeda, led by Osama bin Laden. This narrative was accepted almost universally, with a grieving nation eager for answers and unity. However, amid the widespread acceptance of the government's account, a small but determined group of individuals began to question the details and seek alternative explanations.

The early 9/11 Truth Movement emerged from a confluence of diverse voices—architects, engineers, journalists, and ordinary citizens—who refused to accept the official story at face value. These individuals found discrepancies in the official reports, inconsistencies in the timeline of events, and glaring omissions in the explanations provided by the government and mainstream media. Some were survivors of the attacks or family members of the victims, motivated by a deep desire to understand what had truly happened on that day. Others were academics and professionals who used their expertise to analyze the evidence and offer alternative interpretations.

One of the earliest signs that the movement was gaining momentum was the formation of online forums and independent research groups. The internet provided a platform for truth-seekers to connect, share information, and organize grassroots campaigns. Websites dedicated to uncovering the truth about 9/11 sprung up, many of them run by dedicated activists who meticulously documented every piece of evidence that contradicted the official story. These online communities became hubs for debate, information sharing, and the mobilization of efforts to demand transparency and accountability. In these early years, the movement was a patchwork of voices and theories, but the common thread was a refusal to accept the official narrative without question.

Key figures emerged as leaders in the early 9/11 Truth Movement. Among them were Richard Gage, an architect who would later found Architects & Engineers for 9/11 Truth, and David Ray Griffin, a theologian and author who wrote extensively on the topic, dissecting the government's reports and highlighting what he viewed as significant flaws. These early leaders used their professional credibility to lend weight to the movement, emphasizing that their critiques were based on evidence, not ideology or conspiracy. Their work inspired others to join the cause, providing the movement with a sense of legitimacy and purpose.

Despite its grassroots nature, the early 9/11 Truth Movement faced intense opposition and ridicule. The mainstream media often portrayed truth-seekers as fringe theorists, eager to undermine the national unity that was seen as essential in the aftermath of the attacks. This marginalization only fueled the determination of early activists, who saw their work as a vital counterbalance to the uncritical acceptance of the official story. They believed that the truth about 9/11 was too important to be dismissed or suppressed, and they were willing to face the stigma and backlash that came with their quest for answers.

These early efforts laid the foundation for what would become a global movement. While initially fragmented and small in scale, the determination of these pioneers demonstrated that there was a demand for a deeper investigation into the events of September 11. Their willingness to speak out, organize, and challenge the official narrative, even when it was unpopular or dangerous to do so, set the stage for the movement's growth and evolution in the years that followed. In the early 2000s, they were planting the seeds for a broader, more organized campaign that would eventually draw support from professionals, activists, and ordinary citizens around the world who shared a commitment to uncovering the truth.

Challenges and Fragmentation Within the Movement

As the 9/11 Truth Movement expanded beyond its initial base of activists and independent researchers, it began to face significant challenges and internal fragmentation. While the movement's core objective was unified—questioning the official narrative of the 9/11 attacks—its diverse membership brought with it a variety of viewpoints, methods, and levels of skepticism. This diversity, while initially a strength, also became a source of division, as different factions emerged with differing interpretations of the events and theories about what truly happened on September 11, 2001.

One of the primary challenges the movement faced was the proliferation of competing theories. While some focused on the structural anomalies of the Twin Towers and Building 7, suggesting controlled demolitions, others pointed to alleged intelligence failures or complicity at the highest levels of the U.S. government. There were also theories that emphasized the role of financial motives, such as insurance fraud or the manipulation of stock markets in the days leading up to the attacks. Each of these theories attracted its own group of supporters, and while they shared a common goal—demanding truth and transparency—their differences often led to disagreements and fragmentation within the movement.

The emergence of extreme views and misinformation also contributed to the fragmentation. As the movement grew, it attracted people with varying levels of credibility, some of whom presented ideas that were outside the bounds of verifiable evidence. While the majority of truth-seekers aimed to ground their claims in facts and logical analysis, others proposed theories involving holograms, advanced military technology, or even extraterrestrial involvement. These more extreme claims created a rift within the movement, as more moderate and evidence-focused members sought to distance themselves from what they saw as unsubstantiated speculation that could discredit their efforts.

This internal conflict was exacerbated by the mainstream media's portrayal of the movement. Journalists and pundits often lumped all truth-seekers together, focusing on the most outlandish claims to discredit the movement as a whole. By highlighting the more sensational and extreme voices, the media framed the entire 9/11 Truth Movement as a collection of conspiracy theorists who lacked credibility. This portrayal created a public perception that made it difficult for those within the movement to present their arguments without being dismissed outright. The stigma associated with questioning the official narrative further discouraged potential supporters, making it challenging to build a cohesive and credible front.

Despite these obstacles, many within the movement worked tirelessly to establish a more unified and credible approach. They aimed to distance themselves from extreme elements and misinformation, focusing instead on verifiable evidence, scientific analysis, and expert testimony. Efforts were made to organize conferences and public events that highlighted credible voices, such as architects, engineers, and former intelligence officials, who could provide expert analysis of the evidence and counter the perception that the movement was merely fringe. Groups like Architects & Engineers for 9/11 Truth emphasized their commitment to scientific rigor, offering detailed critiques of the official reports and presenting evidence that supported their claims of controlled demolition and structural anomalies.

Even with these efforts, achieving unity within such a diverse and often contentious movement proved difficult. Ideological differences remained, and some activists felt that emphasizing scientific evidence alone was too limited a strategy, arguing that broader geopolitical and economic factors also needed to be addressed. Others believed that focusing too heavily on specific technical details risked alienating those who were more interested in the political motivations behind the attacks. As the movement continued to grow, so too did these tensions, making it challenging to present a unified front that could effectively challenge the official narrative and gain wider public support.

Nevertheless, the resilience of the movement's core members allowed it to persevere through these challenges. Despite fragmentation and internal conflict, the movement continued to adapt and evolve, learning from its missteps and refining its approach. While the divisions within the movement were significant, they did not stop its members from working toward a common goal: seeking truth, transparency, and accountability for one of the most significant events in modern history. The movement's ability to navigate these challenges, albeit imperfectly, demonstrated its commitment and tenacity, laying the groundwork for future efforts to build a more unified and impactful campaign for 9/11 truth.

Strategic Shifts and Professionalization of the Movement

As the 9/11 Truth Movement navigated the challenges of fragmentation and public perception, some of its leaders recognized the need for a strategic shift. To gain credibility and counter the narrative that portrayed them as mere conspiracy theorists, they began focusing on a professional, evidence-based approach. This period marked a crucial evolution for the movement, as it sought to establish a more authoritative and organized front to present its case to the public and policymakers.

One of the key strategies during this phase was the emphasis on professional expertise. Leaders within the movement, such as Richard Gage, understood that gaining legitimacy required more than just passionate advocacy; it demanded the involvement of credible professionals who could analyze and present evidence in a scientifically sound manner. Gage, an architect with decades of experience, founded *Architects & Engineers for 9/11 Truth*, a nonprofit organization composed of building professionals committed to investigating the structural anomalies of the World Trade Center's collapse. By gathering a coalition of experts in architecture, engineering, and demolition, the movement aimed to offer a technically rigorous analysis that would stand up to scrutiny from skeptics and the mainstream media.

This professionalization strategy extended beyond architecture and engineering. The movement also sought to include voices from other fields, such as intelligence, aviation, and journalism. Former intelligence agents and whistleblowers who expressed doubts about the official 9/11 narrative were invited to speak at conferences and public events, providing insight into the failures of intelligence agencies before and after the attacks. Pilots and aviation experts analyzed the flight patterns of the hijacked planes, questioning the plausibility of inexperienced pilots maneuvering large commercial jets with such precision. Journalists and independent researchers conducted thorough investigations, challenging the mainstream narrative and exposing gaps in the official accounts. By building a multidisciplinary coalition, the movement aimed to demonstrate that skepticism about 9/11 was not the domain of uninformed outsiders but a legitimate stance supported by professionals with expertise relevant to the events of that day.

Another significant aspect of this professionalization was the use of scientific conferences and public presentations to disseminate findings. Organizations like *Architects & Engineers for 9/11 Truth* hosted events where experts presented their analyses, using detailed simulations, forensic evidence, and peer-reviewed papers to support their conclusions. These conferences attracted not only activists but also academics, journalists, and members of the public interested in hearing alternative explanations from qualified professionals. The movement's focus on scientific presentations aimed to shift the debate away from sensationalism and toward a rational, evidence-based discussion. By adopting this approach, the movement sought to build a foundation that could withstand criticism and gain traction among those who might otherwise be skeptical of its claims.

In parallel with these efforts, the movement worked to produce high-quality documentaries and publications. Films like *Loose Change* became iconic within the 9/11 Truth Movement, compiling footage, expert testimony, and critical analysis of the events surrounding the attacks. These documentaries reached millions of viewers online and became instrumental in spreading the movement's message. By leveraging visual media, the movement was able to present its evidence in a compelling and accessible format that resonated with a broad audience. Additionally, books authored by experts like David Ray Griffin provided in-depth analysis and critiques of the official 9/11 Commission Report, appealing to readers who preferred detailed, written accounts over visual media.

The movement also recognized the importance of building alliances with other activist groups and movements to broaden its base and influence. Many within the 9/11 Truth Movement saw parallels between their cause and other social justice and anti-war efforts. By connecting with groups that opposed the wars in Afghanistan and Iraq or those advocating for government transparency and accountability, the movement aimed to situate the fight for 9/11 truth within a larger context of political activism. This not only expanded its reach but also brought new energy and resources into the fold, allowing for collaborative events and campaigns that drew from a wider pool of supporters.

Despite these strategic and professional advancements, the movement faced ongoing challenges. The media continued to portray it as fringe, and public perception was slow to shift. Critics argued that despite the involvement of experts, the movement's conclusions were biased or unfounded. Yet, the professionalization of the movement created a more resilient foundation, enabling it to withstand such criticisms and continue its work. By organizing, expanding its expertise, and focusing on scientifically sound presentations, the movement laid the groundwork for further efforts to influence public opinion and demand a more thorough investigation into the events of September 11.

In these years, the movement transitioned from a loosely connected network of skeptics into a more coordinated and professional body, capable of engaging with the media, public, and policymakers in a serious and credible manner. This shift would prove crucial as the movement sought to grow its influence and advocate for a new investigation into the attacks, one that would address the questions left unanswered by the official narrative.

Addressing Disinformation and Internal Divisions

As the 9/11 Truth Movement matured and sought greater credibility, it faced two significant obstacles: the spread of disinformation and internal divisions. These challenges threatened to undermine the movement's message and cohesion. To counter these threats, leaders and activists took deliberate steps to distinguish credible evidence from baseless speculation and to unify their efforts around a cohesive strategy.

Disinformation became a prominent concern as the movement gained visibility. Opponents of the movement, as well as individuals seeking to exploit the 9/11 tragedy for personal gain, began spreading false or exaggerated claims about the attacks. Some of these claims included theories that were more sensational than plausible, such as the idea that holograms, rather than planes, had struck the World Trade Center or that no planes were involved at all. These ideas, often amplified through social media, gained traction among certain segments of the movement and the general public, distracting from the core evidence that professionals within the movement were trying to present.

Leaders within the movement recognized that if they did not address these false claims, the credibility of the entire cause would be compromised. Richard Gage and other prominent figures in the movement began to issue statements distancing themselves from unsupported theories, emphasizing the importance of sticking to evidence-based analysis. Organizations like *Architects & Engineers for 9/11 Truth* carefully curated the information they presented, focusing on physical evidence, eyewitness accounts, and technical expertise rather than speculative or unverified claims. By maintaining a commitment to rigorous standards, they aimed to demonstrate that the movement was serious about uncovering the truth, not merely promoting sensationalist narratives.

This effort also led to the development of internal guidelines and standards for those involved in the movement. Conferences, presentations, and publications underwent more thorough vetting processes to ensure that only credible information was disseminated. Documentaries and books aligned with the movement's professional ethos, presenting evidence in a logical, coherent manner. While this approach did alienate some individuals who preferred more speculative theories, it strengthened the movement's ability to engage with the media and the public in a way that positioned it as a credible, serious entity. By weeding out disinformation, the movement aimed to protect its reputation and ensure that its core message—the need for a thorough, unbiased investigation into 9/11—remained clear and focused.

Internal divisions also emerged as the movement evolved, primarily over strategy and the scope of the movement's goals. Some factions argued for a narrow focus on structural evidence and the specifics of the Twin Towers' collapse, insisting that the movement would be more effective if it concentrated on concrete, provable claims. Others believed the movement should expand its focus to include broader issues, such as the motivations of policymakers, the geopolitical consequences of 9/11, and the economic interests driving the response to the attacks. These differences often led to heated debates within the movement's ranks, with some activists feeling that their perspectives were being sidelined or ignored.

To navigate these divisions, leaders in the movement began promoting unity through collaboration and shared purpose.

Conferences and meetings provided platforms for different factions to present their ideas and engage in constructive dialogue. Rather than insisting on a single narrative, the movement allowed for a diversity of opinions while ensuring that all participants adhered to evidence-based analysis. This approach aimed to create a balance where various perspectives could coexist, strengthening the movement by pooling resources and ideas while avoiding fragmentation. Key figures like David Ray Griffin and others wrote extensively on the need for unity, advocating that the ultimate goal—the pursuit of truth—should supersede any internal disagreements.

Efforts were also made to foster transparency and communication within the movement. Online forums, newsletters, and other communication channels were set up to keep supporters informed and engaged. These platforms allowed for open discussions on strategies, evidence, and the best ways to present information to the public. While debates persisted, this openness fostered a sense of community and commitment to the cause, helping the movement stay cohesive despite its diverse viewpoints.

Another challenge that arose from internal divisions was the question of how to approach the mainstream media. Some members of the movement believed that engaging with the media was essential for gaining wider support and legitimacy, while others felt that the media, as part of the establishment, could not be trusted to fairly represent the movement's message. This debate highlighted a deeper philosophical divide: whether to work within existing systems or to entirely reject them as complicit in suppressing the truth.

To address this, the movement adopted a dual approach. While some leaders continued to engage with mainstream media, offering interviews and submitting op-eds, others focused on building independent media channels. Platforms like

YouTube, alternative news websites, and social media pages became vital tools for disseminating the movement's message without the filters of traditional media outlets. By combining these strategies, the movement was able to reach a broad audience, from those already skeptical of mainstream narratives to those who might only encounter 9/11 Truth material through traditional channels.

Despite these efforts, the movement's response to internal divisions was not without challenges. Disagreements still flared up, particularly when different groups felt their voices were being marginalized. However, the emphasis on open dialogue, professionalization, and adherence to evidence helped to mitigate these conflicts, creating an environment where members could focus on their shared goals rather than their differences.

In confronting both disinformation and internal divisions, the 9/11 Truth Movement took critical steps to strengthen its position. By distinguishing credible evidence from baseless speculation and fostering unity amidst diverse perspectives, it aimed to build a resilient and focused movement capable of advocating for the truth in the face of widespread skepticism and opposition.

Building Alliances and Expanding the Movement's Reach

To sustain momentum and amplify its impact, the 9/11 Truth Movement recognized the importance of building alliances with other groups and expanding its reach beyond traditional supporters. This approach aimed to integrate the 9/11 Truth narrative into broader discussions of government accountability, civil liberties, and global geopolitics. By linking its cause with wider movements for transparency and justice, the 9/11 Truth Movement sought to grow its base and gain legitimacy as a credible force for change.

One of the first steps in building alliances involved connecting with other advocacy groups focused on government transparency and whistleblower protection. Organizations such as *Veterans for Peace*, *Civil Liberties Groups*, and even factions of the *Anti-War Movement* were seen as natural allies. Many members of these groups were already critical of the government's response to 9/11, particularly the subsequent wars in Afghanistan and Iraq. By framing the push for a new investigation as part of a broader struggle against unjust wars and unchecked government power, 9/11 Truth activists found common ground with these groups.

Collaborative efforts included organizing joint events, protests, and conferences where the issues surrounding 9/11 could be discussed alongside other pressing political topics. These events created opportunities for the movement to present its evidence to a new audience—individuals who were already skeptical of official narratives and who might be receptive to the idea that 9/11 was more than just a terrorist attack. In these settings, activists could contextualize 9/11 as part of a larger pattern of state misconduct, furthering their argument that the public should demand accountability and transparency.

One of the most significant alliances the movement formed was with whistleblower organizations. Whistleblowers from government agencies like the NSA, FBI, and the military often faced intense pressure to remain silent, and those who spoke out about intelligence failures related to 9/11 were no exception. The movement embraced these individuals, promoting their stories as evidence of a cover-up and using their testimony to bolster its arguments. Figures like Sibel Edmonds, a former FBI translator who claimed to have witnessed crucial intelligence being suppressed, became key allies. The 9/11 Truth Movement amplified such voices, emphasizing their courage and supporting their legal battles when they faced retaliation.

In addition, the movement sought to build bridges with professionals outside of the engineering and architectural fields. Medical professionals, firefighters, and environmental experts were brought in to address the long-term health consequences faced by first responders and New Yorkers due to exposure to toxic dust and chemicals released by the collapse of the towers. This collaboration not only added credibility to the movement but also highlighted the human toll of 9/11 and the government's failure to protect or adequately care for those affected. By expanding its scope to include health and safety issues, the movement aimed to show that its concerns were not limited to abstract theories about structural integrity but also involved real people and their suffering.

To further expand its reach, the movement also engaged with international audiences and groups who were critical of U.S. foreign policy. The invasions of Afghanistan and Iraq, perceived as unjust and destructive by many around the world, created fertile ground for the 9/11 Truth Movement to spread its message. By emphasizing the global consequences of the official 9/11 narrative—such as wars, destabilization, and loss of life—the movement sought solidarity with international activists and peace organizations. Global conferences and online forums allowed activists from different countries to share information and strategies, creating a sense of an international movement united in seeking the truth.

The movement's efforts to build alliances extended into the political realm as well. Some 9/11 Truth activists saw potential allies among elected officials who had expressed skepticism about U.S. intelligence agencies or who had spoken out against the government's handling of post-9/11 policies. Over time, these activists approached legislators to advocate for the declassification of documents, the protection of whistleblowers, and the formation of new investigative bodies to reexamine the events of 9/11. Though these efforts often faced resistance and skepticism from within the political establishment, the movement's persistence led to incremental victories, such as the partial release of classified documents and the inclusion of 9/11-related issues in political debates.

Despite these successes, forming alliances was not without its challenges. The movement had to be careful in its messaging to avoid alienating potential allies who might be wary of associating with a group perceived as promoting conspiracy theories. This required a delicate balance, where the movement emphasized its evidence-based approach and the professional expertise of its members while carefully distancing itself from more speculative or sensationalist elements. By prioritizing collaboration with established and reputable organizations, the 9/11 Truth Movement worked to present itself as a legitimate partner in a broader fight for transparency and accountability.

Through its alliance-building efforts, the movement aimed to create a network of support that extended beyond its initial base. By integrating its message into wider struggles for peace, justice, and government transparency, the movement positioned itself as part of a larger push for systemic change. This strategy not only helped to strengthen its credibility but also expanded its influence, drawing in new supporters who saw the pursuit of truth about 9/11 as a vital component of holding powerful institutions accountable.

Ultimately, the 9/11 Truth Movement's alliances and outreach efforts demonstrated its evolution from a niche group of skeptics into a broad coalition advocating for a reexamination of one of the most pivotal events in recent history. By connecting its cause with wider social and political movements, the 9/11 Truth Movement aimed to ensure that its message would not be ignored and that the call for truth and accountability would continue to gain strength in the face of resistance.

Chapter 19:
Lessons Learned:
Power, Fear, and
Cont

The Politics of Fear as a Tool of Control

In the wake of 9/11, the politics of fear became a powerful tool wielded by the U.S. government to shape public perception and justify sweeping changes to policy and legislation. Fear, as a political instrument, has long been used to manipulate populations, but the scale and intensity with which it was employed after the attacks were unprecedented. The trauma and shock experienced on that day created a collective vulnerability, making Americans more receptive to measures that they might otherwise have resisted. In this atmosphere, the government quickly moved to capitalize on this fear, introducing policies and laws that expanded its power under the pretext of protecting national security.

The Patriot Act, passed just weeks after the attacks, serves as a stark example of how fear can override rational scrutiny. Billed as a necessary measure to protect against future terrorist threats, the act granted sweeping surveillance powers to intelligence agencies, allowed for the detention of individuals without charge, and eroded long-standing civil liberties. The act was pushed through Congress with minimal debate, as lawmakers faced intense pressure to act swiftly. In the emotionally charged climate of post-9/11 America, the narrative that any dissent or hesitation equated to a lack of patriotism or even complicity in terrorism made it politically risky for anyone to oppose the legislation.

The Bush administration's rhetoric amplified the sense of urgency and fear. Phrases like "Axis of Evil" and "War on Terror" painted the world in stark, binary terms: you were either with America or against it. This approach made it easy to justify extraordinary measures, as they were presented as the only viable response to an existential threat. By framing the situation as a clash between good and evil, the government fostered an environment where critical discussion was stifled, and fear became the unifying force to rally public support. The administration's insistence that such measures were temporary and essential for safety placated many who otherwise might have questioned their necessity or implications.

The fear-induced compliance of the American public was not accidental; it was the result of a calculated strategy. In times of crisis, governments often seek to consolidate power, but the scale and rapidity with which this happened after 9/11 was remarkable. The use of fear was not merely a reaction to an unexpected event; it became a means to achieve broader, long-term goals. As citizens, shaken by the images of the collapsing towers and worried about future attacks, surrendered freedoms in exchange for the illusion of safety, the government's power grew.

This dynamic wasn't confined to domestic policy. The fear narrative also became a justification for military interventions abroad. The invasion of Afghanistan was presented as a necessary response to dismantle terrorist networks, and the subsequent invasion of Iraq was rationalized through the claim of weapons of mass destruction—a claim later debunked. In both cases, fear was used as a rallying cry, mobilizing public support for wars that would have otherwise faced greater scrutiny and resistance. By repeatedly invoking the specter of terrorism, the government built a sense of inevitability around its actions, making it difficult for opponents to counter the narrative without appearing unpatriotic.

In examining the politics of fear post-9/11, it becomes clear how effective this tool was in reshaping American society. The atmosphere of fear allowed for policies that expanded state power and reduced individual freedoms, all while maintaining a veneer of democratic legitimacy. The challenge, then, is recognizing how fear can be weaponized and learning from this period to guard against future manipulations. Fear, while understandable in moments of crisis, should not become the foundation upon which freedoms are sacrificed and unchecked power is granted.

The Expansion of State Power Post-9/11

In the immediate aftermath of 9/11, the United States experienced a rapid and profound expansion of state power, reshaping the relationship between the government and its citizens. The fear and uncertainty that gripped the nation provided fertile ground for the government to implement measures that, under normal circumstances, might have faced significant public opposition. Instead, the shock of the attacks created a climate where the public, desperate for protection and security, accepted—even welcomed—these changes.

The most prominent example of this expansion is the USA PATRIOT Act, passed with overwhelming support just 45 days after the attacks. The legislation granted law enforcement and intelligence agencies unprecedented powers, including the ability to conduct warrantless wiretaps, access personal records, and detain individuals suspected of terrorism without due process. While the act was presented as a necessary response to an extraordinary threat, its sweeping provisions raised serious concerns about privacy rights and civil liberties. Critics argued that the legislation's broad language allowed for abuses of power and targeted not just terrorists, but anyone deemed a potential threat, including activists, journalists, and ordinary citizens.

The creation of the Department of Homeland Security (DHS) further illustrated the government's efforts to centralize and expand its control. Formed in response to the perceived need for better coordination and oversight of national security efforts, the DHS consolidated 22 federal agencies under one umbrella, transforming the country's approach to homeland security. While the department's mission was to protect the American people, its creation also marked a significant increase in the federal government's reach. The DHS became a symbol of the state's growing influence, capable of deploying resources and implementing policies that had wide-ranging impacts on everyday life, from airport security measures to immigration enforcement.

The expansion of state power extended beyond legislation and structural changes; it also infiltrated the cultural and social fabric of American life. Surveillance became a norm, justified as a necessary means to prevent future attacks. The National Security Agency (NSA), emboldened by the post-9/11 climate, ramped up its surveillance capabilities, often operating in legally ambiguous territory. Programs such as PRISM, which collected massive amounts of data from electronic communications, remained largely hidden from public view until whistleblowers like Edward Snowden exposed their extent. By that time, however, the surveillance state had already become deeply entrenched, with broad legal and technological capabilities to monitor citizens without their knowledge.

Additionally, the government's efforts to expand its power post-9/11 were not limited to domestic policy. The Authorization for Use of Military Force (AUMF), passed just days after the attacks, gave the president near-unlimited authority to use military force against any entity deemed responsible for terrorism. This resolution became a blank check for the U.S. to engage in military interventions across the globe, far beyond Afghanistan and Iraq. Under the banner of fighting terrorism, the government extended its reach into countries like Yemen, Pakistan, and Somalia, using drone strikes and special operations forces with little oversight or accountability. The AUMF, still in effect years later, remains a testament to how the expansion of power during times of crisis can have lasting and far-reaching consequences.

While the expansion of state power was justified as a temporary and necessary response to an unprecedented threat, the reality has proven otherwise. Over the years, the extraordinary measures put in place after 9/11 have become normalized. The government's powers to surveil, detain, and wage war have not only persisted but, in many cases, have been expanded further. Despite assurances that these measures were temporary, the infrastructure built around the "War on Terror" became a permanent fixture, creating a new status quo in which civil liberties are increasingly sacrificed in the name of security.

The rapid expansion of state power after 9/11 illustrates a fundamental truth about crises: they often serve as opportunities for governments to reshape their authority, sometimes in ways that extend far beyond the immediate need. The fear and urgency following the attacks made it easy to justify these changes, but their long-term impact raises critical questions about the balance between security and freedom. As Americans navigated a transformed landscape, many began to wonder whether the government's response to 9/11 was truly about keeping them safe or about consolidating power that would be difficult, if not impossible, to roll back.

Fear as a Tool for Control

In the wake of 9/11, fear became one of the most powerful tools employed by those in power to maintain and expand their influence. The trauma of the attacks, broadcast repeatedly on television and reinforced by ongoing threats, created a collective sense of vulnerability. This pervasive fear was leveraged not only to justify aggressive foreign policies but also to reshape domestic society, ensuring that citizens would accept, and even support, measures that would have been unthinkable before the attacks.

The use of fear as a means of control is not a new tactic, but the post-9/11 era marked a particularly effective deployment of this strategy. Government officials and media outlets continuously warned of imminent threats, emphasizing the possibility of future attacks and instilling a sense of constant danger. Phrases like "weapons of mass destruction," "terror alerts," and "Axis of Evil" became part of the everyday lexicon, heightening the public's sense of urgency. Color-coded threat levels were prominently displayed on news programs and in public spaces, reinforcing the idea that the country was under perpetual threat. The narrative was clear: the enemy could strike at any moment, and the only way to stay safe was to trust the government's response.

This climate of fear was instrumental in shaping public opinion and justifying government actions. The invasion of Afghanistan in 2001 was met with widespread approval, seen as a necessary response to bring those responsible for the attacks to justice. However, the fear narrative was further utilized to build support for the 2003 invasion of Iraq, despite the lack of evidence connecting Iraq to 9/11. The government's insistence that Saddam Hussein possessed weapons of mass destruction and posed an immediate threat played directly into the fear that gripped the nation. Many citizens, still traumatized by 9/11 and bombarded with ominous warnings, supported the invasion, believing it was essential to prevent another catastrophic event. The media, often echoing official rhetoric without sufficient scrutiny, amplified these fears, creating a unified front that drowned out dissenting voices.

Fear also facilitated the erosion of civil liberties at home. With a populace eager for protection, the government expanded its surveillance capabilities and law enforcement powers under the guise of security. Programs like warrantless wiretapping and the mass collection of phone and internet data became accepted as necessary tools to prevent future attacks. The public's fear of terrorism was so great that many were willing to relinquish their rights to privacy in exchange for a sense of safety. The PATRIOT Act, which granted broad and invasive powers to intelligence agencies, passed with overwhelming bipartisan support and minimal debate, illustrating how effective the fear-driven narrative had become.

The media's role in perpetuating this fear cannot be overstated. News networks, competing for viewership, often prioritized sensationalism over critical analysis. The 24-hour news cycle became dominated by dramatic headlines and constant reminders of the threat level, keeping the public in a state of heightened alert. Images of the burning towers, interviews with terror experts predicting further attacks, and government briefings about the latest security measures were presented with a sense of urgency, ensuring that fear remained at the forefront of public consciousness. This environment created a feedback loop, where fear drove public support for aggressive policies, which, in turn, were reported as necessary and effective, further

deepening the public's sense of reliance on government authority.

Over time, this climate of fear evolved beyond the immediate
aftermath of 9/11. The "War on Terror" became a broad, undefined campaign that extended well beyond the original targets
in Afghanistan. The narrative of an ongoing, endless war against
a shadowy and ever-present enemy was reinforced through constant reminders of potential attacks, real or imagined. Airport
security, once a straightforward process, became an intrusive
and visible reminder of the persistent threat. The introduction
of body scanners, enhanced pat-downs, and no-fly lists became
accepted parts of daily life, justified by the notion that such
measures were necessary to prevent another tragedy. The fear-
driven changes seeped into everyday experiences, from passing
through metal detectors at sporting events to seeing armed
guards patrolling public spaces.

The government's ability to use fear as a tool of control was
effective not only because of the immediacy of the 9/11 attacks
but also due to the psychological impact of such a traumatic
event. The images of that day, seared into the collective memory, created an emotional vulnerability that made it easier for
people to accept the narrative of a world filled with enemies.
The invocation of 9/11 became a powerful political tool, used
to rally support for various policies long after the attacks themselves. In this sense, fear became a means of ensuring compliance, a way to maintain public support for policies that, under
different circumstances, might have sparked widespread resistance.

The deployment of fear post-9/11 serves as a reminder of
how powerful emotions can be harnessed to influence public
behavior and opinion. By keeping the public in a state of heightened anxiety, the government was able to push through measures that fundamentally altered the balance between security

and freedom. This tactic of leveraging fear for control highlights a deeper lesson about the vulnerabilities of democratic societies: when fear takes hold, it can lead to the acceptance of policies that erode the very freedoms that define such societies in the first place.

The Manipulation of Power and Public Perception

The use of fear to control and manipulate public perception post-9/11 was not only a response to a tragic event but a calculated exercise in consolidating power. The Bush administration, along with its allies in the media and other branches of government, used the attacks as a springboard to reshape public consciousness and redefine the nation's priorities. This was not merely about responding to terrorism; it was about leveraging a national crisis to expand the reach of government influence and steer public opinion in ways that would support a broader political agenda.

At the core of this manipulation was the concept of "us versus them." The government, with assistance from the media, crafted a narrative that portrayed America as a nation under siege by a vague, shadowy, and omnipresent enemy: terrorism. This was a strategic move, as it allowed the government to frame almost any foreign policy action, military intervention, or domestic security measure as a necessary step in the fight for survival. The language of patriotism and duty was employed extensively. Phrases such as "freedom," "defending democracy," and "protecting the homeland" became rallying cries that overshadowed critical examination of government actions.

By positioning the United States as a nation fighting an existential threat, the government effectively silenced dissent. Anyone who questioned the motives behind the wars in Afghanistan or Iraq, or who expressed skepticism about the erosion of civil liberties, was painted as unpatriotic or even sympathetic to the enemy. This manipulation of public perception was not accidental; it was a deliberate strategy aimed at maintaining support for controversial policies. Critics of the government were often marginalized or attacked, ensuring that the dominant narrative went unchallenged in the public sphere.

The media played a crucial role in amplifying this manipulation. In the months and years following 9/11, major news networks largely echoed the government's message, creating a monolithic perspective that left little room for alternative viewpoints. This was particularly evident in the buildup to the Iraq War, where coverage focused heavily on the supposed existence of weapons of mass destruction (WMDs) and the threat posed by Saddam Hussein. The media's failure to critically interrogate these claims, combined with its eagerness to align itself with the patriotic fervor of the moment, helped create a sense of inevitability around the war. This lack of critical reporting allowed the government's narrative to dominate, making it easier to rally public support for an invasion based on questionable evidence.

Public perception was also manipulated through the deployment of symbolic gestures and imagery designed to evoke a sense of unity and resolve. The repeated display of the American flag, the constant invocation of the phrase "never forget," and the portrayal of first responders as heroes reinforced the idea of a nation coming together in the face of adversity. While these symbols were powerful in fostering national unity, they also served to bolster the government's position by creating an emotional buffer against critical examination. It became difficult for many people to separate the genuine emotions of grief and patriotism from the policies being pursued in their name. By intertwining the national response to 9/11 with its broader agenda, the government was able to manipulate emotions to gain support for actions that may have otherwise faced significant resistance.

Another aspect of this manipulation was the deliberate obfuscation of information. The government selectively released intelligence, highlighting threats that reinforced its message while downplaying or suppressing data that contradicted its narrative. For instance, reports questioning the presence of WMDs in Iraq were often minimized or ignored, while dubious intelligence, such as the forged documents alleging uranium purchases from Niger, was given prominence. This selective presentation of information was a means of shaping public perception to align with policy objectives, ensuring that skepticism was met with either dismissal or accusations of disloyalty.

The creation of an atmosphere where fear and patriotism were intertwined also made it easier to justify the expansion of government powers. The implementation of the USA PATRIOT Act, which granted sweeping surveillance capabilities and other extraordinary measures, was framed as a necessary response to the threat of terrorism. By fostering a sense of urgency and danger, the government persuaded the public that such measures were essential for their protection. The constant emphasis on the idea that these policies were temporary and solely for the purpose of defeating terrorism helped placate those who might have otherwise resisted such infringements on civil liberties.

The manipulation of power and public perception also extended to the shaping of international alliances and enmities. The "coalition of the willing," as it was called during the Iraq invasion, was marketed as a global effort, but in reality, it was an assembly of allies brought together through diplomatic pressure, promises of aid, and, in some cases, outright coercion. By presenting this coalition as evidence of widespread support for American actions, the government was able to reinforce the narrative of a justified and morally sound campaign, further suppressing domestic and international dissent.

Over time, the manipulation of public perception began to unravel, as evidence emerged that the justification for the Iraq War was based on faulty intelligence. Yet, the damage had been done. The initial success of the manipulation—building public support, passing legislation that expanded executive powers, and framing critics as enemies of the state—demonstrates how effectively fear and patriotism can be used to control a population. Even as the narrative began to crack, many continued to cling to the story they had been told, a testament to the power of emotional manipulation when fear and loyalty are intertwined.

The events following 9/11 reveal a broader lesson about the vulnerabilities inherent in democratic societies. When trauma and fear are leveraged by those in power, they can create an environment where citizens, driven by emotional responses rather than rational analysis, support policies that may ultimately undermine their own freedoms. The manipulation of power and public perception after 9/11 is a clear example of how the interplay of fear, media influence, and nationalistic sentiment can be used to achieve political ends that may have little to do with genuine security concerns.

The Long-Term Consequences of Fear-Based Governance

The manipulation of power and perception following 9/11 had profound and long-lasting consequences that reshaped American society, foreign policy, and the global order. The use of fear as a governing tool not only justified immediate actions, such as military invasions and the implementation of sweeping security measures, but also established a precedent for how governments could harness crises to expand their authority. The impact of these decisions has reverberated through subsequent administrations, demonstrating the lingering effects of fear-based governance and its ability to reshape societies in ways that persist for decades.

One of the most immediate and tangible consequences of the 9/11 attacks was the erosion of civil liberties under the guise of national security. The USA PATRIOT Act, passed with overwhelming bipartisan support in the weeks following the attacks, granted unprecedented powers to law enforcement and intelligence agencies. These powers included expanded surveillance capabilities, warrantless searches, and the detention of individuals without due process. Framed as a necessary measure to protect Americans from further attacks, the legislation was accepted by a fearful public, many of whom believed that extraordinary times required extraordinary measures. Yet, as time went on, the expansive scope of these powers became apparent, revealing a government capable of monitoring its citizens on an unprecedented scale.

This expansion of surveillance and security infrastructure did not simply vanish with the passage of time. Instead, it became entrenched within the system, evolving and adapting to new technological advancements. Programs like PRISM, revealed years later by whistleblower Edward Snowden, demonstrated how the initial measures taken after 9/11 had grown into an extensive surveillance apparatus capable of monitoring virtually anyone, anywhere. What began as a response to terrorism had morphed into a widespread system of data collection and analysis that extended far beyond its original scope. The normalization of these practices illustrates how fear-based governance can create a state where privacy is sacrificed in the name of security, and once such powers are granted, they are rarely relinquished.

The international consequences of this fear-based approach were equally significant. The wars in Afghanistan and Iraq, launched under the banner of fighting terrorism, had long-term repercussions that extended well beyond the removal of regimes or the defeat of specific militant groups. The destabilization of regions, the rise of extremist organizations like ISIS, and the loss of hundreds of thousands of lives are direct outcomes of policies that were shaped by the desire to harness fear for geopolitical gain. The justifications provided for these wars—ranging from the existence of weapons of mass destruction in Iraq to the necessity of nation-building in Afghanistan—were later proven to be misleading or outright false. Yet, the fear generated in the immediate aftermath of 9/11 was sufficient to maintain public and political support for these conflicts, even as their disastrous consequences became evident.

Domestically, the use of fear as a tool to consolidate power also transformed the political landscape. The government's portrayal of a constant and pervasive threat made it difficult for any politician or public figure to challenge policies related to national security without risking their reputation or career. Dissent was equated with disloyalty, and skepticism about the government's narrative was often met with accusations of siding with the enemy. This climate of fear and suspicion stifled meaningful debate and led to the marginalization of those who sought to question the trajectory of U.S. policy. In a democracy, where open discourse and accountability are vital, such an atmosphere undermines the very foundations of the system, creating an environment where power can be wielded unchecked.

The media's role in perpetuating this fear-based governance further illustrates the long-term effects of such manipulation. By uncritically amplifying government narratives and downplaying dissenting voices, the media became complicit in creating a culture where fear was omnipresent. This relationship between the media and the government did not end with the Bush administration; it set a precedent for how future administrations, regardless of political affiliation, could use crises to their advantage. The fear generated after 9/11 was not a one-time event; it became a template for how subsequent events, whether related to terrorism, immigration, or other perceived threats, could be used to rally support and suppress opposition.

Over the years, the legacy of this fear-driven approach became evident in other areas of policy. Immigration debates, for instance, often relied on the same tactics of fear and suspicion that had been honed in the aftermath of 9/11. Policies that restricted the rights of immigrants, particularly those from Muslim-majority countries, were justified using the same language of national security and existential threat. This fear-based governance extended beyond issues of terrorism, seeping into broader social and political realms where fear could be leveraged to achieve specific goals, whether they involved border security, economic policies, or civil rights.

Perhaps one of the most troubling long-term consequences is the erosion of public trust in institutions. As the contradictions and misrepresentations of the post-9/11 era became apparent, many Americans grew increasingly skeptical of the government's intentions. The revelations surrounding faulty intelligence, the abuses at Guantanamo Bay, and the secretive nature of surveillance programs like those revealed by Snowden contributed to a sense of betrayal. This distrust extended to the media, which many perceived as complicit in promoting misleading narratives and failing to hold those in power accountable. The legacy of fear-based governance, therefore, is not only the expansion of state power but also a growing cynicism and polarization within society, as people struggle to discern truth from manipulation.

The consequences of using fear as a tool for governance extend far beyond the immediate aftermath of a crisis. They shape societies, influence policy for generations, and leave lasting scars on the political and social fabric of a nation. In the case of post-9/11 America, the manipulation of fear led to an expanded surveillance state, prolonged military conflicts, and a fractured public trust that continues to affect the country's ability to address crises in a united and informed manner. Understanding these long-term impacts is essential for recognizing the dangers of fear-based governance and ensuring that such tactics are not used to undermine democratic principles and personal freedoms in the future.